Portugal in the European Union

This book examines the involvement of Portugal in the European integration process since the country signed the Accession Treaty in 1985.

The volume elicits how Portugal has grasped opportunities and challenges emanating from its participation in the institutional, regulatory and political frameworks of the European Union (EU), as these have become more intricate as well as intrusive. It scrutinizes the adjustments and transformations that have taken place in Portuguese society, politics and economics as well as in the country's international relations, as engendered by its increasing enmeshment in the Community-building dynamics. It is divided into three main parts:

- Part I focuses on the major changes within the domestic arena, notably on the political, economic and social fronts;
- Part II addresses the adjustments that the Portuguese leadership had to make in order to secure the country's participation in key common policies and strategies;
- Part III is centred on foreign policy and assesses and discusses the impact upon Portugal's international relations.

This book will be of interest to students and scholars of European politics, EU studies, comparative politics and those with a strong interest in Portugal.

Laura C. Ferreira-Pereira is Professor of Political Science and International Relations at the University of Minho, Portugal.

Routledge advances in European politics

1 **Russian Messianism**
Third Rome, revolution, Communism and after
Peter J.S. Duncan

2 **European Integration and the Postmodern Condition**
Governance, democracy, identity
Peter van Ham

3 **Nationalism in Italian Politics**
The stories of the Northern League, 1980–2000
Damian Tambini

4 **International Intervention in the Balkans since 1995**
Edited by Peter Siani-Davies

5 **Widening the European Union**
The politics of institutional change and reform
Edited by Bernard Steunenberg

6 **Institutional Challenges in the European Union**
Edited by Madeleine Hosli, Adrian van Deemen and Mika Widgrén

7 **Europe Unbound**
Enlarging and reshaping the boundaries of the European Union
Edited by Jan Zielonka

8 **Ethnic Cleansing in the Balkans**
Nationalism and the destruction of tradition
Cathie Carmichael

9 **Democracy and Enlargement in Post-Communist Europe**
The democratisation of the general public in fifteen Central and Eastern European countries, 1991–1998
Christian W. Haerpfer

10 **Private Sector Involvement in the Euro**
The power of ideas
Stefan Collignon and Daniela Schwarzer

11 **Europe**
A Nietzschean perspective
Stefan Elbe

12 **European Union and E-Voting**
Addressing the European Parliament's internet voting challenge
Edited by Alexander H. Trechsel and Fernando Mendez

13 **European Union Council Presidencies**
A comparative perspective
Edited by Ole Elgström

14 **European Governance and Supranational Institutions**
Making states comply
Jonas Tallberg

15 **European Union, NATO and Russia**
Martin Smith and Graham Timmins

16 **Business, The State and Economic Policy**
The case of Italy
G. Grant Amyot

17 **Europeanization and Transnational States**
Comparing Nordic central governments
Bengt Jacobsson, Per Lægreid and Ove K. Pedersen

18 **European Union Enlargement**
A comparative history
Edited by Wolfram Kaiser and Jürgen Elvert

19 **Gibraltar**
British or Spanish?
Peter Gold

20 **Gendering Spanish Democracy**
Monica Threlfall, Christine Cousins and Celia Valiente

21 **European Union Negotiations**
Processes, networks and negotiations
Edited by Ole Elgström and Christer Jönsson

22 **Evaluating Euro-Mediterranean Relations**
Stephen C. Calleya

23 **The Changing Face of European Identity**
A seven-nation study of (supra) national attachments
Edited by Richard Robyn

24 **Governing Europe**
Discourse, governmentality and European integration
William Walters and Jens Henrik Haahr

25 **Territory and Terror**
Conflicting nationalisms in the Basque country
Jan Mansvelt Beck

26 **Multilateralism, German Foreign Policy and Central Europe**
Claus Hofhansel

27 **Popular Protest in East Germany**
Gareth Dale

28 **Germany's Foreign Policy Towards Poland and the Czech Republic**
Ostpolitik revisited
Karl Cordell and Stefan Wolff

29 **Kosovo**
The politics of identity and space
Denisa Kostovicova

30 **The Politics of European Union Enlargement**
Theoretical approaches
Edited by Frank Schimmelfennig and Ulrich Sedelmeier

31 **Europeanizing Social Democracy?**
The rise of the party of European socialists
Simon Lightfoot

32 Conflict and Change in EU Budgetary Politics
Johannes Lindner

33 Gibraltar, Identity and Empire
E.G. Archer

34 Governance Stories
Mark Bevir and R.A.W Rhodes

35 Britain and the Balkans
1991 until the present
Carole Hodge

36 The Eastern Enlargement of the European Union
John O'Brennan

37 Values and Principles in European Union Foreign Policy
Edited by Sonia Lucarelli and Ian Manners

38 European Union and the Making of a Wider Northern Europe
Pami Aalto

39 Democracy in the European Union
Towards the emergence of a public sphere
Edited by Liana Giorgi, Ingmar Von Homeyer and Wayne Parsons

40 European Union Peacebuilding and Policing
Michael Merlingen with Rasa Ostrauskaite

41 The Conservative Party and European Integration since 1945
At the heart of Europe?
N.J. Crowson

42 E-Government in Europe
Re-booting the state
Edited by Paul G. Nixon and Vassiliki N. Koutrakou

43 EU Foreign and Interior Policies
Cross-pillar politics and the social construction of sovereignty
Stephan Stetter

44 Policy Transfer in European Union Governance
Regulating the utilities
Simon Bulmer, David Dolowitz, Peter Humphreys and Stephen Padgett

45 The Europeanization of National Political Parties
Power and organizational adaptation
Edited by Thomas Poguntke, Nicholas Aylott, Elisabeth Carter, Robert Ladrech and Kurt Richard Luther

46 Citizenship in Nordic Welfare States
Dynamics of choice, duties and participation in a changing Europe
Edited by Bjørn Hvinden and Håkan Johansson

47 National Parliaments within the Enlarged European Union
From victims of integration to competitive actors?
Edited by John O'Brennan and Tapio Raunio

48 Britain, Ireland and Northern Ireland since 1980
The totality of relationships
Eamonn O'Kane

49 **The EU and the European Security Strategy**
Forging a global Europe
Edited by Sven Biscop and Jan Joel Andersson

50 **European Security and Defence Policy**
An implementation perspective
Edited by Michael Merlingen and Rasa Ostrauskaitė

51 **Women and British Party Politics**
Descriptive, substantive and symbolic representation
Sarah Childs

52 **The Selection of Ministers in Europe**
Hiring and firing
Edited by Keith Dowding and Patrick Dumont

53 **Energy Security**
Europe's new foreign policy challenge
Richard Youngs

54 **Institutional Challenges in Post-Constitutional Europe**
Governing change
Edited by Catherine Moury and Luís de Sousa

55 **The Struggle for the European Constitution**
A past and future history
Michael O'Neill

56 **Transnational Labour Solidarity**
Mechanisms of commitment to cooperation within the European Trade Union Movement
Katarzyna Gajewska

57 **The Illusion of Accountability in the European Union**
Edited by Sverker Gustavsson, Christer Karlsson, and Thomas Persson

58 **The European Union and Global Social Change**
A critical geopolitical-economic analysis
József Böröcz

59 **Citizenship and Collective Identity in Europe**
Ireneusz Pawel Karolewski

60 **EU Enlargement and Socialization**
Turkey and Cyprus
Stefan Engert

61 **The Politics of EU Accession**
Turkish challenges and Central European experiences
Edited by Lucie Tunkrová and Pavel Šaradín

62 **The Political History of European Integration**
The hypocrisy of democracy-through-market
Hagen Schulz-Forberg and Bo Stråth

63 **The Spatialities of Europeanization**
Power, governance and territory in Europe
Alun Jones and Julian Clark

64 **European Union Sanctions and Foreign Policy**
When and why do they work?
Clara Portela

65 The EU's Role in World Politics
A retreat from liberal internationalism
Richard Youngs

66 Social Democracy and European Integration
The politics of preference formation
Edited by Dionyssis Dimitrakopoulos

67 The EU Presence in International Organizations
Edited by Spyros Blavoukos and Dimitris Bourantonis

68 Sustainability in European Environmental Policy
Challenge of governance and knowledge
Edited by Rob Atkinson, Georgios Terizakis and Karsten Zimmermann

69 Fifty Years of EU–Turkey Relations
A Sisyphean story
Edited by Armagan Emre Çakir

70 Europeanization and Foreign Policy
State diversity in Finland and Britain
Juha Jokela

71 EU Foreign Policy and Post-Soviet Conflicts
Stealth intervention
Nicu Popescu

72 Switzerland in Europe
Continuity and change in the Swiss political economy
Edited by Christine Trampusch and André Mach

73 The Political Economy of Noncompliance
Adjusting to the single European Market
Scott Nicholas Siegel

74 National and European Foreign Policy
Towards Europeanization
Edited by Reuben Wong and Christopher Hill

75 The European Union Diplomatic Service
Ideas, preferences and identities
Caterina Carta

76 Poland within the European Union
New awkward partner or new heart of Europe?
Aleks Szczerbiak

77 A Political Theory of Identity in European Integration
Memory and policies
Catherine Guisan

78 EU Foreign Policy and the Europeanization of Neutral States
Comparing Irish and Austrian foreign policy
Nicole Alecu de Flers

79 Party System Change in Western Europe
Gemma Loomes

80 The Second Tier of Local Government in Europe
Provinces, counties, départements and landkreise in comparison
Hubert Heinelt and Xavier Bertrana Horta

81 **Learning from the EU Constitutional Treaty**
Democratic constitutionalism beyond the nation-state
Ben Crum

82 **Human Rights and Democracy in EU Foreign Policy**
The cases of Ukraine and Egypt
Rosa Balfour

83 **Europeanization, Integration and Identity**
A social constructivist fusion perspective on Norway
Gamze Tanil

84 **The Impact of European Integration on Political Parties**
Beyond the permissive consensus
Dimitri Almeida

85 **Civic Resources and the Future of the European Union**
Victoria Kaina and Ireneusz Pawel Karolewski

86 **The Europeanization of National Foreign Policies towards Latin America**
Lorena Ruano

87 **The EU and Multilateral Security Governance**
Sonia Lucarelli, Luk Van Langenhove and Jan Wouters

88 **Security Challenges in the Euro-Med Area in the 21st Century**
Mare Nostrum
Stephen Calleya

89 **Society and Democracy in Europe**
Oscar W. Gabriel and Silke Keil

90 **European Union Public Health Policy**
Regional and global trends
Edited by Scott L. Greer and Paulette Kurzer

91 **The New Member States and the European Union**
Foreign policy and Europeanization
Edited by Michael Baun and Dan Marek

92 **The Politics of Ratification of EU Treaties**
Carlos Closa

93 **Europeanization and New Member States**
A comparative social network analysis
Flavia Jurje

94 **National Perspectives on Russia**
European foreign policy in the making
Maxine David, Jackie Gower and Hiski Haukkala

95 **Institutional Legacies of Communism**
Change and continuities in minority protection
Edited by Karl Cordell, Timofey Agarin and Alexander Osipov

96 **Sustainable Development and Governance in Europe**
The evolution of the discourse on sustainability
Edited by Pamela M. Barnes and Thomas C. Hoerber

97 **Social Networks and Public Support for the European Union**
Elizabeth Radziszewski

98 The EU's Democracy Promotion and the Mediterranean Neighbours
Orientation, ownership and dialogue in Jordan and Turkey
Ann-Kristin Jonasson

99 New Democracies in Crisis?
A comparative constitutional study of the Czech Republic, Hungary, Poland, Romania and Slovakia
Paul Blokker

100 Party Attitudes Towards the EU in the Member States
Parties for Europe, parties against Europe
Nicolò Conti

101 The European Union and Occupied Palestinian Territories
State-building without a state
Dimitris Bouris

102 Portugal in the European Union
Assessing twenty-five years of integration experience
Edited by Laura C. Ferreira-Pereira

103 Governance and European Civil Society
Governmentality, discourse and NGOs
Acar Kutay

Portugal in the European Union

Assessing twenty-five years of integration experience

Edited by Laura C. Ferreira-Pereira

Routledge
Taylor & Francis Group
LONDON AND NEW YORK

First published 2014
by Routledge
2 Park Square, Milton Park, Abingdon, Oxon OX14 4RN

and by Routledge
711 Third Avenue, New York, NY 10017

Routledge is an imprint of the Taylor & Francis Group, an informa business

British Library Cataloguing in Publication Data
A catalogue record for this book is available from the British Library

Library of Congress Cataloging in Publication Data
Ferreira-Pereira, Laura C.
Portugal in the European Union : assessing twenty-five years of integration experience / Laura C. Ferreira-Pereira.
pages cm. – (Routledge advances in European politics)
Includes bibliographical references and index.
1. European Union.–Portugal. 2. Portugal–Politics and government–1974– I. Title.
HC240.25.P8F47 2014
341.242'209469–dc23 2013030682

ISBN: 978-0-415-58053-3 (hbk)
ISBN: 978-1-315-81802-3 (ebk)

Typeset in Times New Roman
by Wearset Ltd, Boldon, Tyne and Wear

FCT
Fundação para a Ciência e a Tecnologia
MINISTÉRIO DA EDUCAÇÃO E CIÊNCIA

MIX
Paper from responsible sources
FSC www.fsc.org FSC® C013056

Printed and bound in Great Britain by
TJ International Ltd, Padstow, Cornwall

Contents

Figures

Tables

Contributors

Pedro Tavares de Almeida is Professor of Political Science at Universidade Nova de Lisboa, and has written extensively on political elites and elections. Recent books include *Who Governs Southern Europe?* (with A.C. Pinto and N. Bermeo, Frank Cass, 2003).

André Azevedo Alves holds a PhD in Government from the London School of Economics and is currently a Lecturer at the Catholic University of Portugal's Institute for Political Studies where he is also the Coordinator of the Institute's Research Centre and a member of the core team of its PhD programme in Political Science and International Relations. His main research interests and publications are in public policy analysis, political economy, rational choice theory, and ethics with a particular emphasis on applications to public administration and regulation.

Michael Baum is Associate Professor and Chair of the Political Science Department at the University of Massachusetts Dartmouth. He serves as co-chair of the Iberian Studies Group at Harvard University (2000–present), an executive board member of UMass Dartmouth's Center for Portuguese Studies (1997–present), and an affiliate of UMass Dartmouth's Women's Studies Program (2004–present). His teaching and research focuses on comparative politics, contemporary Portugal, transitions to democracy, political economy, and development theory.

Sérgio Caramelo, is invited Associate Lecturer at the ISCTE-Lisbon University Institute, and Research Fellow at the Centre for Territorial Studies. His teaching and research focuses on political geography, prospective evaluation, strategic planning, regional planning and territorial cooperation. He has coordinated various projects on social intervention at a local scale, the evaluation of structural programmes and the strategic developments of Iberian border regions. His most recent publications are: 'Transborder Management Models and Territorial Articulation Processes in the European Mainland', *Society and Territory*, 41, 2008; 'European Union, Border and Territory', *Campo das Letras*, 2007; and 'Diffusion and Implementation of Supranational Spatial Planning Initiatives in Europe', *Polígonos*, 13, 2003.

David Corkill is Professor of Iberian Studies at Manchester Metropolitan University. He has published widely on the Portuguese and Spanish economies and on the impact of immigration on the Iberian labour markets. His most recent publications are: *Spain: A Modern European Economy* (with R.J. Harrison) (Ashgate, 2004); 'Portugal's changing integration into the European and global economy' in S. Syrett (ed.) *Contemporary Portugal: Dimensions of Economic and Political Change* (Ashgate, 2002); 'Aspects of the Portuguese economy during the late Estado Novo', *Portuguese Journal of Social Science*, 2, 2003, pp. 61–72; and 'The double centenary commemorations of 1940 in the context of Anglo-Portuguese relations' in T. Pinto Coelho (ed.) *Portuguese Discoveries in the English-Speaking World 1880–1972* (Editorial Colibri, Lisbon, 2006).

Laura C. Ferreira-Pereira is Professor of Political Science and International Relations at the University of Minho, where she has served as the head of the Research Unit in Political Science and International Relations and editor of the journal *Perspectivas-Portuguese Journal of Political Science and International Relations.* She taught previously at the Technical University of Lisbon. Her main research interests include European Foreign Security and Defence Policy, International Relations of the European Union (with particular emphasis on its strategic partnerships), Portuguese Foreign, Security and Defence Policy and International Organizations in post-Cold War Europe. Her work has been published in *Journal of Common Market Studies*, *International Politics*, *Cooperation and Conflict*, *Journal of European Integration*, *European Integration online Papers*, *Perspectives on European Politics and Society*, *Journal of Contemporary European Studies*, *European Security* and *Global Society*. Her monograph *The Militarily Non-Allied States in the Security Architecture of Post-Cold War Europe* was published by Peter Lang in 2007. Since 2004, she has been a member of the Standing Group on International Relations of the European Consortium for Political Research (SGIR-ECPR). She is a founding member of the European International Studies Association (EISA) and Associate Editor of the *European Review of International Studies* (ERIS).

Miguel Glatzer is Assistant Professor of Political Science at La Salle University. His research focuses on the politics of globalization, democracy and inequality in comparative perspective. He is the co-editor of *Politics Matters: Globalization and the Future of the Welfare State* (University of Pittsburgh Press, 2005) as well as *Portugal: Strategic Options in a European Context* (Lexington Books, 2003) and has also published in the journal *South European Society and Politics*. His most recent work is on the politics of taxation and inequality. In addition to courses on Europe, Latin America, China and India, his teaching interests include civic education, the media, globalization, social movements and the US military.

Paulo Gorjão is Director of the Portuguese Institute of International Relations and Security (IPRIS) and editor of the *Portuguese Journal of International*

Affairs (PJIA). He lectures at Lusíada University. He is author of several peer-reviewed articles, published by academic journals such as *Asian Survey*, *Civil Wars*, *Contemporary Southeast Asia*, *Democratization* and *International Relations of the Asia-Pacific*.

A.J.R. Groom is Emeritus Professor of International Relations at the University of Kent. He is Visiting Professor of Politics at Canterbury Christ Church University and a regular lecturer at Sciences Po Paris and the *Diplomatische Akademie* Vienna. He was formally editor of *Global Society* and has published 16 volumes as editor or author and over 160 chapters and articles. He was Executive Secretary of WISC (World International Studies Committee) until 2008. He is a former board member of the Academic Council of the United Nations System and on the Executive Committee of the European Consortium for Political Research. He has served as Vice-President of ISA (the International Studies Association) and Chairperson of BISA (the British International Studies Association). He was also the founder of the European Standing Group for International Relations. After being awarded his doctorate by the University of Geneva, he was made Doctor of Social Science *honoris causa* by the University of Tampere in 2000. He has supervised 44 successful doctoral theses.

Maria Helena Guimarães is Associate Professor at the University of Minho, Jean Monnet Professor since 2002 and Fulbright Visiting Scholar at American University in Washington, D.C. (2011). Her research interests include political economy of European integration, internal market governance, EU negotiation processes and international political economy. She has published in peer-reviewed American, Brazilian and Portuguese journals, and her last article appeared in *Business and Politics* (with M. Egan, 2012). She published *Political Economy of International Trade* (Principia, Portugal, 2005), has co-edited *Market Integration* (Emerald, UK, 2010) and has chapters in several edited books. She has received research grants from the European Commission, the American government and the Luso–American Foundation, among others. She has served as member of the Fulbright screening panel in Portugal, was Chair of the School of Economics and Management of UMinho, and served on various University governing bodies. She has organized a number of international summer courses on European Union issues, supervised numerous successful graduate theses on European integration and served on the examining boards of master and PhD theses at several Portuguese universities.

Manuel Laranja has been Director of the Innovation Agency in Portugal, Advisor on Innovation Policy for the Secretary of State of Economic Affairs, and more recently advisor to the Cabinet of the National Coordinator of the Lisbon Strategy and the Technological Plan, and to the Secretary of State for Energy and Innovation. He currently occupies a teaching position at the Higher Institute of Economics and Management, Technical University of Lisbon (ISEG/UTL). He has published several books and international articles.

Paul Christopher Manuel is Professor of Political Science at Mount St. Mary's University in Maryland, where he directs the Institute for Leadership. An author, co-author, or editor of seven books and numerous scholarly articles, he writes on religion, politics and comparative public policy, with a regional focus on Portugal. Manuel previously served as professor and chair of the politics department, as well as the executive director of the New Hampshire Institute of Politics, at Saint Anselm College. Manuel also served as a visiting scholar, an affiliate, and a co-chair of the Iberian Studies Group at the Minda de Gunzburg Center for European Studies at Harvard University. He has been a member of the National Screening Panel for the US Graduate Fulbright Competition for the Iberia programme. Manuel is currently a research fellow at the Berkley Center for Religion, Peace and World Affairs at Georgetown University.

Alfredo Marques is a Professor at the Faculty of Economics of the University of Coimbra. During his academic career he has combined several responsibilities. He started by teaching growth and development theories. He then became an official of the European Commission in Brussels in the field of competition policy (responsible for regional state aid). Later he devoted himself to teaching, researching and consulting in the field of the Economics of Integration. In this specific domain his publications comprise a handbook and several articles focusing on regional and competition policies and on the European monetary union. He was president of the Coordination and Regional Development Commission of the Centre of Portugal (in the framework of which he was in charge of managing Structural Funds in this Region) from 2005 to 2012.

Diogo Moreira is PhD candidate in Political Science at the Institute of Social Sciences, University of Lisbon. He was a member of the INTUNE Project and has published on political parties in Portugal and on attitudes towards the European Union.

Arminda Neves was Deputy Coordinator of the Lisbon Strategy in Portugal between 2005 and 2011. She holds a PhD in Management with specialization in Management and Public Policies – Public Governance and is invited Professor at the University of Évora. Among her recent publications, the books *Gestão na Administração Pública* (Editora Pergaminho, Lisbon, 2002) and *Governação Pública em Rede: Uma Aplicação a Portugal* (Editora Sílabo, Lisbon, 2010) stand out.

Rui Novais is Researcher at Communication and Society Research Centre of the University of Minho. His PhD featured East Timor as a case study and he has co-edited the book *Timor-Leste: Da Nação ao Estado* (East Timor: From Nation to State) (Editions Afrontamento, Porto, 2006).

António Costa Pinto is Senior Researcher at the Institute of Social Sciences of the University of Lisbon and Professor at the University Nova of Lisbon. He is a political scientist and historian who has published extensively on Portuguese history and politics.

Miguel Rocha de Sousa is Assistant Professor of Economics at University of Évora (UE), head of the BA in International Relations, and deputy head of the PhD in International Relations and Legal and Political Theory. He is a researcher and deputy head of NICPRI-UÉ (Research Unit in Political Science and International Relations). His areas of research are international organizations, political economy, land reform, economic growth and development, macroeconomics of the euro, co-integration and economic literacy. He is an associate of SEDES (Socio and Economic Development Association), and IPSA (the International Political Science Association), where he belongs to RC35 (Research Committee 35), whose goals are to study technology and development. In July 2012 he became president of this RC35. He is also an associate of AEA (the American Economic Association).

Sebastián Royo, political scientist, is Associate Dean and Professor of Government at Suffolk University in Boston, and director of the Suffolk University Madrid campus. Royo's articles and reviews on comparative politics have appeared in *Comparative Political Studies*, *European Journal of Industrial Relations*, *PS: Political Science and Politics*, *West European Politics*, *South European Society and Politics*, *Democratization*, *Mediterranean Quarterly*, *SELA*, *FP*, *Perspectives on Politics*, and other publications. His books include *From Social Democracy to Neoliberalism: The Consequences of Party Hegemony in Spain, 1982–1996* (St Martin's Press, 2000), *A New Century of Corporatism? Corporatism in Southern Europe: Spain and Portugal in Comparative Perspective* (Praeger, 2002), *Spain and Portugal in the European Union: The First Fifteen Years* (with Paul Christopher Manuel: Frank Cass, 2003); *Portugal, Espanha e a Integração Europeia: Um Balanço* (Imprensa de Ciências Sociais, 2005); and *Varieties of Capitalism in Spain* (Palgrave Macmillan, 2008). He writes a regular column for the Spanish daily *Cinco Dias*. His research interests include Southern European and Latin American politics and economic institutions. Royo is an affiliate at the Minda de Gunzburg Center for European Studies at Harvard University, where co-chairs the Iberian Study Group.

Nuno Severiano Teixeira is Professor of International Relations at the Faculty of Human and Social Sciences of the University Nova de Lisboa. He has been a Visiting Scholar at the Institute for European Studies, Berkeley University of California; and a Visiting Professor at Georgetown University. He was the former Director of the Portuguese Institute of International Relations (IPRI, Lisbon) and of the Institute of National Defence. He has published extensively on Portuguese foreign policy and the history of European integration. His most recent publications are: *The International Dimension of Democratizations* (Routledge, 2008) and *Southern Europe and the Making of the European Union* (Columbia University Press, 2002). Nuno Severiano Teixeira served as Minister for National Defence between 2006 and 2009.

Carlos Zorrinho was Secretary of State for Energy and Innovation in the Ministry of the Economy, Innovation and Development and National Coordinator for the Lisbon Strategy and the Technological Plan between 2005 and 2011. He leads the Socialist Parliamentary Group in the Portuguese Parliament. He holds a PhD in IT Management and is a Full Professor in the Department of Business Administration at the University of Évora.

Foreword

On the European crisis

I took on the request to write this foreword with the conviction that, today more than ever, we must renew the public debate on the destination of the European project and on the future of Portugal in Europe. In this sense, this work is a good contribution, although we all bear in mind the risks we are taking when writing on the current European situation, given the times of uncertainty we are experiencing.

It is impossible to anticipate safely what is coming our way. Europe is, according to the words of its most important political leaders, going through the biggest crisis since the end of the Second World War and important decisions will need to be taken in order to react to a situation of unbearable uncertainty and instability. Regardless of what happens to the Euro, we are definitely in a new stage of the European project, which will mean the revision of Treaties, or even the drawing up of a new treaty, with all of the imponderables of this process. What will take place then is something that no one can quite predict at the moment. Nevertheless it is fairly obvious that the rhythm and the form of the integration process will be quite different from that which one would have imagined before the crisis, and this will have a considerable impact on European geopolitics.

Anyone who has some experience and knowledge of the European Union and the way its institutions make their decisions cannot help but feel restless. We have entered unknown territory with new and unexpected situations, within a process where political voluntarism prevails, according to the old 'bicycle metaphor' that inspired Delors. It is necessary to keep pedalling to avoid falling off, but where to, if a common will and a clear destination cannot direct our movements in the fog of an unexpected crisis, for which none of us was prepared? In a way, the European Union is lost within its own institutional and political maze, which it has been creating over the last decades. Beyond the latent lack of confidence in the relations between markets and governments or the growing tension between technocrats and politicians, which are difficult to manage, is the undisguised lack of trust of the people and the citizens as far as following elites and other leaders is concerned. If it is certain that the 'elitism' that has so far supported the European project will be questioned, the issue is finding out whether there may be another 'modus' in this chaotic situation in which we find ourselves, which might save us from the abyss. Will the referendum, to which some rulers intend to resort because of their democratic instinct, resist 'market pressure'? What happened in Athens is a disquieting sign of how the categories for representation and political legitimation are so easily put in jeopardy by the 'state of emergency' that nowadays dominates democracy in Europe.

It seems evident to us that, regardless of the political and institutional forms developed within the scope of a potential revision of the Treaties, the European people and their rulers either concentrate on a common collective goal, or all the demons of history, which are already wandering around them, will inexorably end up imposing themselves and dominating our lives and the future of Europe.

It is quite evident that the financial crisis and the recession that followed it are far from being resolved and are now confronting us with new problems, which have surprised both economists and politicians. The crisis of 2008/2009, the first globalization crisis, had a brutal impact worldwide. The collapse of the financial system and the immediate impact it had upon the real economy only saved was by the coordinated intervention of states, whether by means of automatic stabilizers or the new public investment programmes, or even by intervention within the private sector, in order to avoid the insolvency of the banks that were at risk. In any case, in most developed countries, the necessary intervention by the governments was made at the cost of more public debt. Ultimately, to solve a problem created by the excess of indebtedness, mostly in the private sector, the states had to increase their deficits and their debts – it is within this context that the problem of sovereign debt in Europe has arisen, much like in the USA, which actually has an even greater level of debt than the Eurozone.

In Europe the situation is more serious, however, because the crisis exposed the fragility of a common currency in an imperfect monetary union. The weakness of the Euro is what the markets seem to distrust ever more. The reductionist perspective of centring the crisis on the fiscal and budgetary problems of the periphery and hiding its systemic and structural dimension was a mistake, as may be seen by the dynamic of the crisis in late 2011 and early 2012. The financial markets struggle with the uncertainty that hovers over the future of the Euro and the whole Zone is feeling its effects. This is why it is an urgent necessity to act rapidly to create the proper political and institutional conditions that will restore confidence in the common currency. Its implosion would have terrible consequences for the whole financial system and the world economy. Thus, the stability of the Euro has become the most important issue for international politics at the end of 2011 and it remains at the centre of the international agenda for 2013.

It is very important to bear in mind that the European crisis occurs and evolves within a context of a complex and dangerous process of transformation of the international system. The financial crisis of 2008 and the great recession that followed it exposed the imbalances of unregulated globalization of the past twenty years. Its correction demands a hard and painful macro-economic readjustment exercise on a global scale, which will end up imposing a new political order worldwide. The establishment of a multipolar order, which will ensure the balance and stability of the international system, will not be made without difficulties or risks, and will take place in an environment of great tension and conflict, much like those through which we are living now. We all know that a global confrontation would put at risk the survival of humankind, which imposes huge responsibility upon governments and politicians in general and particularly, in the current circumstances, upon Europe. It is very hard to conceive a new order and a new geopolitical balance without a Western centre of reference and the latter will not be possible without European stability which inevitably means the European Union: a 'project of civilization' in the words of Habermas.

Confronted with the current crisis, the European Union has entered a period of many and important decisions. The urgent refounding of the Euro will determine the redefinition of the European project, as it has been implemented since the very thorny and ambiguous commitment reached in the Maastricht Treaty, and later renewed in Nice and in Lisbon, after the frustrating rejection of the European Constitution solemnly signed in Rome.

Maastricht tried to answer the implosion of the Soviet Union, fulfilling two essential goals: to accommodate the new Germany and to create the conditions for the reorganizing and stabilizing the geopolitical space of central and Western Europe. The Euro was, as we all know, the trade currency of reunification. It was the price that Germany was deemed to have to pay for its reunification. Eventually, the country accepted this *sine qua non*, but it also established its own conditions. These are the conditions that are at stake today and this is why Germany must have a decisive word in solving the crisis, thereby assuming the leadership role that it has largely forged for itself. However, it is clear that Germany will do so by imposing on other states a set of conditions involving additional guaranties that are considered indispensable in the face of the new and challenging responsibilities that are expected to be assumed by that country's authorities. Yet another problem is that of the acceptance of German leadership by its European partners.

It remains certain that the financial markets cannot endure the uncertainty, which has arisen as far as the sustainability of the Euro is concerned and, as a consequence, investors are running away from the European debt markets. Pressure on the Treasury bonds of the central countries will hasten decisions to avoid the implosion of the Eurozone and to renew confidence in the preservation of a common currency. There seems to be no alternative. Either the Euro will collapse, at least in its current configuration, or the Eurozone will become a 'unifying' core around which an integrating circle of the European Union should be organized. Today that is for twenty-seven countries but a wider circle may be considered in the future. It is obvious, even today, that the joint integration, of the twenty-seven at the same pace, is already a pipe dream. This will leave the United Kingdom in a very uncomfortable situation, bearing in mind the critical role it played in the European balance of power, which has helped to mould the integration process over the last thirty years or so, both in its enlargement and deepening phases. Such a balance of power will definitely be questioned should the refounding process of the Euro proceed. Thus deciding the basis for a new commitment between the unifying core and the integrated circle, today of twenty-seven, will be a sensitive and complex operation, politically, institutionally and technically. Its negotiation and ratification will be a difficult and troubled process, generating great internal tensions and under the permanent threat of the guillotine of the 'Markets'.

The options with which Portugal is faced, within this context, are extremely delicate. In our current situation, we have no access to the markets that would normally allow us to finance the economy and the State. Under an assistance programme of severe austerity, which will probably be prolonged, the country's margin for manoeuvre is necessarily very limited. Leaving the Eurozone is an option that will attract ever more support, although it would have dramatic consequences at an economic, social and strategic level. It is nevertheless good that we remain cognisant of the huge difficulties that await us should we decide to resist and maintain our position in the Eurozone, the unifying core of the EU.

Without a new proactive impulse, supported by a big public debate on the future of Europe and its place in the world, fed by a dose of 'European idealism', it is very likely that the last utopia of the twentieth century, the European utopia, as Eduardo Lourenço would say, will be over, much as all the other utopias of the century, a tragedy both for Europe and the world.

Luís Amado
Portuguese Minister of Foreign Affairs, 2006–2011
October 2012

Introduction

Laura C. Ferreira-Pereira

On 1 January 2011, twenty-five years had elapsed since Portugal – one of the oldest nation-states in Europe – became a fully-fledged member of the then European Community (EC). This temporal landmark in itself warrants a monograph with the purpose of presenting a cogent portrait of Portugal's quarter-of-a-century engagement in the European integration project. What is more, although Portugal can be said to be an old member state of the European Union (EU), it has traditionally been a long neglected country and hence there is a putative dearth of Anglophone literature devoted to the country's integration experience.

Among the few books that have been written for an Anglophone readership on the country's engagement in the Community-building process since 1 January1986,[1] three can be mentioned here: *Portugal: A European Story*, edited by Álvaro Vasconcelos and Maria João Seabra (2001); *From Isolation to Integration: 15 Years of Portuguese and Spanish Accession*, edited by Sebastián Royo and Paul Christopher Manuel (2003); and *The Developing Place of Portugal in the European Union* written by José Magone (2004). They are now outdated in terms of content since essentially they cover the first ten to fifteen years of the Portuguese integrative venture. Moreover, some of these scholarly works concentrate on the Iberian experience, rather than Portugal's trajectory, and tend as their unique selling point to offer a picture of Portugal as it stood at the *fin-de-siècle* in the political, social and foreign policy domains, rather than to give an assessment of the impact of EU membership on Portugal since 1986.[2]

This lacuna in the specialized literature covering the twenty-five year period of Portuguese membership in the EU has stimulated a collective intellectual effort to produce a study designed to scrutinize the process of change and adaptation undergone by the country's society, politics, economics and external relations as a result of the increasing enmeshment in the multidimensional dynamics of European integration. Indeed, this book sets out to provide a wide-ranging analysis and reflection on what have been the most significant changes in Portugal as a result of EU membership while echoing a range of authoritative views on how EU membership has affected the country. While addressing mainly the change and weakening of domestic autonomy in looking at the reorganization of the national economy and political system, it also considers the fundamental questions of the adaptation of foreign policy, including the post-accession relationship with neighbouring Spain and relations with former colonies. Furthermore, it raises issues relating to the transformation of society, citizenship and (national) identity whilst highlighting the EU–domestic interface resulting from the increasing penetration of the EU's activities into the nooks and crannies of domestic social life. The multifaceted nature of adaptation and change generated by EU membership is, in essence, the overarching central theme running through the book. The country's fully-fledged participation in the European project has left no stone unturned in its national institutions, agencies, political actors and policy processes, including external relations.

In this perspective, the current volume is taken up with eliciting how Portugal has grasped opportunities and challenges emanating from its participation in the institutional, regulatory and political frameworks of the EU as these became more intricate, as well as more intrusive in terms of state sovereignty. The wide range of topics covered in the chapters of this book ultimately unravel a diverse panorama of the choices and constraints that faced successive Portuguese governments for whom the consolidation of the country's EU member state status became an indisputable overriding national interest-oriented goal. For twenty-five years, the EU underwent successive deepening and enlarging exercises, which required continuous adjustments from individual member states like Portugal. Equally important, especially after the end of the Cold War, has been the expansion of EU foreign policy and security objectives resulting in a greater role in the provision of security, not only on the Old Continent, but also on the world stage. Charting the particular experience of Portugal, as a small and peripheral Southern European state with an authoritarian past, enables us to cast light on the general transformational process that this country had to undergo in order to meet a multitude of needs and expectations stemming from the increasing dynamics of integration. Its transformation is also the result of receiving substantial structural funds as one of the 'convergence countries'. Whilst space limitations do not permit every aspect of the complex and multifaceted nature of the impact of EU membership in Portugal to be explored, we believe that the principal issues and discussions are given due consideration.

This book is divided into three main parts, which reflect its multidisciplinary approach, with contributions and inputs mainly from the fields of history, economics, political science, comparative politics and international relations. The first part undertakes a systematic analysis of the major changes occurring within the domestic arena, notably in the political, economic and social spheres, while the second part addresses the adjustments that the Portuguese leadership had to introduce in order to participate in key European common policies and strategies. Finally, the third part, centred on foreign policy, appraises the extent to which a deepened participation in European foreign and security policy has had an impact upon Portugal's international relations. This last part also incorporates a chapter focused on what can and should be learned from the Portuguese experience, especially by the Eastern European states that joined the European venture in 2004 and 2007, and a contribution that examines how the relations between Portugal and Spain have evolved between 1986 and 2011. In the conclusion, we draw out a number of points that derive largely from the preceding chapters, which point towards a balance against the backdrop of a comparative analysis between the Portuguese trajectory and the experiences undergone by other former Western colonial powers.

While focusing on diverse policy levels and sectoral policies, all the chapters attempt to advance understanding of the Portuguese experience of integration in taking as a methodological point of departure for both empirical enquiry and analytical endeavour the following questions: What were the most important challenges faced by Portugal in adapting to a (specific) European policy or strategy in its experience of EU integration? What were the most important opportunities that Portugal faced in its process of policy adjustment, in particular, and as a result of EU integration, in general? What were the tangible contributions made by Portugal in the specific policy being considered and at the level of the European (political and economic) project as a whole? And, how is the country's approach best characterized (e.g. passive, reactive, pro-active, fully committed, half-hearted)?

Underpinning most of these questions there is a concern to avoid sweeping unsubstantiated generalizations about the Europeanization of major Portuguese sectoral policies, including foreign policy, by offering a thorough analysis based on sound empirical evidence. Here the focus is particularly on what the Europeanization literature designates as 'downloading' or 'top-down' dynamics encapsulated in the adaptation of national legislation to provisions enshrined in the EU treaties. For example, legislative changes required by the latter generated important amendments to the political system (see Manuel, Chapter 1). That being said, we further outline the 'uploading' or 'bottom-up' dynamics reflected in and resulting from the various endeavours undertaken by the Portuguese authorities during the country's Presidencies of the Council of the EU, namely in the domains of trade and Common Foreign and Security Policy/Common Security and Defence Policy (CFSP/CSDP) (Guimarães; Ferreira-Pereira, Chapters 7 and 10 respectively).

Although the present book provides insights into the very different aspects with which the notion of Europeanization may be connected, the chapters are not informed by a concern to develop this concept. Hence Europeanization does not feature in all contributions. This is because this book's main goal is not to be an addition to the academic debate on the notion of Europeanization, but rather to become an addition to the existing literature on the meaning of European integration for Portugal – and for other Southern European member states for that matter – in scrutinizing the country's integration into the EU on the different aspects under discussion through the perspective offered by its twenty-five years of membership.

As this study suggests, the formulation and pursuit of the 'European option', which led to the Portuguese application to the EC, was a by-product of the post-1974 leadership's choice of democracy that eventually dictated the demise of the colonial empire. The accession process (i.e. ranging from its application for membership in 1977 to its formal accession in 1986), therefore, evolved separately from, but in an interactive way with the democratic consolidation process. To be sure, it was accompanied by consistent endeavours to shift paradigms not only in internal politics, by replacing the old authoritarian rule by democratic principles and institutions along with the adoption of the market economy system. This was also the case with foreign policy given the need for the country to enter into and adjust itself to post-imperial role, something that called for a new self-identity reflecting the country's place in Europe and in the world. For a democratic Portugal, membership in the EC became the overriding new and clear-cut foreign policy goal that would enable the country to regain respectability, credibility, status and prestige after decades of international isolation and ostracism. This was to be pursued in a steadfast fashion as a way of reinventing the Portuguese presence in the five continents by means of drawing on longstanding historic, cultural and linguistic affinities.

Despite this book not providing a detailed analysis and elucidation of the pre-accession period, it acknowledges the explanatory relevance of the eminently historical issues that conditioned this phase to understanding the early years of Portugal's participation in the EC. It also has implications not only for the political system and diplomatic relations (see Teixeira and Manuel, Chapters 2 and 1 respectively), but also for the economic field and citizenship development (see Corkill; Baum and Glatzer; Moreira *et al.*, Chapters 3, 5 and 4 respectively). There is a depiction of the road towards the consolidation of the country's democratic regime, which put an end to the Portuguese exceptionalism encapsulated in the expression 'Europe ends at the Pyrenees'. It can be seen, too, in the consensual observation that European economic support after 1986 contributed to the successful consolidation of the democratic regime (see Manuel, Chapter 1). These historical issues are crucial to an appraisal of the main elements of change, and also continuity, in the country's European experience of integration throughout the period under review.

The significance of accession to the EC to the break with dictatorship, colonialism and isolationism and to the subsequent development of the main features characterizing contemporary Portuguese politics, economics, society and the country's place in the world politics should be seen against this backdrop. Incidentally, both membership to the EC and the European strategy endorsed by the country after accession have traditionally been capitalized upon by governing elites to further deepen and enhance Portugal's adherence to liberal democracy and a market economy. This was particularly successful during the first ten to fifteen years of the country's membership, which were marked by a pro-European consensus both across the political party spectrum and public opinion. In the case of the latter, euro-optimism was instrumental in nature to the extent that it was based largely on the perception of material benefits springing from economic growth, rising incomes, and investment in health, education and social security system (see Moreira *et al.*; and Royo, Chapters 4 and 14 respectively). Such optimism was caused by the utilitarian outlook of the EU which started gradually to be curbed with the prospects of the Eastern enlargement with all that this prospect entailed in terms of decreased financial support for Portugal (see Moreira *et al.*, Chapter 4). With the impact of the economic and financial crisis, national support for the EU reached its lowest levels in 2011. The enormous cuts that affected all public policies put the core structures of the national welfare state system under unprecedented strains. Brussels' institutional constellation ceased to be seen as the guardian of the national welfare state system, and was instead perceived as being responsible for its rapid and eventually inexorable decline. Under these circumstances, trust in European institutions to secure continued economic growth and good standards of living suffered a considerable blow.

When assessing the first two-and-a-half decades of the country's membership of the EU, it can be said that the attitude of the Portuguese towards the integration experience is positive. On the basis of the positive attitude prevailing in the mid-1990s, António Guterres' government made every effort for the country to meet the convergence criteria and to join the Economic and Monetary Union (EMU) as a co-founder in 1999. The replacement of the escudo by the euro as the new currency brought with it immediate advantages, namely access to international finance, an increase in external investment and low rates of interest for both business and private consumers. Yet participation in the Eurozone, besides the appreciable constraints it entailed in terms of economic autonomy, created the conditions for increasing indebtedness which, combined with the erosion of Portuguese economic competiveness and deep-rooted structural problems, exacerbated the country's economic difficulties (Corkhill, Chapter 3).

Besides the economic and monetary domain, both agriculture and trade are sectors within which the impact of the European integration process has been particularly profound. This is due to the supranational nature of both the Common Agriculture Policy (CAP) and the Common Trade Policy, and the need for Portugal to endorse systematically the continual expansion of the respective *acquis*. As some contributions of this volume highlight, Portugal has endeavoured to find room to incorporate its major views and interests in the policy decision-making process. However, policy flows have been mainly from Brussels to Lisbon. The result of this has been the emergence of a more open and internationalized economy (Guimarães and Rocha de Sousa, Chapters 7 and 6 respectively). That said, in the case of trade, Portuguese authorities have attempted to reflect national interests and preferences in the EU agenda regarding commercial relations with African, Carribean and Pacific (ACP) countries while contributing to the advancement of European interests in Latin America. The EU Presidencies of 1992, 2000 and 2007 became paradigmatic of such endeavours and, in general, have been successful. It is also worth noting that the country has been rather effective in its attempts to protect the interests of traditional industries, notably of the textile industry. All in all, considering the limited negotiating resources and the small share of extra-EU trade in the country's total trade, Portugal's trade diplomacy in the framework of the Common Trade Policy merits a positive evaluation (Guimarães, Chapter 7).

Given its backward position in the 1980s, participation in the CAP has historically been seen as a major concern and challenge from the early days of EU membership given the existing weaknesses of the Portuguese agricultural sector, standing in contrast with those prevailing in countries such as France and Germany who conceived the CAP's original design. Although the CAP reform of 1992 brought about some successful results, a general assessment of the country's participation in the CAP is equated with a lost opportunity for Portugal's agrarian development. From 1986 until the Eastern enlargement, the Portuguese stance can be characterized as being weak and passive. The entry of twelve new states that were included in the 'cohesion range' has increased competition for funds while challenging both authorities and farmers to reinvent a national strategy and outlook so as to reflect the new circumstances (Rocha de Sousa, Chapter 6).

The relative economic success resulting from Portuguese participation in EU can be attributed to the support that the country received through European structural funds as part of the 'cohesion group' of the poorer European states, namely Greece, Ireland, Portugal and Spain (Corkill; Marques, Chapters 3 and 8 respectively). An assessment of the structural funds' impact reveals not only positive effects that would not have happened otherwise without this financial programme, but also some important lost opportunities. Generally speaking, the European funds, of which Portugal has been one of the main beneficiaries since their inception, have allowed it to overcome its low level of development compared to the European average. In the first periods of intervention, this was achieved by means of considerable investments in diverse infrastructures for collective use whose chronic deficit represented an impediment to economic progress. Nevertheless, the lack of qualified human resources was not addressed in the first place, at the same time as the need for basic infrastructure. Thus, the initial (limited) convergence with European standards proved not to be sustainable given the continued structural problems at level of employment and labour productivity, which eventually contributed to a failure of structural funds during the third Community Support Framework (2000–2006). Eventually, the missed opportunity to channel the financial support to implementating the major goals of the Lisbon Strategy, that is knowledge, innovation and competitiveness, took their toll when the financial and economic crisis started to affect the country from 2008 (Marques, Chapter 8).

Portugal's European engagement is linked to the Lisbon Strategy signed at the 2000 Spring EU Council, under the country's Presidency of the Council of the EU. The Portuguese authorities made efforts to form a consensus about the Lisbon Strategy. They also played an important role throughout all stages of its development, especially in the preparatory works for the 2008–2010 cycle, which took place, yet again, under the Portuguese Presidency, undertaken in the first semester of 2007. The implementation of both policies and instruments launched in Portugal under the umbrella of the Lisbon Strategy had some positive influence in a number of domains, such as the recognition of skills and lifelong learning, social inclusion, and renewable energies. (Neves *et al.*, Chapter 9).

This has helped further to reinforce convergence with European norms, something that was sought throughout the twenty-five years of EU accession and can be identified in such policy areas as family structure, gender roles, welfare state developments and their respective impact on inequality. The incremental adoption of European standards has fostered a change in attitudes and patterns of behaviour by means of which the Portuguese gained a more cosmopolitan outlook and identity. This should also be seen in regard to a considerable growth in the numbers of foreign immigrants, which albeit not being necessarily a direct consequence of EU membership, took place against its backdrop. This development has changed the historical portrayal of Portugal as a 'country of emigrants' (Baum and Glatzer, Chapter 5).

The third part of the book attempts to illuminate the extent to which participation in the EU has helped national authorities to reshape foreign policy, which has undergone important transformations. Two major factors account for this: first, the country's fruitful experiences during the Presidencies of the Council of the EU in 1992, 2000 and 2007; and second, both the extension and the reinforcement of the EU's foreign and security policy profile, which has called for the country's involvement in a plethora of new institutions, agencies, mechanisms and tools. It is clear that after 1986, as the democratic consolidation took root, and the more so after the end of the Cold War, the centrality of the EU became one of the major tenets of Portugal's international strategy. Of course, foreign policy activities outside the realm of the EU continued to be carried out, as demonstrated in the critical role played by national authorities in the foundation of the *Comunidade de Países de Língua Oficial Portuguesa* (Community of Portuguese-Speaking Countries – CPLP), in 1996. This also applies to the politico-ethical voluntarism reflected, throughout the 1990s, in the prioritization of the self-determination of East Timor in the foreign policy agenda and the defence of the Timorese cause in both European and international fora (see Gorjão; and Novais, Chapters 12 and 11 respectively). On the other hand, engagement in NATO's structures and activities remained a cornerstone of the country's security and defence policy, despite the progress that has been made in the context of the EU's CFSP and CSDP (see Ferreira-Pereira, Chapter 10). Incidentally, the Euro-Atlanticist outlook of Portuguese foreign policy that gradually crystallized after 1986, and remains unchallenged to date (2012), should be understood against this backdrop.

As the EC has evolved into the EU, its emergence as a foreign and security policy actor gave a new dimension to Portuguese foreign policy. In fact, the development of the CFSP and CSDP opened new horizons for the country in terms of international engagement, something that represented a source of rejuvenation of the national security and defence policy (Ferreira-Pereira, Chapter 10). Yet, the years of European integration have not, fundamentally, transformed the country's core foreign policy priorities. As the evolution of its engagement in the growing CSDP dynamics evinces, Portugal continues to attach considerable importance to the zealous safeguarding of state sovereignty while perceiving military defence as a national *chasse gardée* and collective defence as the Atlantic Alliance's *domain privé* (ibid.). Furthermore, the Lusophone world, especially the Portuguese-speaking states in Africa, saw its prominence renewed

(Gorjão, Chapter 12). In this perspective, this volume provides additional insight pointing to a limited Europeanization of Portuguese foreign, security and defence policy. All things considered, however, there can be no doubt that as a result of the experience of twenty-five years of integration, Portugal's foreign policy has moved away from a strict Atlantic posture typified by a somewhat exclusive emphasis placed upon relations with NATO and the United States to gain a more flexible and inclusive Euro-Atlanticist stance (Teixeira; and Ferreira-Pereira, Chapters 2 and 10 respectively).

It is a commonplace to observe that the country's deepening participation in the EU has considerably expanded both its diplomatic network and the geographical focus of its national foreign policy activity. On the other hand, this has influenced significantly both the country's self-perception and how it is perceived by and relates itself to third states, notably its allies, partners and neighbours. In this respect, relations with the former colonies and the neighbouring Spain are cases in point.

The post-1986 period has witnessed the normalization of politico-diplomatic relations between Portugal and its former colonies. Eventually, it also saw the relationship with Portuguese-speaking countries being upgraded and taken to a multilateral level with the creation of CPLP. This bound the former colonies into a privileged partnership based on common historical and language roots, with all partners standing on an equal footing. Rather than diverting Portuguese authorities' attention from the former colonies, deepened participation in the EU moved them to make the most of its renewed post-colonial relations within the CPLP's realm to reinforce the country's role as *the* Lusophone interlocutor in Europe. Hence, Portugal's status as a EU member helped the authorities to reassess and redefine relations with both African former colonies and Brazil, while adding weight to Portugal's diplomatic efforts to play a tangible role in the independence of East Timor. Interestingly enough, as the recent past has shown, the country's leverage in the eyes of its European peers became especially dependent upon its ability to manage strategically relations with the rising countries of Brazil and Angola (Gorjão, Chapter 12)

When it comes to rapport with Spain, Portugal's European venture as of 1986 has fostered a fundamental transformation in relations between the two states by inaugurating a new paradigm of bilateral relations that historically have been marked by mutual suspicion, strategic caution, pragmatic separation and diverse tensions. The replacement of the non-aggression pact by a friendship and cooperation agreement, which materialized during the EC membership negotiating process of the Iberian countries, paved the way for an increased common understanding and positions. The latter were initially informed by and structured around the common ambition of EC membership that both Portuguese and Spanish authorities wanted to achieve as speedily as possible. Later, taking stock of the favourable conditions created by the experience of integration, they paved the way for a deeper coordination at multiple levels as the principle and routine of Luso–Spanish Summits developed deep roots along with the search for common agreement on European matters. The first decade of membership saw the normalization of relations and increased coordination on European issues, notably the European Regional Policy, the CAP, the Single Market and relations with Africa and Latin America. Over time, practical coordination and integration as reflected in cross-border transport infrastructure gradually transformed an historical border of mutual control, containment and mistrust into a relatively porous border of mutual advantage. The same applied to the economic border that both EU accession and the bilateral trade agreements helped to blur thereby diffusing the fear of Spanish economic colonization of Portugal. Economic interdependence – once feared – became a welcome reality (Caramelo, Chapter 13).

Portugal's twenty-five-year long experience of integration allows one to draw more lessons that may be applicable not only to newcomers from Central and Eastern Europe and acceding countries (i.e. Croatia), but also to those on the road to membership, notably, the candidate countries (such as Iceland, Serbia, Montenegro and the Former Yugoslav Republic of Macedonia). These lessons relate to both challenges and opportunities springing from engagement in the European project, in general, and in the EMU, in particular. Salient is the role played by the democratic imperative inherent in EU membership for the sustainability and consolidation of democratization processes as well as the significance of participation in both the EU's decision-shaping and decision-making processes. The strategic importance of cultivating flexibility in coalition-building dynamics while looking for ways to advance 'win–win' formulae is something that allows states to be perceived as constructive and credible players in the European game. The acknowledgment of the 'price' attached to fully fledged participation in the European integration process is translated into costs, risks and unintended consequences, including the need to garner public support to carry out economic and social policies bringing with it painful effects in the short-to-medium term. The notion of nominal convergence and the importance of securing real economic convergence, and the critical role played by political stability, are important. Linked to the Portuguese experience from the country's ordeal in coping with the current economic and financial crisis are additional potential lessons that can be drawn by future EMU applicants (Royo, Chapter 14).

When this book was being finalized, the eye of the international economic and financial storm, which started with the collapse of the Lehman Brothers in 2008, had hit Portugal very fiercely with unprecedented implications while opening scenarios of political instability, social unrest and general angst, not to say, hopelessness, about the future. This has led some to advocate the country's abandonment of the Eurozone. Analysing the unfolding of the financial turmoil, which only began to be addressed by the Portuguese government during 2011, falls outside the temporal remit of the present book (i.e. 1 January 1986–1 January 2011). However, its initial phase and repercussion, as well as the extent to which this has stirred the political leadership to broach new and continuing problems and challenges, underpin the place of Portugal in the European integration process and its continued commitment to the EU. In fact, both the Foreword and Chapter 15 reflect the first strong impressions and concerns related to the effects of the economic hardship.

Between 2008 and 2011, the government led by the Socialist José Sócrates seemed to have failed to see the writing on the wall that hinted at a deep economic and financial storm of unprecedented magnitude and unforeseen and devastating results. The austerity packages undertaken in 2010 and 2011, against the backdrop of the Greek and Irish bailouts and the growth of the wider spreads on sovereign debt to unsustainable levels, made it impossible to avoid the country's bailout by the international community in the form of a financial assistance programme of €78 billion led by a Troika composed of the European Central Bank (ECB), the European Commission and the International Monetary Fund (IMF). To be sure, the economic, financial and budgetary crisis in Portugal was the corollary of a cumulative process of a decade or so of grim overall conditions marked by economic stagnation, high levels of public deficits, a persistent current account negative balance, growth of public social expenditure, excessive increase of wages with low productivity growth and erosion of international competitiveness. (Alves, Chapter 15). These circumstances indeed set the scene for Portugal being caught in the eye of the economic and financial storm – a process that was still in a state of flux with unforeseeable outcomes at the time the writing of this book was completed.

However, from October 2011, implementating the Memorandum of Understanding on Specific Economic Policy Conditionality, which had been agreed upon with the Troika the previous May, has been the main driving factor in the policy of the government led by the Social Democrat Pedros Passos Coelho. So far, the measures with the most impact have been a range of tax increases and public sector wage cuts affecting both workers and pensioners that are likely to be maintained for the duration of external assistance programme. As these lines were being written there were expectations that the Portuguese economy would continue to stagnate in recession, and that unemployment would reach a record height, with all that this implied in terms of potential for political and social instability.

Notes

1 As for books written for Lusophone audiences, one can find a few titles that tend to cover both the pre-accession period and the first twenty years of Portugal's integration experience. One can also include in this category studies that focus mainly on a comparative analysis between the EU membership of Portugal and Spain. See Leitão (2007), Lobo and Lains (2007) and Pérez and Lobo-Fernandes (2007).

2 Since the writing of this book there have been two additions to the existing literature on the Portuguese democratization and the European integration processes with the perspective offered by its two decades and a half or so of membership. These are Pinto and Teixeira (2012) and Royo (2011). The former's contributions rest on providing detailed information about how Portuguese institutions (i.e. government, parliament, courts and interest groups) have dealt with the reality of European integration, and how popular and elite attitudes have adapted themselves to this process. As for the latter, while addressing issues related to Portugal's integration into the European Union, it is more concerned with offering a comprehensive appraisal of the development of Portuguese politics, economy and society since the Carnation Revolution of 1974 and the transition to democracy.

Bibliography

Leitão, Nicolau Andresen (ed.), *20 Anos de Integração Europeia (1986–2006): O Testemunho Português*, Lisbon, Editora Cosmos, 2007.

Lobo, Marina Costa and Lains, Pedro (eds) *Em Nome da Europa: Portugal em Mudança (1986–2006)*, Estoril, Principia, 2007.

Magone, José *The Developing Place of Portugal in the European Union*, New Brunswick, Transaction Publishers, 2004.

Pérez, Rafael García and Lobo-Fernandes, Luís (eds), *España y Portugal: Viente años de integración europea*, Santiago de Compostela, Tórculo Edicións, 2007.

Pinto, António Costa and Teixeira, Nuno Severiano (eds), *The Europeanization of Portuguese Democracy*, New York, SSM-Columbia University Press, 2012.

Royo, Sebastián (ed.) *Portugal in the Twenty-First Century: politics, society, and economics*, Lanham, MD: Lexington Books, 2011.

Royo, Sebastián and Manuel, Paul Christopher (eds), *From Isolation to Integration: 15 Years of Portuguese and Spanish Accession*, London, Frank Cass, 2003.

Vasconcelos, Álvaro and Seabra, Maria João (eds), *Portugal: A European Story*, Estoril, Principia, 2001.

Part I

Twenty-five years' experience

The evolution of Portuguese politics, economics and society

1 Portuguese exceptionalism and the return to Europe

The April 25, 1974 coup and democratization (1974–2010)[1]

Paul Christopher Manuel

Napoleon is said to have once quipped that "Africa begins at the Pyrenees" or "Europe ends at the Pyrenees," given the Moorish conquest and their 700-year rule of the Iberian Peninsula. This notion of Spanish and Portuguese exceptionalism resonated with the European political and economic elite for some two hundred years. There was a widespread belief that Portuguese society and government existed outside of European understandings of society, politics and authority relations. This belief could draw some support from the fact that even at the start of the twentieth century, the political views still dominating Portuguese political discourse involved a rejection of the democratic and liberal revolutions of the modern era (see Payne 1976, Robinson 1979, Manuel 2002, Royo and Manuel 2003). In the 1960s some social science scholars even wondered if the Roman Catholic country could ever become democratic, because its hierarchical political culture rejected the fundamental Enlightenment values of equality, individualism and the general will (see Almond and Verba 1965). Portugal was accordingly viewed among the European political and economic elite as existing at the outer orbit of the European existential space, trapped in the historical and philosophical vacuum of overseas exploration and lusotropicalism[2] (see Freyre 1942, Martins 1969, Birmingham 1993).

Portugal's return to Europe was complex, multi-dimensional, and featured a wide variety of players. During the turbulent days following the Carnation Revolution of April 25, 1974, one political slogan particularly resonated with the hopes and dreams of the Portuguese people: *A Europa Connosco* (Europe is with us). This slogan – coined by the Socialist Party to help gain electoral support in the 1975 and 1976 elections – spoke to both a generalized hope to end the country's historical isolation from the rest of Europe, and a European future of peace and prosperity for Portugal. In many ways, Portugal's successful transition to democracy, and its subsequent adhesion to the European Union, were two concrete steps that helped to fulfill the existential hopes pregnant in that slogan.

Perhaps the starting point of the process took place on April 28, 1974 when Socialist leader Mário Soares arrived in Lisbon from his long political exile in Paris, on what he called the *comboio da liberdade*, or the liberty train. He knew that a dramatic change had occurred when he was greeted by huge crowds at each train stop – at one stop, the train driver even waited for Soares to tell him when it was time to depart (Soares 1976: 24). Lisbon was full of admirers who looked to Soares with great hope and anticipation. Arguably, more than any other single individual, Mário Soares's articulated vision of a socialist and European Portugal eventually captured the imagination of most Portuguese, and helped propel his party to electoral success over the Communists and other rivals in the following years. He subsequently made relevant policy decisions as Prime Minister and as President, which deepened the democratization and the Europeanization process of the country, and resulted in its economic integration into the European Union (Manuel 1996a: 17–70).

Democratic waves

Placing democratic development on a timeline, Samuel Huntington has usefully noted that there have been three main periods of democratic expansion since the eighteenth century, which he refers to as "waves." Huntington's first long wave lasted some ninety-eight years, from 1828 to 1926, and includes the development of democratic regimes in Britain, France, Italy, the United States, and Argentina. This first wave suffered a setback in the period 1922 to 1942, when several formerly democratic countries adopted fascist governments, including Portugal, Spain, Italy, Germany, and Argentina. For the most part, these were elite-driven, fragile, democratic institutions, with little connection to, or support from, civil sectors. Yet, the democratic procedures they introduced into policy-making processes – limited as they were – were a marked improvement on the authoritarian governmental structures that preceded, and followed, this democratic interlude. After World War II, Huntington notes the development of a second democratic wave. This short wave lasted from 1945 until 1962 and includes Japan, West Germany, Italy, and India. This wave was reversed for a second time, and from 1958 to 1975 several countries abandoned democratic forms of government in favor of military regimes, including Brazil, Argentina, and Chile. The third wave stated in 1974 with the creation of new democracies in Portugal, Spain, Greece, then moving on to Latin America in the 1980s, and to Eastern Europe after the events of 1989 (Huntington 1993: 13–26).

Portugal was very slow in accepting democratic values, institutions, and procedures during the first wave; in 1910, towards the end of this wave, the Portuguese First Republic was finally established by reformers. Although problematic, the reformers sought to effectuate political and economic reforms in line with Enlightenment and democratic principles (see Wheeler 1978). The First Republic unfortunately suffered through years of governmental instability, economic hardships, and the burden of World War I, and was overthrown by a military coup on May 28, 1926. The military sought to restore political order and economic stability, and eventually established the anti-modern, anti-European *Estado Novo* regime, under the leadership of António de Oliveira Salazar (see Kay 1970 and Figueiredo 1976).

Under Salazar, Portugal maintained some of the vestiges of the First Republic. He held the title of Prime Minister, and regularly scheduled elections for the

National Assembly and the Presidency were held throughout his rule. But this was not a democracy: this was a corporative system of government, which limited the actual impact of elections (Manuel 1995: 21–23). For instance, voter registration procedures kept the electorate small, and members of the National Assembly were not allowed to influence public policy significantly. Yet, officially recognized political parties were allowed some measure of free speech to debate policies during the brief period leading up to the election (see Georgel 1985).

The most contested election during the Salazar era took place in 1958, when General Humberto Delgado, known as the *General sem medo* (General without fear) ran a robust campaign against the Salazar-backed candidate, Admiral Américo Tomás. Delgado was a feisty candidate, and even promised to dismiss Prime Minister Salazar if elected. Delgado basked in the huge anti-Salazar election rallies he held around the country. He was finally defeated in what may have been a rigged election.[3] Following this electoral challenge, Salazar decided to do away with the system of direct presidential elections. Delgado continued his anti-Salazar movement, and attempted to overthrow the regime by military coup on a few occasions. He was killed in 1965 by members of Salazar's secret police (Marques 1976: 212–235).

Salazar was finally removed from office in 1968 when he slipped into a coma after having fallen in his bathroom. His successor, Marcelo Caetano, was overthrown on April 25, 1974 by young military officers – an event that marks the commencement of Huntington's third wave. Portugal appeared finally to be on the brink of adopting and consolidating institutional reforms consistent with the democratic and liberal revolutions of post-1789 Europe.

The revolution of April 25, 1974

Juan Linz has insightfully observed that the Portuguese transition to democracy involved a rupture (*ruptura*), or break from the fascist past, compared with the gradual reform process (*reforma*) that took place in Spain in the 1970s. Whereas various sectors of Spanish political and civil society engaged in a gradual transition punctuated by a series of pacts, or agreements, among the various players, junior military officers in Portugal, calling themselves the Armed Forces Movement (MLA) simply overthrew the dictatorship on April 25, 1974. This military action led to the quick eradication of the former regime, a rupture from the past, and required that a new regime be made from scratch (Linz 1977: 237–296).

The development of the MLA is a complicated story (Bandeira 1976: 1–56). In brief, the prolonged and seemingly interminable colonial struggle in Africa put great strains on the Portuguese military, especially the junior officers. Many had been forced to spend ten or more years in Africa, which disrupted their families and careers. The formation of the Armed Forces Movement started principally in response to the professional grievances of junior officers, notably their demand for the repeal of Decree Law 373–73 (which allowed the *milicianos*, or conscripted officers, to count all of their service toward seniority, moving ahead of professional junior officers). When the Caetano administration appeared both disinterested and antagonistic toward their demands, the MFA decided that regime change was the only way to repeal Decree Law 373–73, end the colonial war, and offer a new political model for Portugal. The officers responsible for the planning and execution of the April 25, 1974 Carnation Revolution, known as the "April Captains," promised the Portuguese people a political program known as the three "Ds," meaning democracy, development and decolonization (Bruneau 1974).[4] However, the members of the Armed Forces Movement themselves could not agree as to the content of these terms (Manuel 1995: 26–37).

During the 1974–1976 revolutionary process, known as the PREC (or the *Processo Revolucionário em Curso*), the MFA divided into four main ideological factions, one in favor of the creation of a West European Social Democratic state, another advancing an Eastern Bloc Communist model, a third group preferring the establishment of a Cuban-style socialist state, and a traditionalist vision seeking gradually to reform the pre-existing authoritarian model. This internal MFA conflict controlled the final outcome; the victorious faction was able to shape the new form of social and political organization. All of the players sought to implement the "three Ds," but the actual policy preferences varied considerably, depending on their proposed political model (Manuel 1995: 55–83; also see Maxwell 1997).

Mário Soares was the leading civilian political leader advancing a West European style social democratic model, while Communist Party leader Álvaro Cunhal supported the Eastern Bloc Communist system of government. Of note, these two leaders had known each other for a very long time. In his youth, Soares studied at the Colégio Moderno in Lisbon, founded by his father. Álvaro Cunhal was employed as a teacher at the Colégio, and actually taught geography to the young Soares. They both opposed the dictatorship of António de Oliveira Salazar, and were each imprisoned and exiled (Soares in Paris, Cunhal in Moscow). Soares subsequently became a political opponent of Cunhal (Manuel 1996a: 4–6)

The eyes of Europe were upon Portugal during the PREC. Jean-Paul Sartre, the great French existential philosopher, visited Portugal in the spring of 1975. Sartre was given a very warm welcome by hoards of young university students. At one of his press conferences, Sartre told the students that he considered the Portuguese revolution to be one of the most important events in post-war Europe, and called upon them to build West Europe's first socialist state (Sartre *et al.* 1975: 32–34). Another development of European-wide consequence took place on November 6, 1975. Appearing on a French television station, Álvaro Cunhal and Mário Soares debated the future of Portugal for almost four hours. During this robust back-and-forth, Cunhal praised the equality of the Eastern bloc countries, and suggested that their political system would be a good model for Portugal. Soares countered by arguing that the person of Joseph Stalin separated the Communists from the Socialists, not Karl Marx and/or Vladimir Lenin. Soares railed against a "socialism of misery" common to the East. Citing the examples of Germany and Sweden, Soares instead proposed a democratic, prosperous and equitable political, social and economic system for Portugal.

What is perhaps most interesting is that this Communist–Socialist debate was very current in the 1970s, when the reform communist ideology of Eurocommunism was gaining electoral strength throughout Europe, and especially in Italy.[5] The political dynamic in Portugal served to illustrate larger issues for all Europeans. The decision to appear on French television – hence a window to a greater European audience – was a dramatic break from the isolation of the Salazar/Caetano years, and opened the floodgate to deeper and more European interest and investment into Portugal. The April 25, 1974 Revolution clearly represented a significant break from the past and to new possibilities with Europe (see Gallagher 1983).[6]

The six provisional governments in office from 1974 to 1976 tried to strike a balance between macroeconomic challenges and the immediate needs of the Portuguese. The continuing political instability and regional actions for social revolution precluded stable economic growth; causing great anguish and turmoil among the population (see Bermeo 1986). With each new austerity measure taken by the regime in Lisbon, young militants would take direct action against the policy. In the end, rather than bringing law, order, and progress, the MFA's own internal divisions became a source of the political, economic, and social upheaval (Manuel 1995: 55–130).

By the spring of 1976, Prime Minister General Vasco Gonçalves, who had been in favor of the construction of a East European communist state with Álvaro Cunhal, and Major Otelo Saraiva de Carvalho, who had been in favor of the creation of an MFA–*Povo* (MFA–People) alliance, had been politically outmaneuvered and discredited by the MFA moderate group known as the "Group of Nine." These moderate officers had gained control of the Council of the Revolution by July of 1976, and enjoyed the widespread support of political society, including Mário Soares's Portuguese Socialist Party, the Popular Democratic Party (PPD) led by Francisco Sá Carneiro, and Freitas do Amaral's Party of the Social Democratic Centre (CDS). Only the Communist Party, which enjoyed about 10 percent of electoral support, regretted this turn of events, but it too eventually accepted the new democratic rules and institutions. In time, all of the more militant and leftist anti-democratic elements were forced out of the political process.

The defeat of both leftist and rightist anti-democratic elements facilitated the Europeanization of the political regime (Linz 1977: 237–296). That is, in spite of the serious differences of opinion among those who survived the transition, there were no significant anti-democratic political forces in Portugal after 1976. Those remaining political forces represented a narrow ideological spectrum, and subsequent party formation followed the overall European model (Corkill 1993 and Manuel 1996a: 10–11). The pro-European victors adopted the classical ideas of social democracy, abandoning Marxist ideology and supporting the liberalization of the economy and integration with Europe.[7]

There are currently six major ideological expressions among political society in Portugal. On the left, there are three organizations: the Portuguese Communist Party, (PCP, *Partido Comunista Português*), the Left Bloc (BE, *Bloco de*

Esquerda), and the Green Party (PEV, *Partido Ecologista* or "*Os Verdes*"). The center–left is occupied by the Socialist Party (PS, *Partido Socialista*). The center-right is taken by the Social Democratic Party (PSD, *Partido Social Democrata*), and the Centrist Social Democrat Party, also called the People's Party, is on the right (*Centro Democrático e Social/Partido Popular*) (Manuel 1996a: 4–6).

Of these six political parties, only two have governed since 1976: the Socialist Party and the Social Democratic party. Together, they comprise the center-left and center-right sides of the political spectrum, and combined they represent a more moderate, centrist elements of the population. The Social Democrat Party (PSD) is very strong in the central and northern regions of the country, representing a more conservative electorate. The Socialist Party (PS) enjoys strong support in the cities and in the central and southern regions. The PS essentially supports a reformist capitalist agenda, not an anti-capitalist one, and is significantly more progressive on cultural issues than the PSD. We can identify similar patterns throughout Europe. In Spain, for instance, the Spanish Socialist Workers Party (PSOE) on the left, and the Popular Party (PP), on the right, function similarly to the PS and PSD in Portugal. The same general pattern of ideological and political party formation holds in Italy and France as well.

Key institutional elements of Portuguese democracy

The Portuguese Constitution of 1976, and its subsequent revisions of 1982 and 1989, created a dual-executive, or semi-presidential regime in Portugal. The dual-executive institutional arrangement contains elements from both presidential and parliamentary systems. This system was first designed by French President Charles de Gaulle, with the creation of the Fifth Republic Constitution in 1958. In contrast to the well-known French system of approximate constitutional parity between the President and Prime Minister in many areas, the Portuguese dual-executive model can be better described as a parliamentary system with a separately elected, presiding executive officer. In Portugal, the law-making function is under the jurisdiction of the Prime Minister and the National Assembly. Portugal has a unicameral legislature, called the *Assembleia da República*. Small and homogeneous unitary nation-states frequently prefer one legislative body to two, such as Sweden and Greece – whereas a bicameral legislature exists in Spain. There is a 230-seat parliament, with four-year terms, and twenty-two multi-seat constituencies.[8]

The constitution grants the President independent authority and legitimacy outside of the National Assembly. He is expected to monitor the activities of the government, and has veto power. In the event of a serious deadlock in the National Assembly, the President has the constitutional power to ensure governmental balance and accountability. The President may dismiss the Prime Minister, appoint a new Prime Minister or call for new elections. He also serves as the Commander-in-Chief. The President is elected by universal suffrage to a five-year term, and no president may serve more than two consecutive terms.

Any President is also permitted to run for a third and final term, as long as it is not consecutive with the previous terms (*Constituição da República Portuguesa* 1990: 228–231). Although these powers seem to provide the Portuguese President with substantial leverage, his or her actual power is somewhat less than what it may seem.[9]

Like many European democracies, Portugal functions under a multi-member constituency, proportional representation system for the election of members to the National Assembly. Legislative seats are allocated in proportion to the votes received by each party, based the d'Hondt method.[10] Proportional representation systems encourage the formation of coalition governments among the various political parties, especially if no single party enjoys an absolute majority of seats. A coalition among political parties is a solution to this problem, when two or more parties agree to a common legislative program (Manuel and Cammisa 1998: 26–35).

Five milestones on the road to Portuguese democratization

The development of democratic institutional norms has taken time. Portugal has had to pass several milestones – or significant events – on the road towards the consolidation of its democratic regime. These are, namely, the issues of getting the new dual-executive arrangement up and running, establishing civilian control of the military, achieving integration into the European Economic Community, building electoral alliances across ideological differences, and the peaceful alternation of power. Let us now turn to each of these five milestones, in chronological order.

The first milestone involved getting the new Constitutional dual-executive system to actually function. As in France, the dual-executive arrangement embodied in the post 1976 Portuguese Constitutional regime was complicated, and there was some potential for serious institutional deadlock should the Prime Minister not accept the directives of the President. Following the June 1976 Presidential elections, President Ramalho Eanes, a military hero of the transition, and the leader of the now defunct *Partido Renovador Democrático* (Democratic Renewal Party, or PRD) was elected President. Mário Soares was elected as the first Constitutional Prime Minister, presiding over a minority Socialist government. The two executives needed to figure out how their constitutional roles would interact, as their actions were establishing the very foundation of the new democracy.

In the National Assembly, Prime Minister Soares had to deal with frequent challenges from the opposition to his legislative initiatives. Each time his government stalemated with the other parties, overall power and authority shifted to the President. After two years of Socialist minority rule and general governmental instability, President Eanes became widely perceived as the savior of the democratic system from the political parties.

Throughout this period, Soares did not seek to block Eanes from intervening in parliamentary affairs. Rather, he used his considerable political skill to build confidence in the workings of the new constitutional regime during this period of economic hardship (Manuel 1996a: 25). The frequently tense – but overall functional – working relationship between the President and Prime Minister at the dawn of the new constitutional arrangement was absolutely critical for the institutionalization of new democratic norms. Their success at developing their respective constitutional roles represents the accomplishment of the first milestone.

The second milestone dealt with the removal of the military from the political equation. When the Movimento das Forças Armadas (MFA) left active politics in 1976, they sought to institutionalize their revolutionary role with the creation of a non-elected body known as the Council of Revolution, which was granted the constitutional power to veto any law passed by the legislature that it alone determined to be anti-revolutionary. The Council was composed solely of military officers, chosen by the military, which stood over the elected politicians. The Council was charged with protecting the revolution, and in particular, defending the constitutional language, which set the overall goal of the democratic regime to create a classless society. This situation was entirely undemocratic, and was eventually remedied with the 1982 Constitutional amendment abolishing the Council.

In the 1979 parliamentary elections Portuguese voters opted for the conservative Democratic Alliance platform of Francisco Sá Carneiro, the leader of the PSD, who had formed a conservative alliance with the CDS. Sá Carneiro became Prime Minister in January 1980, and immediately sought to implement reforms to liberalize the economy, and move Portugal away from socialism. However, before he could get much accomplished, Sá Carneiro died in a plane crash in 1980, and Francisco Pinto Balsemão, also from the PSD, became Prime Minister.[11]

Balsemão reached out to Mário Soares, and gained his support to amend the 1976 Constitution significantly. Soares had frequently been frustrated by President Eanes's role during the first constitutional government, and was very much in favor of enhancing the constitutional powers of the Prime Minister. In 1982, with the support of the CDS, the PSD and the PS, the National Assembly amended the Constitution by abolishing the Council of the Revolution. This amendment also limited the President's ability to veto legislation or dissolve parliament. The overall goal of creating a classless society was finally eliminated in the 1989 Constitutional revision (Manuel 1996a: 37–50, 64).

To their credit, the members of the Council of the Revolution accepted this amendment, and left politics for good (Graham 1993: 82–88). They subsequently formed themselves into an old officers' club, known as the "Association of April 25."[12] The removal of the military from the political equation, and the associated assertion of the supremacy of civilian rule, were clearly necessary steps for the creation of a genuine democracy. The 1982 Constitutional amendment was a vital step in the Europeanization of the new Portuguese political regime.

The third milestone was reached when Portugal finally joined the European Economic Community, now called the European Union, on January 1, 1986. Portugal had been a marginal player in Europe for the first six decades of the twentieth century. Of course, it was a member of the North Atlantic Treaty

Organization, given the regime's strong anti-communist stance, and the strategic importance of Lajes Air force base in the Azores. Portugal also joined the European Free Trade Association in 1959. Yet, to all intents and purposes, the country was essentially blocked from any meaningful dialog by the leading European states, given their displeasure with Portuguese authoritarianism. The European Economic Community only allowed democratic states to become members – a requirement which kept the Salazar/Caetano regime out of the European organization. Following the events of April 25, 1974, and the subsequent transition to, and consolidation of, democracy in Portugal, all of this changed, and membership in the EEC became a possibility. The new financial resources that became available after 1986 both stabilized the economy and led to the creation of a modern infrastructure. These funds represented 3.3 percent of gross domestic product (GDP) in Portugal from 1994 to 1999. Political will was clearly an essential ingredient for the establishment of democracy in Portugal. Subsequent European economic support significantly aided the successful consolidation of the new democratic regime (Manuel and Royo 2004: 1–31).

The fourth milestone involved coalition-formation and alliance-building across the ideological spectrum. This was accomplished during the 1986 Presidential election, which was the first presidential election since 1976 without an important military candidate. There were four major candidates competing in that election. A coalition of center-right forces (CDS and PSD) supported Diogo Freitas do Amaral, the founder and leader of the CDS. Amaral pledged a return to conservative and reformist policies, and essentially to roll back the progressive policies adopted under the Socialist regimes, and adopt the policies of economic liberalization inspired by Prime Minister Thatcher's economic reforms in the United Kingdom. The united right confronted a divided left: Mário Soares, former Prime Minister Maria de Lourdes Pintasilgo and Francisco Salgado Zenha, all Socialists, sought the Presidency. Of note, Zenha was viewed as an anti-Soares candidate, and enjoyed the support of both outgoing President Eanes and the Communist Party.

The first round of voting took place on February 6, 1986, and produced a stunning result: Freitas do Amaral came within three points of an outright victory, with 47 percent of the total votes cast. Soares came in a distant second (25 percent), followed by Zenha (21 percent) and Pintasilgo (7 percent). Portugal uses a two-ballot procedure for its presidential election, which means that if no candidate wins over 50 percent of the vote on the first ballot, a second ballot is held between the two most popular candidates. In the run-off election on February 16, 1986, Soares emerged victorious with 51 percent of the vote. (Manuel 1996a: 60–64). A united coalition of left-wing forces barely defeated the united coalition of right-wing forces. The slight margin of victory has been partially credited to a belief among voters that Soares' connections could help Portugal deepen its relationship with Europe and the wider world. In this regard, the International Socialist Movement afforded the Socialist Party a strategic advantage in the elections. Mário Soares had well known friendships with many European Socialist leaders, including Harold Wilson of the United Kingdom,

Olof Palme of Sweden, François Mitterrand of France and Willy Brandt of Germany. The Socialist Party argued that these connections would help bring Portugal back into a European framework.

The 1986 Portuguese election also fits into a larger European dynamic. The 2002 French Presidential elections is a case in point. Like Portugal, France also uses a two-ballot electoral system. Among the sixteen political parties presenting presidential candidates in 2002, the two candidates expected to face off in the second round of voting were incumbent President Jacques Chirac of the conservative Rally for the Republic party, and his erstwhile rival, Socialist Prime Minister Lionel Jospin. As expected, Chirac did obtain the most votes in the first round of voting, with 19.88 percent of the vote. However, Jospin, with 16.18 percent, finished just behind the far right-wing candidate, Jean-Marie Le Pen of the National Front Party, who received 16.86 percent of the ballots.

The surprising electoral strength of Le Pen stunned even the most seasoned political observers. Indeed, his third-place finish behind Le Pen humiliated socialist Lionel Jospin, who immediately decided to resign from politics, stating, "I assume full responsibility for this defeat and I will consequently retire from politics after the end of the presidential elections."[13]

In 2002, Jacques Chirac faced Jean-Marie Le Pen in the second round of voting. Running on a law-and-order platform, Le Pen tapped into the fears and anxieties of a significant percentage of the French electorate. Among his promises, Le Pen sought to curb immigration into France, place a ban on the building of mosques, and build more prisons. The prospects of an elected French government closing its borders to the outside world, rounding up thousands of immigrants, and curtailing the free expression of religion, all in the name of law and order, disturbed lovers of democracy everywhere. Many French citizens wondered how they could ever adopt such xenophobic policies in the land that offered the world the universalistic and democratic principles of *liberté, égalité, fraternité* during their revolution of 1789.

This presidential election did indeed make history: for the first time in modern French politics, communist, socialist and other leftists joined the Gaullists and others on the right in an anti-National Front alliance. Many simply voted against Le Pen, and found Chirac acceptable because his policies functioned within the French democratic tradition of universal rights. Some left-wing voters actually wore clothes-pegs on their noses in the voting booth as a protest against the "stench" of having to choose, in their view, a lesser evil. Arguably, at the end of the day, the good sense of the majority acted as a check to the fears of the minority: the broad-based electoral coalition enabled Chirac to win re-election by an impressive margin (82.21 percent compared with 17.79 percent). In his victory speech, the President reaffirmed France's commitment to its democratic and universalistic principles:

> We have lived through a time of grave concern for the nation, but tonight, in a massive surge, France has reaffirmed its attachment to the values of the republic. I hail France, true to itself, true to its lofty ideals, true to its universal and humanist mission.[14]

Combined, the 1986 Portuguese Presidential Elections and the 2002 French Presidential elections offer us a revealing window into the perils and possibilities of a political system predicated on the rule by the people. In order for the system to work sometimes, individuals and groups with very different ideological views must cooperate. Coalition-formation among competing ideological factions for a greater goal is an essential milestone in the consolidation of democracy in any country, especially those functioning under the d'Hondt method of allocating parliamentary seats.

The fifth milestone involves the peaceful alternation of power among competing political parties. The new Portuguese democracy has performed well in this area. The office of the presidency has provided both stability and accountability since 1976. There have been four different presidents from three different parties elected to office in the past thirty-four years; namely President Ramalho Eanes (1976–1985) of the PRD; President Mário Soares (1986–1996) of the PS; President Jorge Sampaio (1996–2006) of the PS; and President Aníbal Cavaco Silva, of the PSD, who was elected in 2006 and remains in office at the time of writing (2012).

There has been similar success in the National Assembly, where Portugal's two leading parties – the PS and the PSD – have alternated power since 1976. In the most recent elections in 2009, Prime Minister José Sócrates and his Socialist Party garnished 36.6 percent of the vote, down from 45 percent in the previous elections in 2005, giving the party ninety-six seats in the 230-seat parliament, from their previous total of 121 seats. Under the leadership of Manuela Ferreira Leite, the PSD won seventy-eight legislative seats in 2009, up from seventy-five seats in 2005, with 29.1 percent of the vote. Smaller parties at both ends of the ideological spectrum have also won some electoral support, and parliamentary seats as well. In 2011, the PSD reclaimed a majority in the National Assembly. Pedro Passos Coelho led the PSD to victory over the incumbent Prime Minister José Sócrates and the Socialist Party, with 108 seats and 38.7 percent of the vote. To form a governing majority, the PSD joined forces with the People's Party, led by Paulo Portas, who had won twenty-four legislative seats with 11.7 percent of the 2011 vote. President Aníbal Cavaco Silva, also a member of the PSD, was also elected to a second term in 2011.[15]

These five accomplished milestones have resulted in the creation of the new democratic state in Portugal. Following Joseph Schumpeter's minimalist institutional definition of democracy, we can realistically refer to the contemporary political regime in Portugal as a functioning democracy in the larger European tradition because it has both adopted and then institutionalized three foundational criteria: first, free and fair elections, in which adult citizens have been included, have been held on a regular basis since 1976; second, these elections have been open for all offices, including the highest and most powerful political roles; and third, basic civil and political rights are respected in Portugal (see Schumpeter 1943, reprinted 2008). Civil society has developed robust democratic structures in the years since 1974, and the prospects for continuing democratic governance are excellent (Hamann and Manuel 1999: 71–99).

To be sure, democracy is practiced imperfectly in Portugal as well as in most of the countries that fulfill these three criteria. Even so, Schumpeter's minimalist institutional definition captures the political essence of what a democracy does, and as such, is a useful way to understand Portuguese democracy. These criteria – which have become the standard of the West European democratic regimes – eluded Portuguese politics throughout the forty-eight year Salazar/Caetano regime, and indeed, had never been formally part of the Portuguese body politic before April 25, 1974.

Conclusion

Portuguese exceptionalism is no more. The return to Europe and the associated democratization of the Portuguese political system can be understood as a much-needed corrective to both Portuguese authoritarianism and its associated notions of lusotropicalism: that is, democracy and Europe have replaced corporatism and the Portuguese overseas empire as two of the key defining elements of contemporary Portuguese identity.[16] In the thirty-five years since the April 25, 1974 Carnation Revolution, the Portuguese political system has developed new mechanisms for debate, elections, and policy adoption. Portugal is currently completely integrated into Europe as a member of the European Union, with a democratic government and a developing economy. Whatever the merits or faults of the current democratic system in Portugal, it is certainly time to place the old adages that "Africa begins at the Pyrenees," or that "Europe ends at the Pyrenees" in the rubbish bin for good.

Notes

1 The author wishes to thank Andrew Martin of the Minda de Gunzburg Center for European Studies at Harvard University for his very useful comments to a draft version of this chapter.

2 The term "lusotropicalism" was coined by the Brazilian sociologist Gilberto Freyre. It describes the belief that the Portuguese had a singular civilizing mission in the Portuguese Empire. The Salazar regime used this theory as a justification for waging the colonial wars. For more information see Gilberto Freyre (1942).

3 A. H. de Oliveira Marques notes:

> Although no guarantees of electoral freedom were granted, and no poll control by the opposition was accepted, Delgado decided to fight to the end. Official figures gave him one-fourth of the vote (he won in several places, including a number of towns in Mozambique), but he always claimed to be the real winner.
>
> (Marques 1976: 222)

4 The Carnation Revolution (*Revolução dos Cravos*) was a largely bloodless military action, best known for a photo of a young child placing a carnation into the gun of a soldier. Some Portuguese people will still wear carnations on April 25 to celebrate the event.

5 The Eurocommunism movement in the 1970s was inspired by the writings of Italian Socialist Antonio Gramsci. This movement supported West European democratic institutions and criticized the human rights abuses of Soviet communism.

6 The November 1975 Soares–Cunhal debate is available on YouTube at www.youtube.com/watch?v=Gen8NmL5g70 and www.youtube.com/watch?v=yYbEUMyjtts&feature=related (accessed 13 March 2011).

7 In spite of regularly scheduled elections, Portugal was clearly not democratic under the Salazar/Caetano regime. For the purposes of this chapter, we will adopt Joseph Schumpeter's minimalist institutional definition: to be considered a functioning democracy, a regime must hold regularly scheduled free and fair elections, in which all adult citizens have been included; these elections must be for all political offices, including the highest; and a country must respect the basic civil and political rights of its citizens (see Schumpeter 1943, reprinted 2008). If these conditions are met, then one could safely refer to a political regime as democratic.

8 There are eighteen districts on the continent, one for the Azores, one for Madeira, one for Portuguese living in Europe and one Portuguese living elsewhere.

9 President Sampaio removed the wayward government of Pedro Santana Lopes in 2004, and called for new elections, even though Santana Lopes enjoyed an absolute majority in the National Assembly. So this power is used; but it is not a frequent occurrence.

10 Variations of this system are used in many countries, including Austria, Belgium, Finland, Portugal, and Spain.

11 The circumstances of the plane crash have led to speculation that Sá Carneiro was killed by the remaining far left-wing elements of the MFA, but nothing has even been conclusively proven.

12 Associação 25 De Abril, at http://www.25abril.org/a25abril/ (accessed October 1, 2013).

13 Available at http://news.bbc.co.uk/hi/english/world/europe/newsid_1899000/1899029.stm (accessed September 30, 2013). Also see http://news.bbc.co.uk/hi/english/world/europe/newsid_1943000/1943193.stm (accessed March 13, 2011).

14 Available at http://news.bbc.co.uk/hi/english/world/europe/newsid_1899000/1899029.stm (accessed March 13, 2011).

15 This overall pattern is similar to Spain. The Partido Socialista Obrero Español (PSOE, or the Socialist Workers Party) and the Partido Popular (or People's Party, PP) have dominated Spanish politics since the 1976 democratic transition. Prime Minister Jose Luis Rodríguez Zapatero of the PSOE was first elected in 2004, and was re-elected in 2008. The People's Party, led by Mariano Rajoy, regained a legislative majority with their victory in the 2011 elections, with 186 seats and 44.6 percent of the vote. Spanish civil society has since become accustomed to democratic procedures (see Pérez-Diaz 1993).

16 "Fátima, fado, and football" arguably remain as three other defining characteristics of what it means to be Portuguese today: *Fátima* refers to the believed apparitions of the Blessed Virgin Mary to three shepherd children at Fátima in 1917; *fado* is a Portuguese musical form characterized by sad, soulful sounds and lyrics; *football* refers to the national pastime of soccer.

Bibliography

Almond, Gabriel A. and Sidney Verba (1965) *The Civic Culture: Political Attitudes and Democracy in Five Nations, An Analytic Study*. Boston: Little, Brown and Company.

Bandeira, Antonio Rangel (1976) "The Portuguese Armed Forces Movement: Historical Antecedents, Professional Demands, Class Conflicts," *Politics and Society* 6: 1–56.

Bermeo, Nancy G. (1986) *The Revolution Within the Revolution: Workers' Control in Rural Portugal*. Princeton, NJ: Princeton University Press.

Birmingham, David (1993) *A Concise History of Portugal*. Cambridge, UK: Cambridge University Press.

Bruneau, Thomas (1974) "The Portuguese Coup: Causes and Probable Consequences," *The World Today*, July: 277–288.

Chilcote, Ronald (2010) *The Portuguese Revolution: State and Class in the Transition to Democracy.* New York: Rowman & Littlefield Publishers.

Constituição da República Portuguesa: As Três Versões Após 25 de Abril 1989/1982/1976 (1990) Lisbon: Porto Editora.

Corkill, David (1993) "The Political System and the Consolidation of Democracy in Portugal," *Parliamentary Affairs*, October: 517–532.

Costa Pinto, António (2003) *Contemporary Portugal: Politics, Society, and Culture*. New York: East European Monographs.

Figueiredo, Antonio de (1976) *Portugal: Fifty Years of Dictatorship.* New York: Holmes and Meier Publishers.

Freyre, Gilberto (1942) *O Mundo que o Português Criou*. Rio de Janeiro: Livraria José Olympio Editoria.

Gallagher, Thomas (1983) *Portugal: A Twentieth Century Interpretation.* Manchester: University of Manchester Press.

Georgel, Jacques (1985) *O Salazarismo.* Lisbon: Publicações Dom Quixote.

Gildea, Robert (1994) *The Past in French History.* New Haven, CT: Yale University Press.

Graham, Lawrence S (1993) *The Portuguese Military and the State.* Boulder, CO: Westview.

Hamann, Kerstin and Paul Christopher Manuel (1999) "Revisiting Portuguese Civil Society," *South European Society and Politics* 4 (2), Summer, 71–99.

Huntington, Samuel (1993) *The Third Wave: Democratization in the Late Twentieth Century.* Oklahoma, OK: University of Oklahoma Press.

Kay, Hugo (1970) *Salazar and Modern Portugal.* London: Eyre and Spottiswoode.

Kayman, Martin (1970) *Revolution and Counterrevolution in Portugal.* London: Merlin Press.

Linz, Juan J (1977) "Spain and Portugal: Critical Choices." In David S. Landes (ed.) (1977) *Critical Choices for Americans: Western Europe.* Lexington, MA: Lexington Books, 237–296.

Manuel, Paul Christopher (1995) *Uncertain Outcome: The Politics of the Portuguese Transition to Democracy.* Landover, MD: University Press of America, 1995.

Manuel, Paul Christopher (1996a) *The Challenges of Democratic Consolidation in Portugal: Political, Economic and Military Issues, 1976–1991.* Westport, CT: Praeger Press.

Manuel, Paul Christopher (1996b) "Regime Change, Elite Players and Foreign Policy in Portugal, 1960–1991," *Perspectives on Political Science*, 25 (2), Spring, 69–73.

Manuel, Paul Christopher (2002) "Religion and Politics in Iberia: Clericalism, Anticlericalism and Democratization in Portugal and Spain." In Clyde Wilcox and Ted Jelen (eds) (2002) *The One, the Few and the Many: Religion and Politics in Comparative Perspective*. Cambridge, UK: Cambridge University Press, 71–96.

Manuel, Paul Christopher and Anne Marie Cammisa (1998) *Checks and Balances? How a Parliamentary System Could Change American Politics*. Boulder, CO: Westview Press.

Manuel, Paul Christopher and Sebastián Royo (2004). "Reconsiderando as relações económicas e a cidadania política na nova ibéria da nova europa: algumas lições do 15 anniversário da adesão de Portugal e Espanha à União Europeia." In Sebastián Royo (ed.) *Portugal, Espanha e a Integração Europeia: Um Balanço*. Lisbon: Instituto De Ciências Sociais, Universidade de Lisboa, 1–31.

Marques, A.H. de Oliveira (1976) *History of Portugal.* Second Edition. New York: Columbia University Press.

Martins, Oliveira (1969) *A History of Iberian Civilization.* New York: Cooper Square Publishers.

Maxwell, Kenneth (1997) *The Making of Portuguese Democracy.* Cambridge, UK: Cambridge University Press.

Opello, Walter C. Jr (1991) *Portugal: From Monarchy to Pluralist Democracy.* Boulder, CO: Westview Press.

Payne, Stanley G. (1976) *A History of Spain and Portugal*, 2 volumes. Madison, WI: University of Wisconsin Press.

Pérez-Diaz, Víctor (1993) *The Return of Civil Society: The Emergence of Democratic Spain.* Cambridge, MA: Harvard University Press.

Robinson, Richard (1979) *Contemporary Portugal: A History.* London: Allen and Unwin.

Royo, Sebastián and Paul Christopher Manuel (eds) (2003) *Spain and Portugal in the European Union: The First 15 Years.* London: Frank Cass Publishing House.

Sartre, Jean-Paul, Pierre Victor and Philippe Gavi (1975). "A Revolucão Portuguesa," *Vida Mundial*, 854, 27 March: 32–34.

Schumpeter, Joseph (2008) *Capitalism, Socialism and Democracy.* New York: Harper Perennial Modern Classics. First printing in 1943.

Soares, Mário and Dominique Pouchin (1976) *Portugal: Quelle Revolution? Entretiens avec Dominique Pouchin.* Paris: Caleman Levy.

Wheeler, Douglas (1978) *Republican Portugal, A Political History.* Madison, WI: University of Wisconsin Press.

2 Portugal and European integration (1974–2010)[1]

Nuno Severiano Teixeira

1 Introduction

Two political factors conditioned the integration of Portugal into the process of European unification between 1945 and 1974: the dictatorial nature of Salazar's regime and its tenacious resistance to decolonization.[2] It was only following the institutionalization of democracy, as well as the process of decolonization, during 1974–75, that the first serious steps were taken to follow a strategy of integrating Portugal into what was then the European Economic Community (EEC).

Portugal did not experience the same levels of international isolation as neighbouring Spain following the Second World War. Its status as a founding member of the North Atlantic Treaty Orgnanization (NATO), participation in other international organizations, such as the Organization for European Economic Co-operation (OEEC) and the European Payments Union (EPU), as well as incoming funds from the Marshall Plan – albeit on a relatively small scale – are all examples of the country's international acceptance.

Excluded from and mistrustful of the Treaty of Rome, which paved the way for the EEC, and following positions adopted by the United Kingdom, Portugal's membership of the European Free Trade Association (EFTA) came across as an important economic aim for the dictatorship throughout the 1960s.[3] Negotiated on terms favourable to Portugal, which saw the majority of its economic activities largely protected, the EFTA agreement laid the seeds of the 1960s' economic growth and a significant increase in commercial relations with Europe. It also boosted the emergence of interest groups less involved with the colonies. However, the development of a pro-European outlook was essentially a consequence of the decolonization process and the institutionalization of democracy.

Following a complex transition process, the integration of Portugal into the EEC became a strategic objective, with simultaneous political and economic overtones. Democratic consolidation and Portugal's integration in the European economic space were to become inseparable.

2 Democracy and European integration (1974–86)

The 25 April military coup in 1974 paved the way for the institutionalization of Portuguese democracy. Portugal's transition occurred at the height of the Cold War, at a time when there were few international pressures for democratization. The rupture provoked by the Portuguese military coup accentuated the crisis of the state, fuelled by the simultaneous process of democratization and decolonization of the last significant European colonial empire.[4] Powerful tensions, which incorporated revolutionary elements, were concentrated in the first two years of Portugal's democracy. During 1974–75, Portugal also experienced a high level of foreign intervention, ranging from diplomatic pressure to the creation of political parties and social organizations (such as the trade unions and interest groups), as well as the anti-left strategies of the so-called 1975 'hot summer'. Portugal was a constant topic of discussion at international fora, from NATO and the EEC, to the institutions of the Soviet Bloc.

The military coup took the international community, particularly the United States, by surprise.[5] Faced with intense social and political mobilization from the left, and concerned with the flight of the country's capital and economic elite, the moderate parties obtained only limited success in implanting themselves and were only able to function during the crisis due to incoming financial and technical support from leading US administration figures and European party organizations, the latter often serving as guarantors to the former.

2.1 Transition to democracy and decolonization

The EEC observed Portugal's transition with discretion, although it gave ambiguous signals that, politically it clearly favoured the emergence of a pluralist democratic system, whilst simultaneously granting limited economic assistance. Soon after the first democratic elections, in 1975, the European Council announced that it was prepared to open economic and financial negotiations with Portugal, though stressing that, 'in accordance with its historical and political traditions, the European Community can only support a pluralist democracy'.[6]

The first significant international challenge for the new-born Portuguese democracy was to dispose of its colonial empire. The second was to open Portugal to the world and reestablish diplomatic relations with all countries, bringing an end to the international isolation enforced by the deposed regime.[7] Decolonization and the reestablishment of diplomatic relations did not, as such, constitute a new strategic direction for Portugal's foreign policy; rather, in the midst of the strenuous conflicts during the process of democratization there was another silent battle taking place, one that was concerned with the international strategic choice for the new democracy.

The transitional period was characterized by a political ideological conflict concerning the country's foreign policy goals, which translated into the practice of parallel diplomatic actions by various institutional agents – something that reflected the absence of a clear foreign policy.

Despite the conflicts, hesitations and indecision, the provisional governments, and in particular those with a preponderance of military ministers, tended to favour adopting a 'Third World' approach to foreign policy and promoted the formation of privileged relations with the country's former colonies. This was the final manifestation, albeit in a pro-socialist form, of the thesis so close to Salazar's heart – Portugal's 'African vocation'.

The consolidation of democracy, which began in 1976 with the election of the first constitutional government, can be characterized by the clarification of the choice of Portuguese foreign policy, and by the unequivocal positioning of Portugal in the world as a Western country, albeit simultaneously Atlanticist and European. These two visions were to become the basic strategic foreign policy vectors for the new democracy. The Atlanticist outlook was predicated on the permanence of historical characteristics of Portuguese foreign policy, and played an important role in directing Portugal externally, as well as stabilizing it domestically. The establishment of fruitful bilateral relations with the United States and the strengthening of its multilateral participation within NATO were the clearest expressions of the new democracy's international position.

Once having overcome the Third World temptations of the revolutionary period, Portugal unreservedly adopted the 'European option' from 1976 onwards. It should be noted this choice was a strategic decision and a political project, rather than the merely pragmatic and economic stance it had been under the authoritarian regime.

2.2 Democratic consolidation, European option and accession to the EEC

Contacts between Lisbon and the European institutions were initiated as early as 1974. The European Commission granted Portugal economic assistance while the European Council made its political position clear: it was ready to begin negotiations, on the condition that a pluralist democracy was established. Nevertheless, the country's economic situation, the political instability and continuing uncertainty regarding the destiny of the democratic regime during the transitional period, ruled out any advance on the European front.

The first constitutional government, led by Mário Soares, adopted the 'European option'. The first step in this process occurred in August 1976, when the Portuguese government successfully applied for membership of the Council of Europe. Once a member of this organization, which consolidated the international community's recognition of the new democratic regime, Lisbon began to outline its next decisive step; its membership application to the EEC.

Following a series of successful negotiations in a number of European capitals, between September 1976 and February 1977, the government made its formal application for EEC membership in March 1977. One month later, the European Council accepted the Portuguese application and initiated the formal process laid out in the various treaties, including the mandatory consultation of the European Commission. In May 1978, the Commission presented a favourable report, clearing the way for the formal negotiations to begin in Luxembourg the following October.[8] With the formal application made, and accession negotiations under way, the hesitations and polemics over the nature of Portugal's integration were finally superseded, placing Portugal firmly on the European path.

The government was motivated by, and based its decision to follow this strategic option upon, two main objectives. First, EEC membership would consolidate Portuguese democracy, and second, EEC assistance would guarantee the modernization of the country and its economic development. Several Portuguese economists remained fearful, with the majority expressing grave reservations regarding the impact that EEC membership would have on some sectors of the Portuguese economy.[9]

A complex series of negotiations over seven years ensued after Portugal's application for membership. An earlier step had been taken in September 1976, prior to the country's formal application, with the revision of the 1972 EEC trade agreement through the conclusion of the Additional and Financial Protocols, which Portugal interpreted as representing a form of pre-membership agreement.[10] Despite these prior agreements, formal negotiations on Portugal's membership lasted from October 1978 until June 1985.[11]

There were two important domestic factors that explain why the accession negotiations for such a small country, with a relatively weak economy, were so complex and drawn out. First, Portugal's economic situation, immediately prior to the transition and, more importantly, the economic measures taken during the revolutionary period (in particular, the nationalization of important economic sectors) raised eyebrows. Second, continuous government instability as well the nature of its political and constitutional regime caused concern. After 1976, the democratic regime was undeniably pluralist, and was generally considered as such. However, the 1976 constitution was a product of the revolutionary period, and embedded within it was the Council of the Revolution. It was a democracy, but a democracy under the tutelage of an undemocratic military institution. These factors weighed heavily in the negotiations, and delayed their conclusion.

During the early 1980s, Portuguese democracy overcame all of these objections. The constitution was revised in 1982 in order to abolish the Council of the Revolution and the National Defence Law, and the armed forces finally accepted their subordination to the civilian political authorities. By 1983, democracy in Portugal had been consolidated, thereby clearing the national obstacles preventing the successful conclusion of the entry negotiations.

One external hurdle remained. In the framework of Europe's southern enlargement, the EEC was also conducting accession negotiations with neighbouring Spain, with a much larger economy than that of Portugal, which did not share its history of close relations with European economic institutions. Portugal's diplomatic strategy was to keep its entry negotiations separate from Spain, thus hoping to secure a faster track to EEC accession, as well as the important status of a member state prior to Spain's entry. This tactic was not successful. In fact, as the Community's policy was to negotiate with both Iberian nations simultaneously, it resulted in Portugal's accession being delayed a further two years, until the dossiers on Spain had been concluded.

The accession process culminated with the signing of the Treaty of Accession by the new government, led by Mário Soares, in June 1985. Portugal became a full member of the EEC on 1 January 1986.

3 Europeanization of Portugal (1986–2010)

Portugal's membership of the EEC paved the way for a period of Europeanization of Portuguese society, registering deep changes in both domestic and foreign policy. Such alterations followed significant modifications in the deepening and enlargement process of European integration. Even since the democratic Constitution of 1976, Portugal has experienced a wide political consensus in the foreign policy domain, namely regarding the process of European integration. Except for certain periods of stronger ideological cleavage, there has always been an agreement on this matter among the main Portuguese political parties – the Socialist Party (PS), centre-left, the Social-Democratic Party (PSD), centre-right, and the right-wing Democratic and Social Centre (CDS). Such an agreement is based upon the 'perception of Portugal as a nation simultaneously Atlantic and European', with a reinforcement of the latter dimension over recent decades.[12]

Faithful to its Atlantic roots, Portugal's foreign policy from 1986 reinforced its European vector. The 'European option' played a fundamental role in the consolidation of democracy and in the modernization process of the country. Therefore, it can be said democratization and modernization were the main domestic echoes of Portugal's integration process in Europe over the last quarter of the twentieth century.

Generally speaking, Portugal supported the 1986 Single European Act, the 1992 Maastricht Treaty, and the following treaties deepening the political and economic European integration process. The various governments viewed the Portuguese presence in the European Union as a guarantee of the Commission and Council support for the Portuguese economic and structural development plans, despite realizing that such alterations implied changes at the level of its domestic and foreign policy.[13] This process, however, was not linear. Three core moments highlight Portugal's participation in the European integration process after 1986. First, between 1986 and 1992, as Portugal tried to adjust to the European challenges, policy was characterized by a position of pragmatism and moderation towards the European integration process. Second, from 1992 to 2000, Portugal's participation in the European project reached its peak, with the Portuguese governments placing the country at the forefront of the process of European integration. Finally, from 2000 onwards, there was a return to a more pragmatic position, with Portugal using the tools for European integration to maximize its external role, thus balancing the costs and benefits of the country's presence at the heart of the European Union.

3.1 Prudence and pragmatism: the first years of membership

Portugal joined the EEC when the process of European integration was undergoing a deepening phase. In 1986, the EEC itself was witnessing a period of institutional relaunch, engendered by the signature of the Single European Act, the first revision of the Treaty of Rome in thirty years. Such alterations received a cautious welcome in Portugal, as the political intensification determined by the Single Act raised serious doubts among the political elite about Portugal's capability to meet the new and reinforced demands. The opening of the national economy, traditionally behind when compared to the most Western European partners, implied that Portugal's accession to the EEC would have to be followed by compensatory economic measures.[14] Thus, in terms of political goals, the Portuguese government, led from the end of 1985 by Aníbal Cavaco Silva, followed a clear strategy focused on the credibility of full Portuguese membership, while, at the same time, it tried to profit from economic and social advantages which arose from EEC participation.[15]

Despite the moderation and the pragmatism of the Portuguese position, the first stage of the participation in the EEC was nevertheless marked by one of the base principles of the Single Act. The decision to create a Single Market was intimately connected to the need to promote economic and social cohesion within the communities. As a consequence, southern European countries and Ireland received, with the approval of the Delors I Package (1988), considerable financial compensation to face the consequences of increased liberalization of the European market. This was decisive for Portugal. The Lisbon government was one of the biggest beneficiaries of the implementation of such measures, with direct consequences for the structural transformations carried out in Portugal, as well as the change of opinion in the public perception of Europe and the due implications of the country's place in European integration. If in the early years of membership the dominant perception was one of concern regarding the country's capability of meeting the challenges of joining the EEC, the massive financial transfers rendered clear and visible the advantages of that integration, hence radically changing Portugal's perception of Europe.[16]

From the political perspective, EEC integration forced the Portuguese government to rethink its alignment within intra-European relations. In the first years, Portuguese prudence and the pragmatic posture of the governments under Cavaco Silva made Portugal stick to the Atlantic position, aligning with former EFTA partners. Following a traditional line of its foreign policy, as far as the European integration process was concerned, Portugal remained aligned with the United Kingdom, perceiving Margaret Thatcher's government as a safe and prudent ally to face the growing supranational trends within Europe.

In the autumn of 1989, when the Berlin Wall fell and the communist regimes in central and Eastern Europe collapsed, this traditional line of Portuguese foreign policy was still predominant. However, after the Soviet implosion, German reunification, European enlargement and the deepening of the EEC, decided in Maastricht, Lisbon evolved from a strict Atlantic alignment to a more flexible Euro-Atlantic position. The new Portuguese situation came across during the first part of 1992, when Portugal took on, for the first time, the Presidency of the European Union. At the time, the European question was faced as a new national purpose, with the country truly committed to a new institutional form of the European project: Political Union.[17]

3.2 Euro-enthusiasm: a decade of convergence

The 1992 the Portuguese presidency of the European Union undoubtedly marked the change to a new stage of Portugal's integration process in Europe. The Portuguese success, namely highlighted in the agreement to reform the Common Agricultural Policy, definitely contributed to movement away from the conservative positions of the early years of Cavaco Silva's governments, initiating a period of enthusiasm for Portuguese participation in the European integration project. While the European Union entered a new stage after the signature of the Maastricht Treaty, Portugal revealed itself as a 'good student' of the European Communities, truly committed to the European process.[18]

It left behind the conservative, traditionally Atlanticist and, until then, dominant trend in strategic and diplomatic culture, which saw the Atlantic link and the exceptional relationship with the United States and other Portuguese-speaking countries as the Portuguese foreign priority. With the end of the Cold War, Portugal's international position evolved into a Euro–Atlantic one, reflecting the Europeanization process of Portuguese strategic orientation. Such a situation was clearly visible in 1995, and was reinforced until the end of the decade. The participation, throughout the 1990s, in peace missions such as in the Balkans, clearly reflects the change in traditional Portuguese foreign policy. It equates the full assumption of the status of a European country and the clearest stage of Europeanization, not just for foreign policy, but also for Portugal's defence policy, as, for the first time since 1914–18, Portuguese armed forces took part in military operations on the European continent.[19]

Clearly taking on a Europeanist tone, traditional to the political line of the party since 1976, the socialist government led by António Guterres, saw the Monetary Union Project as the main Portuguese goal regarding European integration.[20] The Lisbon government took on the goal of placing Portugal at the lead of the integration process, as the only way to maintain a peripheral country right at the centre of the decision-making process made by the Union.[21] Such a strategy implied the immediate Europeanization of Portuguese public policies, in all fields, reflected in the prompt adoption of legislative changes required by the European Union's treaties, namely the Amsterdam Treaty of 1997. In this sense, one could observe the incorporation of the political values of the European Union at all levels of Portuguese policy. The peak of such a strategy was reached in 1998. Despite the atavistic financial indiscipline of the countries from Southern Europe, Portugal met all the conditions and was accepted into the restricted group of European states admitted to Single European Currency, the Euro. Portuguese diplomacy also reached another of its flagship goals (of its democratic regime) with the resolution of the East Timor issue. After the occupation of the former Portuguese territory by Indonesia in 1975, the United Nations Security Council's condemnation was not enough to reverse the occupation. Throughout the 1990s, a growing awareness within the international community raised the question of East Timor, as a consequence of the changes in the international system and due to the persistence of Portuguese diplomacy. The sense of belonging to the European Union was a determining factor, as it allowed Lisbon to increase its international role, thus enabling East Timor's population to exert its right to self-determination by means of a political transition process regulated by the UN.[22]

Portugal's second presidency of the EU, in the first half of 2000, characterized the entrance of the country into the new millennium, with the European goal setting the priority of its national interests. During the presidency, unlike 1992, the Portuguese government reflected the image of a perfectly integrated country within the European project, able to mobilize its peers for the development and improvement of the Union. In the European Council of March 2000, the Portuguese presidency managed to secure approval of the Lisbon Strategy, a declaration of principles seeking to place the European Union economically in the lead worldwide within a decade. Through the promotion of social, educational and environmental policies, the Lisbon Strategy strove to turn the European economic area into a more competitive one, better prepared for the challenges of globalization.

Although enunciating important goals for the affirmation of Europe in the twenty-first century, the aims approved in Lisbon were not entirely achieved, partly because the implementation method permitted a move away from traditional communitarian integration formulae, by introducing non-binding obligations. In fact, in 2000, most European countries were far more interested in improving the EU's institutional system, in order to adapt Brussels for the eastern enlargement. The Intergovernmental Conference in Nice, in 2000, destined to solve the questions left open by the Amsterdam Treaty, ended up by also setting the beginning of the pressure, led by the big member states, in order to have their weight acknowledged and increased in the European institutions' decision-making process. Culminating in this period of Europeanist euphoria, the Nice IGC enabled Portugal to perform a leadership role among the small and medium European states while defending their interests, *vis-à-vis* the wishes of the big powers to reinforce their own importance in the voting process. This role was paramount in the negotiations for institutional reform, arguably one of the most active moments of Portugal's participation within the European integration process.[23]

At the external level, the Portuguese Presidency aimed at reinforcing the EU's international presence, benefiting from Portugal's privileged relations with regional areas traditionally related to its national interest. On one hand, there was the approval of the Mediterranean common strategy whereas on the other hand, the launch of the EU–India strategy followed the Lisbon Summit. Finally, regarding Africa, the presidency's external priority, two main goals were achieved: the replacement of the former Lomé Convention by the Cotonou partnership agreement in the framework of the relations between EU and ACP (African, Carribean and Pacific) countries; and the organization of the first ever EU–Africa Summit, which took place in Cairo.

3.3 Return to pragmatism: a decade of divergence

The conclusions reached in the Nice Treaty, in 2001, coupled with eastern enlargement, signalled the beginning of a decline in Portuguese enthusiasm for the European integration process. At this point, internal and external factors contributed to a more realistic perception by the Portuguese of their membership to the European Union. From 2001, Portugal returned to a phase of internal political instability, with the resignation of Prime Minister António Guterres and the call for early elections. The country's total commitment to the presidency of the European Union and the leadership of the small and medium countries in the Nice Treaty negotiating process contributed to the socialist government's neglect of the internal political front. Parallel to this, political instability was accompanied by an aggravated economic and financial situation nationwide, partly due to a decrease in internal consumption and a loss of export competitiveness.[24]

In the international arena, major political and strategic changes occurred after 11 September 2001, namely the transatlantic crisis and the European division caused by the 2003 Anglo–American intervention in Iraq. For Portugal, however, it was the EU's eastern enlargement to former countries of the Soviet Bloc that mostly affected the Portuguese perception of the European integration process. Nevertheless, at this time, there were no significant alterations, either in the course of these EU trends, or in the Portuguese Government's European policies, led by Prime Minister Barroso's social democrat cabinet, between 2002 and 2005.

From a geopolitical perspective, such a broadening contributed to moving the centre of gravitation to the east, thus accentuating Portugal's peripheral place within the European context.

From the economic perspective, the new member states were far more attractive for multinational corporations, aiming to benefit from low labour costs and qualified human resources available in central and eastern European countries. Portugal was, unquestionably, one of the countries most affected by the delocalization of companies to the East. To this situation another element was added, namely competition with the new members for European structural funds, where Portugal was clearly left behind.[25]

At this point, it should be noted that Portugal's financial constraints deriving from the Economic and Monetary Union, and its adhesion to the Euro, as well as continuing economic issues, were aggravated from 2008 onwards due to the global financial crisis. For the first decade of the twenty-first century, Portugal's GDP would diverge compared to the EU average, and even to its cohesion partners, In 1999 Portugal's GDP *per capita* ranked at 68 per cent of the EU GDP *per capita*, whereas in 2008 it amounted only to 64 per cent.

Despite these various difficulties, during the first decade of the twenty-first century, Portugal did not go back to the plain and simple scepticism characteristic of the early years of Cavaco Silva's government. With the Socialist Party returned to power in the 2005 elections, and notwithstanding the European crisis and the French and Dutch veto of the European constitution, the Portuguese attitude was governed by responsible realism. The Portuguese presidency of the European Union in 2007 exemplified Portuguese political maturity in the European integration process. This was felt both at the internal level of the Union and in its international presence. At the internal level, Prime Minister José Sócrates' government's priority was centred upon the conclusion of the political process to reform the European Union, an effort sealed with the signature of the Lisbon Treaty, 13 December 2007. At the international level, the Portuguese presidency's priorities were centred upon the reinforcement and diversification of the EU's external action, with the holding of the EU–Russia Summit, the second EU–Africa Summit and the first ever EU–Brazil Summit, which created a new strategic partnership.

Such summits contributed to the reinforcement of the global presence of the European Union, but they also favoured the Portuguese national interest by extending the strategic partnerships of the EU to traditional areas of strategic interest for Portugal, namely relations with Africa and Brazil.[26]

4 Conclusion

Portuguese participation in the European integration process brought Portugal both costs and benefits, not only from a political perspective, but also from an economic and social point of view.

From a global standpoint, Portugal's accession to the EEC was fundamental both for the internal consolidation of democracy and the external definition of a new model for playing a part in the international community. Although Portugal was already part of the post-Second World War international system, as a member of UN, NATO, OECD and EFTA, integration into the EEC cemented the Portuguese presence in the international system, thus placing the country in the restrictive club of Western democracies, as both politically stable and economically developed.

From an economic and social perspective, a deep change had occurred throughout more than two decades of Portugal's integration in the EU. The Portuguese economy underwent an accelerated modernization, with a clear impact at the productive structure level, as well as external commerce and social cohesion. Portugal's accession to the EEC took place exactly at the moment when the Communities tried to reinforce the deepening of the European integration, namely with the signature of the Single European Act. In this sense, through structural funds and cohesion policies, the Portuguese economy and society began a process of structural reform, with the goal of macroeconomic stability and an increasingly competitive productive system, which became one of the key consequences of such accession. With all the difficulties and limitations, Portuguese participation in the European integration process was translated, at an economic and social level, during the first decade, by Portugal's convergence with its European partners,[27] and during the second decade and to date (2012), by its divergence from them.[28]

Politically speaking, there was a clear process of Europeanization of both Portuguese institutions and public policies. The transposition of European legislation implied profound changes to adjust public institutions and policies to the mode of functioning of the EU and its decision-making processes.

During the course of this Europeanization process, the costs of sovereignty transfer in the various sectors affected seem to have been widely compensated by the economic benefits achieved. Reflecting this, Portuguese public support for European integration and the country's participation in the European project was evident.[29]

As far as Portugal's foreign policy is concerned, European integration had a tremendous impact, even determining the emergence of a new model for the country's international role. First, it changed the contradicting tension between Europe and the Atlantic. Portugal evolved from a contradicting logic into the logic of complementarity. For Portuguese foreign policy, the Atlantic dimension might mean added value on the Atlantic board and in its post-colonial relations. Second, as it had to be, although the Europe/Atlantic equation was kept, the priorities were inverted. Traditionally Portugal sustained the Atlantic and colonial priority and, whenever necessary, it looked for European compensatory factors. Today, Portugal's priority is Europe, the European Union, and to achieve added value at an international level, it seeks to capitalize on its Atlantic position and its post-colonial relations.

Notes

1 Part of this chapter, regarding the period 1986–2010, was written in collaboration with Daniel Marcos (IPRI-UNL).
2 Teixeira, 1998; Pinto, 2000.
3 Andresen-Leitão, 2001.
4 Maxwell, 1997.
5 Pero, 2001.
6 See Magone, 1997a.
7 MacDonald, 1993; Ferreira, 1993a; Gama, 1994–95.
8 Ferreira, 1995.
9 Cravinho, 1983. See also Tovias, 1990.
10 Ferreira, 1995, p. 28.
11 Alvares, P. and Fernandes, C.R. (eds), 1980.
12 Sebastián Royo (ed.), 2005.
13 Ibid.
14 Pedro Lains, 2007.
15 Martins, 2007.
16 António Goucha Soares, 2007, p. 69.
17 Carlos Gaspar, 2000.
18 Soares, 2007, p. 72.
19 Teixeira, 2006, pp. 71–89.
20 Marina Costa Lobo, 2005, pp. 150–151.
21 Gaspar, 2000.
22 José Júlio Pereira Gomes, 2010.
23 Soares, 2007, p. 77.
24 Soares, 2007, pp. 82–83.
25 Soares, 2007, p. 83.
26 Laura Ferreira-Pereira, 2008.
27 Royo, 2005.
28 Soares, 2011.
29 Lobo, 2005.

Bibliography

Alípio, E.S., 'O processo negocial de adesão de Portugal à EFTA, 1956–1960', Unpublished Master's dissertation. Lisbon: Faculdade de Ciências Sociais e Humanas Universidade Nova de Lisboa, 2001.

Alvares, P. and Fernandes, C.R. (eds), *Portugal e o Mercado Comum, vol. 1: da EFTA aos Acordos de 1972*. Lisbon: Pórtico, 1980.

Andresen-Leitão, N. 'Portugal's European integration policy, 1947–1972', *Journal of European Integration History*, 7 (1), 2001, pp. 25–35.

Castilho, J.T., *A ideia da Europa no Marcelismo 1968–1974*. Oporto: Afrontamento, 2000.

Cravinho, J., 'Characteristics and motives for entry', in Sampedro, J.L. and Payno, J.A. (eds), *The Enlargement of the European Community: case studies of Greece, Portugal and Spain*. London: Macmillan, 1983, pp. 131–148.

Ferreira, J.M., 'Political costs and benefits for Portugal arising from membership of the European Community', in J. da S. Lopes (ed.), *Portugal and EC membership evaluated*. London: Pinter, 1993a.

Ferreira, J.M., 'Características históricas da política externa portuguesa entre 1890 e a entrada na ONU', *Política Internacional*, 6, 1993b, pp. 113–156.

Ferreira, J.M., 'Os regimes políticos em Portugal e a organização internacional da Europa', *Política Internacional*, 11, 1995: 5–39.

Ferreira-Pereira, Laura, 'Portugal e a Presidência da União Europeia (1992–2007)', *Relações Internacionais*, 20, 2008, pp. 131–143.

Gama, J. 'A adesão de Portugal às Comunidades Europeias', *Política Internacional*, 10, 1994–95: 5–19.

Gaspar, Carlos 'Portugal e o alargamento da UE', *Análise Social*, XXXV (154–155), 2000: 327–372.

Gomes, José Júlio Pereira, 'A Internacionalização da Questão de Timor', *Relações Internacionais*, 25, 2010: 67–89.

Griffiths, R.T. and Lie, B., 'Portugal e a EFTA,1959–1973', in *Portugal e Europa: 50 anos de integração*. Lisbon: Centro de Informação Jacques Delors, 1996, pp. 185–206.

Lains, Pedro 'Os caminhos da integração: da autarcia à Europa do Euro', in Marina Costa Lobo and Pedro Laíns (eds), *Em nome da Europa. Portugal em mudança (1986–2006)*, 14–40, Cascais: Princípia, 2007, pp. 14–40.

Lobo, Marina Costa 'A atitude dos portugueses perante a UE: perspectivas sociais e políticas', in Sebastián Royo (ed.), *Portugal, Espanha e a Integração Europeia. Um balanço*, 139–160. Lisbon: Imprensa de Ciências Sociais, 2005, pp. 150–151, 158–159.

Louçã, A., *Hitler e Salazar: comércio em tempos de guerra, 1940–44*. Lisbon: Terramar, 2000.

MacDonald, S., *European Destiny, Atlantic Transformations: Portuguese foreign policy under the Second Republic*, New Brunswick: Transaction Publishers, 1993.

Magalhães, J.C. 'Os movimentos de integração europeia no pós guerra e a participação portuguesa nesses movimentos', in R.T. Guerra, A. de S. Freire and J.C. Magalhães (eds), *Os movimentos de cooperação e integração europeia no pós guerra e a participação de Portugal*. Lisbon: Instituto Nacional de Administração, 1981, p. 45.

Magalhães, J.C., *Portugal na Europa o caminho certo*. Lisbon: Bertrand, 1997.

Magone, J., 'A integração europeia e a construção da democracia portuguesa', in Pinto, A.C. and Teixeira, N.S. (eds), *Penélope: Portugal e a unificação europeia*, 18, 1997a, pp. 51–76.

Magone, J., *European Portugal: The Difficult Road to Sustainable Democracy*. London: Macmillan, 1997b.

Martins, Vítor 'Os Primeiros Anos', in Nicolau Andresen Leitão (ed.) *20 Anos de Integração Europeia (1986–2006). O Testemunho Português*. Lisbon: Edições Cosmos, 2007.

Maxwell, K., *The Making of Portuguese Democracy*. Cambridge: Cambridge University Press, 1997.

Mendes, P.E., 'Portugal e a Europa: Factores de Afastamento e Aproximação da Política Externa Portuguesa', MA Thesis, ISCTE, 2001.

Pero, M. del, 'Kissinger e la politica estera americana nel Mediterraneo: il caso portoghese', *Studi Storici*, 4, 2001: 973–988.

Pereira, Laura Ferreira 'Portugal e a Presidência da União Europeia (1992–2007)', *Relações Internacionais*, 20, 2008: 131–143.

Pinto, A.C., *O fim do Império português: a cena internacional, a guerra colonial e a descolonização, 1961–1975*. Lisbon: Horizonte, 2000.

Royo, Sebastián, 'O alargamento de 2004: lições ibéricas para a Europa pós-comunista', in *Portugal, Espanha e a Integração Europeia. Um Balanço*, 369–413. Lisbon: Imprensa de Ciências Sociais, 2005.

Royo, Sebastián (ed.), *Portugal, Espanha e a Integração Europeia. Um balanço*. Lisbon: Imprensa de Ciências Sociais, 2005, p. 36.

Santos, E., 'Portugal e a adesão à EFTA: primeiro passo para o fim da autarcia', *História*, July–August, 1998: 62–74.

Soares, António Goucha 'Portugal e a Adesão às Comunidades Europeias: 20 anos de integração europeia', in Rafael Garcia Perez and Luís Lobo-Fernandes (eds), *España e Portugal: veinte años de integración europea*, 63–87. Salamanca: Tórculo Edicións, 2007, pp. 69, 72, 77, 82–83.

Soares, António Goucha, 'A Política Europea de Portugal', in Teresa Ferreira Rodrigues and Rafael Gárcia Pérez (eds), *Portugal e Espanha. Crise e convergência na União Europeia*, 195–219, Lisbon, Tribuna, 2011, p. 210.

Teixeira, Nuno Severiano 'A Democracia, a Defesa e as Missões Internacionais das Forças Armadas', in Nuno Severiano Teixeira (ed.), *Os Militares e a Democracia*, 71–89. Lisbon: Edições Colibri, 2006.

Teixeira, N.S., 'Between Africa and Europe: Portuguese foreign policy, 1890–1986', in A.C. Pinto (ed.), *Modern Portugal*. Palo Alto: SPOSS, 1998, pp. 60–87.

Teixeira, N.S., 'From neutrality to alignment: Portugal in the foundation of the Atlantic Pact', *Luso-Brazilian Review*, 29 (2), 1992: 113–127.

Telo, A.J., *Portugal e a Nato*. Lisbon: Cosmos, 1996.

Telo, A.J., *A neutralidade portuguesa e o ouro Nazi*. Lisbon: Quetzal, 2000.

Tovias, A., *Foreign Economic Relations of the European Community: the impact of Spain and Portugal*. Boulder, CO and London: Lynne Rienner, 1990.

Xavier, A., *Portugal e a integração europeia*. Coimbra, Almedina, 1970.

3 The Portuguese economy

The impact of European Monetary Union membership

David Corkill

It is now a quarter of a century since Portugal signed up for membership of the European integration project. Since 1986 the country's experience with the process has been uneven, although the immediate post-accession years did bring positive economic progress as Portugal took advantage of EU funds and world market conditions to begin the modernization of its economy and make some headway in catching up with its more affluent European partners. After 2002, the process stalled and convergence went into reverse, leading to an extended period of low-to-zero economic growth. This chapter will seek to explain this worrying transformation by examining Portugal's relationship with Europe, draw up a balance sheet of Portugal's economic experiences as a member of European monetary union (EMU) and the Eurozone and assess the challenges that lie ahead if the country is to return to the path of growth, particularly in the light of the serious global economic recession since 2008.

A European future?

It is hard to overestimate the attractions that Europe held out for a country that had lived most of the twentieth century relatively isolated from its neighbours under an authoritarian regime. As long as the Salazar and Caetano dictatorships clung on to the empire, long after other European powers abandoned their overseas colonies, Portugal could not join the European mainstream. Once Portugal pulled out of its overseas commitments and the empire no longer played such a key ideological, political and economic role, the void that remained had to be filled (Royo, 2007: 689). There could only be one realistic answer to the choice between standing alone or joining the European Community (EC). In political terms, a closer relationship with Europe made practical sense in order to ensure stability and prevent serious internal divisions. Indeed, for a decade after the 1974 revolution, the political imperative took precedence over economic concerns. It was undeniable that trade patterns had been transformed during the 1960s and 1970s with Europe emerging as a far more important trading partner than the colonies or the rest of the world (Corkill, 1993: 89). Central to these developments was membership of EFTA (the European Free Trade Association) from which Portugal received particularly preferential treatment and was able to establish close trade relations with a number of its European neighbours. In one sense, the economy began to be 'Europeanized' long before the application to join the European Community was lodged in 1977 and the accession process got under way. Political leaders and public opinion concurred in giving their support for European integration. Given the evidence this was hardly surprising as initially Europe became synonymous with democratic political freedoms and then later gradually came to be associated with economic growth and prosperity. Amidst the prevailing mood of optimism the expectation was that the benefits would outweigh the costs by some considerable distance.

The boom years under Cavaco Silva

The years prior to accession and the decade that followed proved to be a golden period for the Portuguese economy. A positive economic environment included access to a large market, strong growth amongst its major trading partners and access to substantial transfers in the shape of EU funds for which Portugal was now eligible. As a result, Portugal became one of Europe's fastest growing economies with consecutive years of impressive increases in GDP accompanied by low levels of unemployment. Indeed, during the late 1980s the GDP growth rate averaged 4.4 per cent, a very strong performance in comparative international terms. Foreign investment was a key driver in this growth, attracted by the new-found stability, relatively low labour costs and the availability of capital. Multinationals regarded Portugal as an attractive export platform particularly in areas that included motor vehicle manufacture, electronics and tourism. Another factor in the growth performance was the contribution made by private consumption as household expenditure, fuelled by low interest rates, the liberalization of the financial system and greater competition, grew strongly. Domestically, it can be said that during the Cavaco Silva years (prime minister, 1985–95) the modernized banking system presided over a credit boom fuelled by consumer demand.

Instead of restraining expenditure in order to prevent overheating, government spending kept on an upward path and public sector employment expanded relatively unchecked. Together with low unemployment levels and assertive trade unions, wage rises became a feature in both the state and private sectors. Not surprisingly, inflationary pressures were ignited as more resources were channelled into the less productive and inefficient state sector. These developments impacted adversely on productivity and the ability to compete internationally. The inability to cope with burgeoning domestic demand led to a rising import bill whilst inflation eroded the competitiveness of Portuguese goods and services. Given the fierce discounting from cheap labour economies in Asia and North Africa, textile and clothing manufacturers in particular felt the pinch, leading to factory closures and redundancies. At the same time, the current account deficit had risen above 10 per cent of GDP by 2000. The lack of fiscal control ensured that in 2001 the public deficit fell foul of the SGP (Stability and Growth Pact) limit set by the European authorities at 3 per cent. In 2001, the budget deficit reached 4.1 per cent of the GDP in clear breach of the EU's SGP and under its terms Brussels initiated proceedings against Portugal. Thus, at the very moment when government intervention might have alleviated some of the worst aspects of the downturn that began in 2001, any policy based on stimulus was inappropriate. Rather than encouraging consumer demand the government was forced to focus on austerity measures and tax increases. As a result, Portugal began to suffer from its worst recession since the mid-1970s and came to be categorized as in former Finance Minister Ernani Lopes' phrase, 'an ailing economy' (*The Economist*, 5 November 2009).

Membership of the 'poor four' Cohesion Group

Portugal's poor economic performance since 2002 stands in marked contrast to Spain's remarkable success story, which enabled it to become the eighth largest economy in global terms. The contrast with the boom economies of Ireland and Spain prior to the global recession made uncomfortable reading for the Portuguese, as did its relative performance against the group of countries known as the Cohesion Group, comprising four of the poorer countries (Greece, Ireland, Portugal and Spain) who all qualified for additional structural funds from Brussels to assist in the catching up process with the advanced EU economies. Partly as a result of this funding Portugal did appear to be making some progress in this regard. There had been a false dawn when, much trumpeted at the time, Portugal overtook Greece to move off the bottom of the European averages for GDP per capita measured against the EU average in the late 1990s, only for the country to slip back again by 2006 behind not only Greece but accession newcomers Czech Republic, Malta and Slovenia as well (*The Economist*, 2007).

Portugal and the Eurozone

Portugal has taken part in all the major staging posts in the European Union economic project, including the single market, the ERM–euro and the enlargement process. Portugal signed up to the monetary union project at its inception in 1998. In January 1999, in a remarkable leap of faith, Portugal declined to adopt the stance taken by its old EFTA trading partners, the UK, Denmark and Sweden, and became a co-founder of the Eurozone, replacing the escudo with the new currency, the euro. In practice, joining the single currency brought a number of immediate advantages. Primary among these was stability in relations with its trade partners based upon membership of a major international currency zone. As a result, Portuguese business gained access to international finance and exchange rate fluctuations were eliminated. An indicator of the greater confidence engendered by Eurozone membership was the surge in external investment as Portugal abandoned its insular and introverted economic gaze. In particular, interest rates dropped significantly and both business and private consumers were able to borrow at low rates of interest and avoid the punitively high rates that had prevailed in the past. Consequently, company as well as family borrowing increased dramatically, along with debt levels. As a result imports were sucked in and the balance of payments was severely prejudiced.

What explains the problems Portugal is facing? How did Spain and other member states benefit from the funds provided by European Union membership while Portugal appears to have squandered many of the opportunities derived from involvement in a major trading and currency bloc? In seeking to find the explanation, a combination of factors must be taken into account. The most common one is that Portugal entered the EMU at an overvalued conversion rate. Some of the subsequent problems with trade and growth can be explained by this initial decision, which had such an impact on exports, growth prospects and the current account deficit. Second, the EU enlargement process posed particular problems for Portugal given the level of development, structure and export specialization of the east European accession states. Lower production and labour costs meant that the new members became direct competitors for trade and investment. In addition, Portugal was buffeted further by fierce competition for its traditional exports from non-EU countries such as China and India.

Thirdly, the new challenges faced by Portugal were exacerbated by the failure to introduce deep and wide-ranging structural reforms. In particular, the areas felt to be in need of reform were education, health and social policy as well as the public administration. Efforts in these vital areas have been half-hearted and limited because of lack of political will and social consensus. EU membership brought a greatly improved infrastructure and may have created a modern consumer society but Portugal remains an EU country with worrying social inequalities. The road, rail and port network have been upgraded but little has been done to assist and modernize the beleaguered manufacturing and fishing industries. In particular, education and training suffered from neglect at a time when a globalized marketplace required upgraded skills and knowledge. This failure to invest adequately in the country's future stands out as the most damning indictment of post-1986 governments and the political elite. As a result, the structural reforms that will enable the country to confront the challenges of the twenty-first century have yet to be implemented.

This feeling that Portugal has squandered a great opportunity has generated a mood of pessimism. Above all, the expectations generated by EU membership remain unfulfilled. Certainly it is true that the EMU and the euro contributed to existing structural imbalances that successive governments have failed to tackle and indeed in some cases have exacerbated through their actions. Even one of the undoubted success stories of closer integration, namely the creation of an Iberian market for trade and investment, has turned out to be a double-edged sword. Despite concerns about the dominance of Portugal's neighbour, the stimulus to cross-border economic relations has brought undoubted benefits. Spain is now Portugal's single most important export market and its major source of imports. However, overdependence on a single trade partner carries inherent dangers. The severity of the economic crisis in Spain and the likelihood that it will be among the last of the leading economies to emerge from recession exposes Portugal's reliance on its neighbour. The motor vehicle industry in particular suffered from the sharp decline in demand from its Spanish customers and the reliance on Spain's labour market to absorb Portuguese migrant workers caused particular difficulties. An example is Portugal's vital textile industry, which has long been the key to Portugal's prosperity, employing 180,000 workers and accounting for 12 per cent of total exports by value. It took a hammer blow when the recession hit and many firms faced bankruptcy. In 2009, exports dipped 6 per cent, partly because of the slump in demand from the biggest importer, Spain.

The Eurozone economic crisis, 2009–10

At the core of the crisis for Portugal has been the failure to control public accounts and the subsequent persistent loss of competitiveness. What made matters worse was that just as the Portuguese started to come to terms with the need for remedial action and the requirement for fiscal reforms to cut the deficit, the impact of the financial crisis in Greece, known as 'the ouzo effect', made matters even worse. Despite protestations from the Prime Minister, José Sócrates, that the state of his country's finances could not be compared to those of Greece and that the economy was in no worse a position than Ireland, the UK and the USA, the acronym PIIGS began to be applied with the general assumption that Portugal, Ireland, Italy, Greece and Spain were all in the same boat and suffered from economic problems of a similar magnitude. The credibility of the Portuguese argument was undermined somewhat by the proposed regional finance initiative that would see an increase in funds devoted to Madeira and the Azores (Mallet and Wise, 2010).

Portugal breached the European Stability and Growth Pact as early as 2001 and the budget deficit continued to rise to a record level equivalent to 9.3 per cent of GDP by 2009. Meanwhile, public debt shot up to 85.4 per cent of GDP. Given the longevity of the problem the deficit cannot be blamed entirely on the global recession, and structural factors clearly played a part. It was during the 'boom years' in the late 1980s when private consumption and investment were at their height that Portugal failed to make the transition to a restructured, more productive economy. The erosion of competitiveness can be traced back to the late 1980s and since then productivity has failed to keep pace with wage rises. Consequently, the productivity gap in relation to the Eurozone has widened. In part this is explained by the quality and efficiency of the investment undertaken, hampered as it was by insufficient matching funds and poor planning. As one commentator points out 'there is no substitute for the domestic implementation of reforms, which should proceed further in areas such as labour, product and capital markets' (Royo, 2007: 692). There is general agreement that only greater investment in technology, a more educated workforce, less state regulation and more flexible labour laws can restore Portugal's competitive position.

The Growth and Stability Pact

Central to the measures contained in the Growth and Stability Pact – *Programa de Estabilidade e Crescimento* (PEC) – the plan designed to ensure fiscal discipline among member states – was a reduction in government expenditure and more efficient tax collection. To critics the combination of a salary freeze, poor employment prospects, higher taxes and expenditure cuts would do little to stimulate economic growth that is forecast to be among the lowest in the Eurozone, averaging little more than 1 per cent (Diário de Notícias, 2010). The government is relying on improved export volumes (helped by the devaluation of the euro against the dollar) coupled with lower imports to provide the necessary growth to reduce the deficit. However, the fall in export demand due to the sluggish recovery among its trading partners in the Eurozone may make this extremely difficult to achieve despite the compensation of opportunities provided in some of the fast-growing economies in Latin America, Asia and Africa. As part of its austerity programme announced in March 2010, the minority Socialist government expected to cut expenditure by reducing employment subsidies and other economic assistance measures. The government attempted a delicate balancing act by trimming the budget while limiting tax rises to the upper echelons of earners. Not surprisingly, the measures alienated public sector workers and led to strike action. The crisis has forced the authorities to tackle the pension issue. Non-contributory pension schemes will be frozen and the pension age for public employees will rise. The deficit will be reduced further by raising receipts from more privatizations, including remaining government stakes in REN (the power grid operator), EDP (electricity), TAP (the national airline) and GALP (oil and natural gas), among others.

In many respects the crisis was not unexpected and it was quite predictable which countries would be worst affected. By adopting a strong currency with low interest rates (down from 16 per cent in the 1990s to 4 per cent in 2001) and by allowing a gradual erosion in its unit labour cost advantage, Portugal exposed itself to just such a crisis and, unwittingly, ensured that the price to be paid for the failure to tackle its longer-term structural problems would be a relatively high one. Ultimately, it condemned Portugal to at least a decade of low growth that held out little or no prospect that per capita income convergence with its partners could recommence. Coupled with the competition to its traditional exports generated by the EU's eastern expansion and the liberalization of world trade in general, it proved difficult to reverse the erosion of Portuguese competitiveness. Nor did the government have at its disposal the means to combat its economic and fiscal problems. In the past, escudo devaluations and emigrant remittances helped to redress the imbalances but these were now ruled out. In the Eurozone Portugal is far more reliant on the actions of the European Central Bank at a time when the mechanisms for managing such a crisis do not exist, or have previously never been tested.

Unemployment and the labour market

In comparison to Spain where unemployment has regularly topped the European league tables and peaked at over 24 per cent in the mid-1990s, Portugal has maintained relatively low levels of joblessness at below the EU average since 1986. However, labour market conditions deteriorated markedly after 2001 as evidenced by two important features, namely rising unemployment and increases in the number of Portuguese opting to leave the country and become economic migrants. The sluggish progress of the economy after 2001 expressed itself in declining productivity growth and a poor record in employment creation. Often the first to suffer from the contraction in economic activity was the immigrant community, which experienced a 50 per cent increase in joblessness during 2008–09. According to IEFP (Instituto do Emprego e Formação Profissional) figures, Brazilian migrants were the worst affected, followed by Ukrainians, Cape Verdeans and Angolans. Nor were Portuguese nationals immune from this downturn in employment and, according to Eurostat, the overall unemployment rate rose from 7.7 per cent in 2005 to over 10 per cent by the end of 2009 when the number of registered jobless rose from 416,000 to 524,000 – an increase of over a quarter on the previous year (Eurostat, 2010).

Despite the gloom, it is unnecessary to be wholly pessimistic. As in the past, Portugal retains a remarkable resilience and adaptability that will stand it in good stead even during adverse economic circumstances. There is some evidence that Portugal may be able to resist the worst aspects of the recession. First, while the reorientation of trade towards Europe was consolidated and extended following entry into the European Community, relations with former colonies were maintained and have gradually begun to bear fruit. Initially, the civil wars that racked Angola, Mozambique, Guinea-Bissau and Cape Verde restricted trade to a minimum. However, the post-conflict recovery of the Portuguese-speaking African countries (*Paises de Língua Oficial Portuguesa*, or PALOPs) has gathered pace and together with the remarkable economic resurgence of Brazil has presented the former colonial power with a unique opportunity to reap the benefits of a close linguistic and cultural heritage and centuries-old ties that had been loosened after 1975. Economic recovery in the Portuguese-speaking world offers new opportunities for business and investment, and Portugal is finally able to build on the 'strategic partnership' with its former colonies that was initially launched in the 1990s. Government credit is available for companies seeking to export to oil-rich Angola, and a development bank funds infrastructure and other projects in the West African country that has posted annual GDP growth rates in excess of 8 per cent (*The Economist*, 2010). In 2008, Angola ranked fourth after Spain, Germany and France as a market for Portuguese exports with trade worth €2.5 billion (EIU, 2009).

If Portugal is to reap maximum benefit from the economic boom in the Portuguese-speaking world, it faces stern competition from countries such as South Africa, China and Brazil. For instance, Portugal ranked only fifth in the list of leading exporters to Mozambique in 2008 and similar trends were repeated with regard to foreign investment. Yet there are areas, such as tourism, where its expertise could assist countries such Cape Verde and Mozambique to emerge as leading destinations for international tourism.

The second factor is that when the 2008 global recession began to bite, Portugal had already been suffering from economic problems since the turn of the century. It meant that the shock was not as severe as in Spain where a once booming economy came to a juddering halt. Portugal avoided a similar fate in part because the economy had already slumped into low-to-negative growth and the labour market was already in a contraction phase. Interestingly, traditional responses to the economic downturn were again evident. Growing numbers of workers chose to emigrate (estimated at 75,000 annually) in search of employment within the EU and, latterly, in Angola. As originally intended, the single market did facilitate worker migration and thousands of unemployed and low-paid took advantage of the free market in labour to seek jobs elsewhere in the EU. In some respects, it provided an uncanny reminder of the labour migration patterns during the era of mass migration in the 1960s and 1970s (principally to France, Germany and Switzerland), with the additional feature that countries like the UK and Spain now offered employment opportunities.

Third, Portugal is less vulnerable than many of its EU partners because its economic growth was not heavily based on the construction industry, which accounts for 6.5 per cent of GDP, half the weight it represents in Spain (12.3 per cent). Portugal did not partake to the same extent in the property boom that was a signature feature of the Irish and Spanish economies over the past two decades and acted as a driver in their impressive economic growth performance. The property market had been relatively flat since 2002 and with no bubbles to burst Portugal's construction industry displayed less vulnerability as a consequence and home-owners were spared the collapse in property values that was such a feature elsewhere (Wise, 2009a). Similarly, Portuguese banks had been far more cautious and conservative than banks elsewhere in Europe and had not exposed themselves to the sub-prime horrors of toxic loans and over-adventurous lending (Wise, 2009b). As a result, despite offering state guarantees worth up to €20 billion in 2008 only one small bank (BPP) required assistance and the government has not been called upon to bail out any of the leading financial institutions, as happened elsewhere.

Public investment took some of the strain from the private sector. It had been a contributory factor to the sustained high growth period during the 1990s and once again infrastructure projects are set to boost demand. During the 1990s Expo-98 and the Vasco da Gama bridge government projects stimulated demand and it is planned that the new €3.1 billion international airport at Alcochete will play a similar role (although some question the urgency of the project given the recession) in tandem with a third bridge over the Tagus and new high speed rail links. In the supplementary budget in January 2009, €2.2 billion of additional spending was announced, including help for the construction industry through a school building renovation project, investment in renewable energy and financial support and credits for SMEs and exporters (EIU, 2009b). However, severe budgetary constraints will limit the extent to which public investment can promote future growth. Certainly the PSD opposition voiced concerns over large-scale public investment projects on the grounds that they involved higher debt levels. The international airport and the high-speed rail links between Lisbon/Oporto and Spain came in for particular scrutiny in this regard. As many of these public projects are not set to begin until 2010–11 their utility in aiding recovery from the current recession is likely to be limited.

A green economic future?

In one area, future prospects look promising and Portugal has emerged as a European leader in renewable energy. Because Portugal imports 86 per cent of its energy needs, minds have been focused on alternatives to fossil fuels. There are two areas where investment in the environment and emerging technologies will maximize the benefits from two of the country's major assets (long hours of sunshine and an Atlantic coastline) and is set to pay dividends in the future. Along with Spain, Portugal can claim the most solar hours in Europe. At the centre of an ambitious energy plan is the world's biggest solar farm at Moura in the Alentejo where 2,500 giant solar panels will tap the sun's energy. The government's target is for 60 per cent of electricity needs to be provided by sun, wind, wave and other clean sources over the next decade.

Portugal is host to one of the largest wind power projects in Europe. The aim is to harness the country's geographical conditions to produce clean energy from wave and wind power. The wind project involves 500 turbines that will double wind power capacity. In 2005, the government pledged €2.5 billion for a wave power plant near Póvoa de Varzim in northern Portugal as well as a hydroelectric dam on the Sabor River in the Douro valley (Tremlett, 2006).

Natural resources are at the centre of the tourist industry, a vital sector for Portugal and one where competition is at its keenest. The year 2009 represented the worst summer season in living memory and the industry responded by cutting prices in order to lure visitors. The Algarve and Madeira were particularly hard hit because they have a high dependence on the UK as a source country where potential tourists were discouraged by the weakness of sterling against the euro. There is every indication that the requirement for a flexible response to rapidly changing market conditions has been grasped, although the floods that afflicted Madeira early in 2010 threatened to undermine the island's tourist-friendly image as 'the garden of the Atlantic'. Further efforts to stimulate tourist expenditure lie behind the plans for more infrastructure investment and the focus that will be placed on cultural and sports tourism: including the new publicity slogan for the north of the country 'The essence of Portugal'.

Conclusion

The global crisis may have exacerbated Portugal's economic problems but it did not cause them. What it did was to reveal the lack of action to correct the country's deep-rooted structural problems. One argument is that the EMU stimulated a boom but created the illusion that reform could be postponed, particularly with regard to indebtedness and competitiveness. It was all too easy to assume that EU membership followed by participation in the Eurozone would suffice to ensure economic growth and prosperity. Yet this was far from being the case. In a small economy the external environment is extremely important and Portugal is heavily reliant on growth among its major trading partners. The failure to generate a consensus around structural reforms and the weakness of minority governments conspired with the electoral cycle to ensure that action was postponed. Portugal was also exposed to the tentative management of the Eurozone during its first major crisis. Unfortunately, mechanisms to deal with the crisis and consensus among member states in support of a coordinated economic and fiscal response were noticeably absent. It was left to national governments to take the initiative and fight their own corners.

Postscript

EU and Eurozone membership initially brought substantial benefits to its less prosperous members but by the late 2000s the costs and limitations associated with membership were thrown into stark relief. In fact, Eurozone membership always carried risk as well as opportunity. Portugal had benefited during the years of strong growth but the economic downturn revealed some of the disadvantages that stemmed from participation in the European economic project. What had been a lifebelt turned out to be more of a straitjacket. During the heady years of high growth the consequences of the Eurozone being treated as one by the financial markets were ignored. The fact that individual governments were able to neglect prudent financial management, at least until the full extent of Greece's public finances became apparent, seemed to matter little. In reality, slow-burning corrosion occurred in public finances whilst Portuguese competitiveness deteriorated alarmingly. Strong wage increases without accompanying growth in productivity played havoc with the country's ability to compete in global markets.

In 2010 the smaller Eurozone economies appeared to be particularly vulnerable to economic and financial collapse. Greece and Ireland both received bailouts from the EU and it was widely expected that Portugal would be the next in line to succumb to the contagion. The prospect that a larger economy, like that of Spain, where the government and private banks own much of Portugal's debt, might possibly default sent a collective shiver throughout the EU and the financial markets. Portugal sailed close to the wind with regard to a possible international financial rescue and many commentators and market speculators believed that it was only a matter of time before the country would seek help from the EU's €750 billion Stabilization Fund. Faced with such an unpromising scenario the Portuguese authorities pledged to consolidate their public finances and reduce the large external deficit from 9.3 per cent of GDP (2009) to 2.0 per cent by 2013 (OECD, 2010: 9). To this end, in May 2010 the government announced public expenditure cuts, including lower pensions and higher taxes, VAT increases and measures to curb tax evasion.

As the country sought to avoid the fate that befell Greece, new obstacles to recovery emerged, notably the rising level of borrowing costs. The upward pressure on interest rates threatened to make it even harder for Portugal to export and undermined future growth potential. In addition, raising funds for future debt repayments is very much determined by the cost of borrowing and Portugal faced the prospect that it could no longer finance the debt markets. During 2011 poor growth forecasts and sharply rising unemployment raised questions about Portugal's ability to refinance its debts and continue to defy pressures from the markets. This was compounded by oil price shocks caused by uncertainty in the Middle East that exposed Portugal's high energy dependence and vulnerability to further rises.

The key problem in the immediate future is that Portugal requires strong economic growth in order to put its financial house in order. Unfortunately, austerity measures, including a 'crisis tax' on wages and companies, whilst deemed necessary to calm the financial markets, did little to enhance growth prospects, as internal consumption can no longer be relied on to drive growth. Any slowdown in economic growth, threatened a slump into a 'double-dip' recession. Like the rest of Europe, Portugal depends on export growth for its recovery and unfortunately cannot rely on a weak Spanish economy, which absorbs a quarter of Portugal's exports when it only has a toe-hold in many of the fast-growth economies in Asia.

What the economic crisis has done is to expose the underlying weaknesses in the Portuguese economy, particularly its reliance on low-technology industries where competition from the Far East and emerging economies is particularly fierce, and even in the more technologically advanced sectors where East European competition is strong (OECD, 2010: 25). Given the difficulties, some economists began to suggest that Portugal should leave the Eurozone and even predicted a major crisis for the single currency.

In March 2011 Portugal became another victim of the Eurozone crisis when the minority government lost a Parliamentary vote on a new package of austerity measures – the fourth in twelve months – and the Prime Minister, José Sócrates, stepped down. Sócrates who continued to maintain that the country did not require a rescue package, blaming Portugal's woes on the global crisis, market speculators and ratings agencies, took a caretaker role until early elections could be held in June. However, political uncertainty (a power vacuum with no certainty that a majority government would be elected) added to gloomy economic news (rising borrowing costs for debt repayments, predictions of further economic contraction) to make resorting to international financial help all but inevitable.

Bibiliography

Corkill, D. (1993) *The Portuguese Economy since 1974*, Edinburgh: Edinburgh University Press.

Diário de Notícias (2010) *Portugal será o país que menos cresce na Zona Euro*, 9 March.

Economist, The (2007) 'A new sick man of Europe', 14 April.

Economist, The (2010) 'Oil, glorious oil', 28 January.

Economist Intelligence Unit (EIU) (2009a) Country Report, Portugal, April.

Economist Intelligence Unit (EIU) (2009b) Country Report, February.

Eurostat (2010) 'January 2010 Euro area unemployment rate at 9.9 per cent EU27 at 9.5 per cent'. Available at http://europa.eu/rapid/pressreleases (accessed 12 March 2010).

Mallet, V. and Wise, P. *Spain and Portugal fight to calm investors*, *Financial Times*, 5 February 2010.

OECD (2010) Economic Surveys: Portugal, vol. 2010/16.

Royo, S. (2007) *Lessons from the integration of Spain and Portugal to the EU*, *Political Science & Politics*, 40, 689–93.

Tremlett, G. (2006) 'Portugal powers ahead as wind champion', *The Guardian*, 2 March.

Wise, P. (2009a) 'Weathering the storm', *The Banker*, 15 May.

Wise, P. (2009b) 'A reliable model for a risk-adverse world', *The Banker*, 4 August.

4 Portuguese elites and European integration

Diogo Moreira, António Costa Pinto and Pedro Tavares de Almeida

When Portugal became a member of the European Economic Community in 1986, expectations were high and largely optimistic. In the context of the polarized Portuguese transition to democracy in 1974–76, when the crucial political divisions corresponded to a conflict 'between democrats and revolutionaries [rather] than between democrats and "reactionaries"' (Alvarez-Miranda, 1996: 202), the European option was an important factor in the break from a dictatorial, isolationist and colonialist past that also assumed an anti-Communist and anti-revolutionary standpoint (Pinto and Teixeira, 2003). As in other southern European transitions to democracy – particularly in Spain – 'the idea that accession to the European Community would help guarantee liberal democracy was more overtly voiced' (Alvarez-Miranda, 1996), and was central to the strategy of the political elites during this period.

The governing elites successfully sought to legitimize the new democratic order by using Europe and EEC membership. In doing so, they adopted a very positive view of European integration, which has had a favourable impact on public opinion. The swift Europeanization of the newly founded parties was also stimulated by their merging with the transnational networks of the European political families. The theme of EEC membership soon emerged in the programmes of the right and centre-right parties, with the Social Democratic Centre (CDS, *Centro Democrático Social*) proclaiming itself as being fully pro-European, and the Social Democratic Party (PSD, *Partido Social Democrata*) adopting a more cautious approach (Barroso, 1983). The CDS, which was affiliated to the European Christian Democratic family, adopted a strongly pro-European strategy right up to accession. The PSD, which was formed by the reformers and 'liberals' of the Dictatorship's final years, first allied itself with the European 'liberal' family, although it defected to the European People's Party in 1996. In 1976, the main slogan of the electoral campaign of the Socialist Party (PS, *Partido Socialista Português*) was 'Europe with us', and the proposal for EEC accession was incorporated into the party's programme.

The arguments in favour of the Community were actively promoted as the means to implement the necessary political and constitutional reforms for democratic consolidation. Only the Communist Party (PCP, *Partido Comunista Português*) remained consistently opposed to EEC membership, and rejected the prospect of accession. This opposition was an important element in its political campaigns between 1977 and 1986. After 1986, the PCP stopped calling for Portugal to withdraw from the EEC, and adopted a more moderate position.

Civil society and the interest groups representing those who would be most affected by EU membership had practically no role to play during any stage of the accession negotiations. European integration was a decision made by the political elite alone, rather than a response 'to popular demand' (Bermeo, 1988: 14) or to pressure from organized interests. The governing elites dominated the negotiating process, with only limited involvement of business associations or organized agricultural interests. Both the Confederation of Portuguese Industry (CIP, *Confederação da Industria Portuguesa*) and the Portuguese Industrial Association (AIP, *Associação Industrial Portuguesa*) supported accession, although to different extents. The CIP wavered between domestic liberalization and protectionism towards the EEC, at the beginning demanding more pre-entry economic aid, and later on showing its opposition to the final agreements. The AIP adopted a more pragmatic 'join and see' position (Lucena and Gaspar, 1991: 899). Nevertheless, despite the CIP's occasional attacks, the hypothesis that the attitudes of these two organizations reflected an attempt to make the government adopt an aggressive negotiating stance rather than any principled opposition appears plausible, especially since these attitudes did not enjoy much support among their affiliates. Several interviews with leading figures of the employers' organizations reveal that their attitudes towards accession were driven by political considerations, with the EEC being presented as the 'guarantor for greater political security that will encourage investment in and modernization of the productive structures in the country'. As regards the two trade union confederations, the political and ideological divisions were much more obvious, with the Communist *Intersindical* standing opposed to accession to the EEC, and the social democratic General Workers' Union (UGT – *União Geral de Trabalhadores*) being firmly pro-European. Formed out of the struggle against communist domination of the trade union movement, and indirectly supported by the PS and PSD, the UGT was rapidly integrated into the European labour movement's international institutions. It was only after accession to the EEC that *Intersindical* moved away from its original opposition to adopt a more pragmatic position.

Portugal's route to EEC membership was promoted by the political elite, with a great degree of political consensus, and without any attempt to assess public opinion through referenda. It was not until after accession had been secured that popular opinion began to exert pressure for more public participation in the reforms that were taking place within the EU. The perception of EEC membership as a positive goal was initially restricted to the political elite. In 1978, shortly after the formal membership application had been submitted, most Portuguese had no opinion on Europe, with over 60 per cent of the population stating that they did not know if EEC membership was essential for the future of Portugal's economy (Bacalhau, 1994). It was not until the early 1980s that the Portuguese became better informed and thus able to express a clearer opinion on the subject. The Eurobarometer survey has regularly recorded Portuguese public opinion since 1980, and its reports have revealed a clear upward trend in support of EEC membership, with a large increase occurring in 1986, the year Portugal finally joined. The proportion of the population believing EEC membership to be a good thing rose from 24.4 per cent in 1980–82 to 64.5 per cent in 1986–90, and finally to over 70 per cent during the early 1990s (Bacalhau, 1994: 269). In 1993, 65 per cent believed that Portuguese economic development had been boosted greatly as a result of EEC membership. As appears to be the case in other southern European countries, there seems to be a strong suggestion that the urban middle classes generally tend towards Europeanism and have only a weak sense of national pride, while the less educated and the rural lower classes generally have weak pro-European sentiments and a strong sense of national pride (Cruz, 1993: 157).

The first ten years of Portugal's membership in the EEC/EU was a 'golden era', with a large degree of pro-European consensus within the party system. There was a wave of economic growth and rising incomes, as well as real social change. Internationally, Portugal used its stronger position as a member of the EU to resolve the tensions prevailing with its former colonies in Africa. The optimism of the 1990s was also marked by Portugal's meeting the convergence criteria for the Euro, and joining it in 1999–2000. This contrasted with the situation at the beginning of the following decade. With the EU's movement towards enlargement and institutional reform, as well as the eventual reduction of financial support from the European Union, Portuguese public opinion became less optimistic (Pinto and Lobo, 2004).

On the whole, Portuguese attitudes towards the EU have been overwhelmingly positive, both in terms of affective and instrumental views. However, it is important to note that the Portuguese consensus is based on a narrow, instrumental view of the benefits of membership for Portugal rather than on wider perceptions of EU as 'a good thing'. As regards attitudes towards the EU as a political system, the evidence is somewhat paradoxical. Whereas the Portuguese have a low participation in the European Parliament elections and are dissatisfied with the way democracy works in the EU, they have increasingly defended the Europeanization of key public policies such as foreign and currency affairs (Pinto and Lobo, 2004: 181). This concurs with the view that Portuguese attitudes are positive, but are formed on an instrumental basis.

Elite attitudes towards EU

Elite surveys are rare in Portugal, and to our knowledge the 2007 IntUne survey is the most comprehensive one that has been conducted so far on European issues.[1] Following the sampling criteria and procedures set up by the IntUne project, the group of interviewees included 80 MPs, 40 business leaders and top officeholders of major interest organizations.[2]

In this chapter we compare the general attitudes of both types of elites, applying the left–right division to differentiate among the group of politicians. Ideologically, we categorized the MPs as follows: the left includes all the respondents who are members of the PCP/PEV (the alliance between the Communist Party and the Green Party[3]) and of the BE (Left Bloc). The centre-left is composed by all respondents who belong to the PS (Socialist Party), the single party in government, with an absolute majority, when the IntUne survey took place. The centre-right aggregates the respondents of the PSD (Social Democratic Party), historically the alternative party of government. The right is represented by all the respondents who are members of the CDS-PP (Christian Democrats/Popular Party). With the significant exception of the Left Bloc, a novelty that emerged in the late 1990s, the other four major parties have been the central actors in the parliamentary arena since the first democratic elections of 1975.

Allegiance to different territorial entities

In order to explore the horizontal dimension of the European citizenship, we have analysed the feelings of attachment of elites to different territorial levels, their evaluation of the benefits produced by membership in the European Union, and their conceptions of what defines the national as well as the supra-national identity.

Regarding the different levels of territorial attachment of the respondents, we find that all Portuguese elite groups consider themselves strongly attached to Portugal as a country, first and foremost, and also strongly attached to their town and village. This perception prevails in all ideological groups. When we look at regional attachment, we find that the consensus is broken. The respondents of the political elite are much more attached to their regions (61 per cent are 'very attached') than those of the economic elite (only 32 per cent are 'very attached') (Table 4.1). Analysing the political groups, the centre-right and the left show, respectively, the highest (65 per cent) and the lowest (38 per cent) proportion of respondents attached to the regions. Finally, a very large majority of the political and economic Portuguese elites feel attached to the EU. However, if one considers only the strongest expression of attachment, the difference with the attachment to the national level is significant. It can also be noted that this supranational allegiance is stronger among the MPs (45 per cent) than the business leaders (38 per cent). From an ideological standpoint, only the left (BE and PCP/PEV) appears to have a relevant number of respondents (24 per cent) who do not consider themselves attached to the EU, which could explain some of the less positive views about the EU that this group will show in this study.

In most mass opinion surveys, when asked about the benefits of the European integration process, the majority of the Portuguese believe that it is a good thing and that Portugal has benefited from it. Thus it should not be a surprise that Portuguese elites overwhelmingly believe that Portugal has benefited from the European integration process. The only exception is the left, as two-thirds of the respondents from the BE and the PCP/PEV claim that Portugal has not benefited from being a member state of the EU.

Table 4.1 Attachment to different communities

		Political elite (%)	*Economic elite (%)*	*Political elite*			
				Left (%)	*Centre-left (%)*	*Centre-right (%)*	*Right (%)*
Attachment to your town/village	Very attached	71	55	50	64	85	75
	Somewhat attached	20	32	25	24	12	25
Attachment to your region	Very attached	61	32	38	64	65	50
	Somewhat attached	32	32	38	31	35	25
Attachment to your country	Very attached	92	90	88	90	96	100
	Somewhat attached	6	10	13	10	0	0
Attachment to the EU	Very attached	45	38	13	45	54	50
	Somewhat attached	51	58	63	55	42	50

Identity

When examining how elites define territorial identities and looking first at the national level – that is, the characteristics that the respondents feel necessary for someone to be seen as truly part of the Portuguese community – Table 4.2 shows that the attribute of being Christian is considered 'not important' by a large majority of both the political elite (74 per cent) and the economic elite (66 per cent). When we turn to a detailed analysis of the political elite, based on party affiliations and ideological self-positioning, we find a significant distinction: most respondents on the left consider the religious attribute irrelevant, while half of the respondents on the right believe it is 'somewhat/very important'.

Identifying with Portuguese cultural values is consensually considered 'somewhat/very important' by both the political (94 per cent) and the economic (95 per cent) elites. Surprisingly, the less favourable attitude in this overwhelming consensus comes from those on the far right of the political spectrum: only 75 per cent considered it 'somewhat/very important'. All the other groups show percentages well beyond the 90 per cent level.

Being born in the national territory is considered a 'very/somewhat important' attribute by 66 per cent of the MPs and 70 per cent of the business leaders. Both the left and the right seem to differentiate themselves from the consensus on this matter. Only 38 per cent of those who are members of the BE or of the PCP/PEV, and 25 per cent of their ideological counterparts on the right, feel that being born in Portugal is considered an important feature of national identity. Parental nationality is also considered important by an overwhelming majority of the political (78 per cent) and the economic (76 per cent) elites. In terms of political groups, only the left diverges from this opinion.

Respect for national laws and institutions is seen as 'somewhat/very important' across the elites (98 per cent of the politicians and an equal percentage of business leaders). The slightly lower importance (95 per cent) given to this element by those who place themselves at the centre-left of the ideological spectrum (in comparison with those on the left, centre-right and on the right) should be noted.

We now turn to the elements of identity that are associated with the supranational level of the European integration process, in an attempt to determine the meaning that the Portuguese elites attribute to the blurry concept of European identity.

Starting with the religious dimension, we find great similarities with the attributes of national identity. Once again, the fact that someone is Christian has little relevance for either the political (16 per cent) or economic (30 per cent) elites. As regards MPs, this appears to be one of the clearest issues in terms of ideological positioning. The left unanimously agrees that religion is not a relevant attribute in terms of European identity, while 50 per cent of the respondents on the right express the opposite opinion.

A more fundamental consensus as to European identity appears when we focus on cultural values. The same proportions (87–88 per cent) of both elite

Table 4.2 Selected elements of national and European identity*

		Political elite (%)	*Economic elite (%)*	*Political elite*			
				Left (%)	*Centre-left (%)*	*Centre-right (%)*	*Right (%)*
Christian	NI	26	34	0	14	50	50
	EI	16	30	0	10	27	50
Identifying with Portuguese cultural values	NI	94	95	100	95	92	75
Identifying with European cultural values	EI	87	88	75	86	92	75
Born in Portugal	NI	66	70	38	67	81	25
Born in Europe	EI	64	60	38	62	73	75
With Portuguese parents	NI	78	76	25	76	92	100
With European parents	EI	54	70	0	55	62	100
Respect for Portuguese laws and institutions	NI	98	98	100	95	100	100
Respect for European laws and institutions	EI	86	100	62	95	77	75
Portuguese citizenship	NI	93	77	88	95	96	75

Notes
* Percentages of those answering 'very important' and 'somewhat important' added together.
NI – Elements of national identity.
EI – Elements of European identity.

groups claim that identifying with European cultural values is an important attribute of European identity.

The fact that someone was born in a European country is seen generally by the political and economic elites as an important attribute of his/her European identity. Once again, this is one of the few items where we can find a clear ideological division among the politicians. Birthplace is considered a relevant characteristic by only a minority on the left (38 per cent) while the remaining respondents hold the opposite position.

Having European parents is another attribute of European identity that is considered important to the majority of the political (54 per cent) and the economic (70 per cent) elites. However, we must emphasize the degree to which the economic elite tends to be much more supportive of this claim *vis-à-vis* its political counterpart. In terms of political groups, the respondents of the BE and the PCP/PEV clearly reject this attribute as an important one. The centre-left tends to follow the general opinion in this matter. Finally respect for European institutions and laws is valued as an important attribute of European identity by all elite groups.

Ever since Linton (1936), the terms ‘ascribed’ and ‘achieved’ contrast the inherited attributes – that is, those not depending on the subject’s will, such as birthplace, race or gender – with those that depend upon the subject’s actions. Parsons (1951) has demonstrated the importance of these two concepts as characterizations of social roles, and they have remained important sociological analytical tools.

It has been pointed out that ascribed and achieved components of national and European identity exist at both the elite and mass levels (Sanders, 2008). Religion, birthplace and parenting are associated with the ascribed dimension of identity, whereas culture, respect for the law, feelings and language are achieved components.

Using factor analysis for the Portuguese elite sample, we find an ascribed component of European identity, with birthplace and parents being a part of the same factor (Table 4.4). Likewise, there appears to be an achieved dimension, with ‘respect for law and institutions’ and the ‘feeling of being European’ being associated in the same factor. Moreover, we find a high and positive interaction with religious and cultural attributes. This seems to indicate that the cultural dimension of European identity in Portugal is strongly associated with Christianity. As we will see shortly, this is not the case with the cultural dimension of national identity.

As regards the components of national identity, birthplace and parents are part of the ascribed component. In the Portuguese elites, the feeling of being Portuguese, mastering the Portuguese language and identifying with Portuguese cultural traditions, elements that constitute the achieved component at the European scale, are also strongly and positively loaded in the same factor. This indicates that likewise, there exists an achieved component of national identity.

Representation

Having explored the horizontal dimension of citizenship, we may now switch our attention to the vertical one. With regards to the dimension of representation, we shall first analyse how trust in European institutions compares with trust in national ones, and then how elites evaluate the representation of national interests in the European sphere, and finally we shall examine their views about the main institutions of the Union.

Trust in a country's political institutions (especially its government and parliament) is one of the issues most frequently debated in Europe, usually in an attempt to compare it with trust in European institutions. Generally speaking, in Portugal, the national government and parliament command low levels of public trust; on the contrary the levels of trust in European institutions are considerably higher (Jalali *et al.* 2008: 13). When we look at the results of the IntUne elite survey, comparing trust in Portuguese institutions with trust in European institutions is possible only for the economic elite. Surprisingly, and in contrast to the findings of mass surveys (such as Eurobarometer), the Portuguese economic elite tends to have more trust in the Portuguese political institutions than the European ones. The institution they trust the most is the Portuguese national government, while the local and regional governments are the institutions they trust the least.

When comparing the trust of MPs and business leaders in European institutions, the former tend to have more trust in the European Parliament and the European Council of Ministers than their economic counterparts. The reverse is true in the case of the European Commission, which is trusted more by business leaders than by Portuguese MPs. This could be a byproduct of the Commission being seen as a less political institution than the other bodies. When we turn to the ideological composition of the political elite, we find that the left shows far less confidence in all the European institutions than the other groups.

The question of whether Portuguese interests are taken enough into account in the EU is also routinely asked in mass surveys (Jalali *et al.* 2008: 36), and the results often show a practically even split in opinion. As to the perspective of the elites, the majority of business leaders (60 per cent) believe that Portuguese interests are not influential in European decision-making, while a thin majority (53 per cent) of the MPs have the opposite opinion.

When we turn to the party affiliation and ideological profile of the respondents, we find that the members of the BE and PCP/PEV unanimously hold the opinion that Portuguese interests have limited influence in Brussels, along with an equal number of the most right-wing respondents. The opposite view is shared by the majority of the respondents of the PS and the PSD, the two mainstream parties that have been the pillars of government in Portuguese democracy.

Another topic that was the subject of the IntUne survey on the Portuguese elites concerned their views about the powers of the three primary actors in the EU: the European Parliament (EP), the member states and the Commission. As

Table 4.3 Powers of the EU institutions

		Political elite (%)	*Economic elite (%)*	*Political elite*			
				Left (%)	*Centre-left (%)*	*Centre-right (%)*	*Right (%)*
The member states ought to remain the central actors of the European Union	Agree strongly	46	38	62	43	38	100
	Agree somewhat	30	38	25	31	35	0
The European Commission ought to become the true government of the European Union	Agree strongly	9	10	0	14	4	0
	Agree somewhat	34	48	0	33	46	25
The powers of the European Parliament ought to be strengthened	Agree strongly	41	28	62	44	35	0
	Agree somewhat	35	36	12	37	38	50

we can see, the Portuguese political elite tends to support fundamentally the role of the Parliament and of the member states in the European political process (Table 4.3). The Commission is seen less positively by MPs, with only 43 per cent believing it should become the true government of the EU. This contrasts with the economic elite where 58 per cent of the respondents are in favour of a much stronger role for the Commission in the European process, although they likewise want the member states to remain the central actors (76 per cent) and advocate the strengthening of the EP's powers (64 per cent).

Looking at the ideological composition of the Portuguese political elite, we find that support for member states as central actors in Europe is stronger within the left and right of the political spectrum than it is in the centre. By contrast, there appears to be much less support at the ideological extremes for the role of the Commission. Regarding the European Parliament, only the right has a more negative view of a possible strengthening of its powers.

Scope of governance

Analysing the topic of the future institutional development of the EU in terms of policy areas, and the question concerning respondents' support for a unified tax system for the EU, the majority of both politicians and business leaders agree that this should be implemented in the next ten years (Table 4.4). When we examine the elements of the political elite closely, we find the strongest support among respondents in the PS, while the more right-wing elements are against it.

Concerning a common social security system in Europe, the political and the economic elites are overwhelmingly supportive of this scheme, but those who are 'strongly' in favour are in a larger proportion among business leaders (32 per cent) than MPs (22 per cent). The results are surprising, since this policy area is an important source of ideological controversies and party antagonisms. We can hypothesize that both the left and the right tend to support a common solution for different reasons. For the left, the transference to the European arena of an egalitarian social security system may be seen as the only way to prevent or compensate for the erosion of domestic welfare benefits. The right may in turn believe that the perceived neoliberal tendencies of the European integration process may undermine the core programmes of the national welfare state.

The responses to the question about a single foreign policy for Europe show a contrast between politicians and business leaders. While the latter are much more enthusiastic in their support (60 per cent 'strongly in favour'), MPs are much more divided in their positive opinion (44 per cent are 'strongly in favour', while 45 per cent are 'somewhat in favour'). It should be noted that the left tends to be strongly opposed to a single European foreign policy, and that on this topic the centre-right is much less enthusiastic than the centre-left (although still somewhat supportive).

The political and economic elites are both in favour of the idea of more help for regions with difficulties, although MPs are much more supportive (75 per cent are 'strongly in favour') than business leaders (58 per cent are 'strongly in

Table 4.4 Are you in favour that in the next ten years, the EU should have…?

		A unified tax system for Europe		*A common system of social security*		*A single foreign policy*		*More help for regions with difficulties*	
		Somewhat (%)	*Strongly (%)*	*Somewhat (%)*	*Strongly (%)*	*Somewhat (%)*	*Strongly (%)*	*Somewhat (%)*	*Strongly (%)*
Political elite		55	15	61	22	45	44	25	75
Economic elite		40	22	48	32	32	60	42	58
Political elite	Left	50	0	50	25	25	0	12	88
	Centre-left	67	17	57	29	38	62	31	69
	Centre-right	42	19	73	15	62	35	15	85
	Right	25	0	50	0	50	0	50	50

favour'). Among politicians, although all groups are unanimously supportive, the right appears to be less warm in its support.

Finally, we shall try to determine the ideal level of governance (regional, national and European) for a series of policy issues according to the perceptions of the Portuguese elites. Regarding all issues, the regional level is overwhelmingly considered inappropriate, an attitude that probably stems from the absence of regional governments in the Portuguese territory (with the exception of the islands of Madeira and the Azores). Thus, we shall aggregate the regional level with the national one. A second aggregate category includes all answers in which a combination of levels, inclusive of the European level, was suggested by respondents as the most appropriate to deal with a given policy issue (Table 4.5).

Starting with the political elite as a whole, there seems to be a divided opinion over what is the best level of government to handle unemployment, with 42 per cent of the respondents considering the national/regional level as the best to deal with this issue, and 38 per cent prefering the European level. The economic elite is less divided, with a majority (58 per cent) preferring the national/regional level. When we look at specific groups, it is once again between the more radical (left and right) and the moderates (centre-left and centre-right) that the great differences emerge: 62 per cent of the left respondents and 75 per cent of the right consider the national level as the most adequate to fight unemployment, while only 33 per cent of the centre-left and 46 per cent of the centre-right consider that unemployment should be resolved at the domestic level.

Immigration policy is seen largely as a European issue. The only discordant position is taken by the left, which is the only political group to advocate by majority (62 per cent) that immigration policy should be dealt with predominantly at the national level.

When we turn to the fight against crime, it is an issue that divides MPs and business leaders, although the majority of both groups consider the European level of governance the best one to handle this issue. Among politicians, there is an extensive gap between the radicals on one hand, and the moderates on the other. For 62 per cent of the left, the national level is the best one; by contrast, 45 per cent of the respondents in the centre-left and 42 per cent in the centre-right believe that the European level is the most appropriate.

Environmental policy is a consensual issue, since both the political and the economic elites overwhelmingly agree that the European level is the most adequate. A reversed consensus occurs with health care, all groups defending the national level as the most adequate – which seems to be somewhat incongruent with the broad support for a European system of social security.

Taxation is a more divisive issue, with half of the respondents of both the political and the economic elites preferring the national level of governance, and the other half the European level.

It has been shown (Lengyel *et al.* 2008) that the elite respondents perceive two distinct sets of topics as to the desired level of policymaking. Unemployment, healthcare and taxation are deemed by the European elites as mainly domestic/national issues. In turn, the environment, immigration and crime are

Table 4.5 At what level should the following policy areas be mainly dealt with?

		National/regional level (%)	*European level (%)*	*Mixed levels including European (%)*
Fighting unemployment	Political elite	42	38	20
	Economic elite	58	35	8
Immigration policy	Political elite	12	68	20
	Economic elite	15	75	10
Environment policy	Political elite	6	71	22
	Economic elite	18	72	10
Fight against crime	Political elite	31	39	30
	Economic elite	35	45	20
Health care policy	Political elite	76	10	14
	Economic elite	70	25	5
Taxation	Political elite	41	39	20
	Economic elite	48	45	8

seen as transnational/supranational issues. At the European level, these dimensions were confirmed by factor analysis. However, if we consider exclusively the Portuguese elite sample, factor analysis does not enable us to infer this dichotomy. This means that in the Portuguese case each topic must be analysed individually.

Conclusion

European citizenship has been defined as a 'compound citizenship' (Cotta 2008), comprising *indirect citizenship*, as a consequence of the already existing national citizenship, and *direct citizenship*, which is the consequence of European institutions and policies. And as in the analysis of national citizenship, we can find two distinct linkages between citizens and policy. A horizontal dimension relates to membership in the European polity, and a vertical dimension connects the citizens with political institutions (Cotta and Isernia 2007).

Within the Portuguese political elite, we have some elements with which we can characterize the horizontal dimension of European citizenship. We find that the level of allegiance to Europe is very high (96 per cent), although it is slightly inferior to the attachment to Portugal itself (98 per cent). As has been argued in the overall analysis of European citizenship (Cotta 2008), it is expected that an indirect model of citizenship will result lower level of attachment. The Portuguese respondents confirm this expectation, with only 45 per cent of MPs being strongly attached to the EU compared to 92 per cent with a strong attachment to Portugal. There may be an instrumental allegiance to Europe, since the Portuguese elites believe overwhelmingly that the country has benefited from European integration.

However the elements of national and European identity, as they are perceived by the Portuguese elites, show considerable divergence from the generic European perception. As argued by Sanders (2008), there exists a mix of ascribed and achieved components in both European and national identities. In the Portuguese case, beyond the above-mentioned components, European identity is seen as possessing an additional cultural/religious component: those who consider European culture as an element of European identity do so because of the religious connotation they attribute to that very European culture.

As to the vertical dimension of European citizenship (that is, the relationship between the members of the polity and its political authorities), it has been argued that there are elements of a direct linkage (via the European Parliament) and of an indirect linkage (through the European Council of Ministers), while the Commission is at the crossroads (Cotta 2008). Like their European counterparts, the majority of Portuguese respondents defend strengthening of the powers of Parliament as well as the role of member states as central actors in the process of Europeanization. In most EU countries, support for the Commission is however much weaker among MPs than among business leaders. This has been interpreted as the resistance of national political elites to the abdication of their role in the guidance of the European process. Actually, the European Parliament is much more connected to national polity (through elections that still have a markedly national character) than the Commission is (Cotta 2008).

This weaker support for the Commission on the part of the political elite corresponds also to a lower level of trust. Portuguese political elites tend to have more trust in the Council of Ministers and the Parliament than they do in the Commission. Portuguese economic elites have the opposite view. They trust the Commission more than the other European institutions, and they also trust the Portuguese political institutions more than their European counterparts. This contradicts the results, on this topic, of mass opinion surveys (Jalali *et al.* 2008: 36). When asked if national interests are taken into consideration in Brussels, the majority of the Portuguese economic elite believe they are not, while the majority of the political elite believe that they are. These differences of opinion could indicate that the economic elite does not feel it has much influence in Brussels, unlike the political elite.

Regarding the scope of governance, it has been argued that the results of the survey in most member states show the existence of two types of topics correlated with different ideal policymaking levels (Lengyel *et al.* 2008). Unemployment, health care and taxation are deemed by the European elites as mainly domestic/national issues. In turn, the environment, immigration and crime are seen as transnational/supranational issues. Although it is not negligible, this dichotomy does not appear to be so relevant in the Portuguese case.

To conclude, we find that the concept of a 'compound citizenship' (Cotta 2008) may be applied to the perceptions of Portuguese elites regarding the EU. Although further study is necessary to refine some of its dimensions, the combination of an indirect European citizenship with a direct one appears to exist in Portugal. And as it has been argued for all EU countries, this European 'compound citizenship' is not in conflict with national citizenship. On the contrary it possesses elements for strengthening their linkage. This would indicate that European citizenship might be analysed separately from national citizenship, while being in fact incapable of dissociating from the components of national identity.

Notes

1 This research was funded by a grant from the INTUNE project (Integrated and United: A quest for Citizenship in an ever closer Europe) financed by the Sixth Framework Programme of the European Union, Priority 7, Citizens and Governance in a Knowledge-Based Society (CIT3-CT-2005-513421).

2 As regards the deputies, the group of frontbenchers interviewed comprised all the six leaders of the party parliamentary groups, most chairs (10 out of 12) of the Standing Committees, and 25 former government members. The business leaders were selected from a list of the 'top 500', ranked according to income, published by the magazine *Exame* in 2006. Most of the interviews (106 out of 120) were face-to-face. The survey was carried out between February and March 2008 for the political elite respondents and between March and May 2008 for the economic elite respondents.

3 A small organization founded in 1982 and orbiting around the Communist Party.

References

Alvarez-Miranda, B. (1996) *Sur de Europa y la adhesión a la Comunidad: los debates políticos*, CIS/Siglo XXI de España, Madrid.

Bacalhau, M. (1994) *Atitudes, opiniões e comportamentos políticos dos portugueses, 1973–1993*, Lisbon.

Barroso, J.M. (1983) *Le système politique portugais face à l'integration européenne: partis politiques et opinion publique*, Associação Portuguesa para o Estudo das Relações Internacionais, Lisbon.

Bermeo, N. (1988) 'Regime change and its impact on Foreign Policy: The Portuguese case', *Journal of Modern Greek Studies*, 6; 14.

Cotta, M. (2008) *A 'compound' model of citizenship? European Citizenship in the eyes of national elites.* Paper presented at the Lisbon IntUne General Assembly, 27–30 November.

Cotta, M. and P. Isernia (2007) *Citizenship in the European polity: questions and explorations*, Report on IntUne Theoretical Framework (www.intune.it/research-materials/theoretical-framework).

Cruz, M. Braga da (1993) 'National Identity in Transition', in *The New Portugal: Democracy and Europe*, ed. R. Herr, Institute of International and Asia Studies, Berkeley, California, pp. 151–62.

Jalali, C., M.C. Lobo and D. Moreira (2008) *Eurobarometer 69: Public Opinion in the European Union*, National Report on Portugal, Lisbon.

Lengyel, G., J. Real-Dato and B. Göncz (2008) 'Intra- and Inter-Elite Consensus and Dissensus on European Policy Making and Policy Priorities', paper presented at the Lisbon IntUne General Assembly, 27–30 November.

Linton, Ralph (1936) *Study of Man*, D. Appleton-Century Co., New York.

Lucena, M. and C. Gaspar (1991) 'Metamorfoses corporativas? Associações de interesses económicos e institucionalização da democracia em Portugal (I)', *Análise Social*, XXVI (114): 847–903.

Parsons, Talcott (1951) *The Social System*, Free Press, Glencoe, IL.

Pinto, A. Costa and M.C. Lobo (2004) 'Forging a positive but instrumental view: Portuguese attitudes towards the EU, 1986–2002', in *Public Opinion and Europe. National Identities and the European Integration Process*, eds A. Dulphy and C. Manigand, Peter Lang, Brussels, pp. 165–81.

Pinto, A. Costa and N. Teixeira (2003) 'From Africa to Europe: Portugal and European integration', in *Southern Europe and the Making of the European Union*, eds. A. Costa Pinto and N. Teixeira, SSM-Columbia University Press, New York, pp. 3–40.

Sanders, David (2008) *European Identity: Evidence from the IntUne surveys of Elite and Mass Publics in 16 European countries*, Paper presented at the Lisbon IntUne General Assembly, 27–30 November.

5 The transformation of Portuguese society

The role of Europeanization

Michael Baum and Miguel Glatzer

Scholars of contemporary Portugal have alternately described Portuguese society and its political economy as 'modern' (Pinto 1998), 'incompletely modern' (Machado and Costa 2000), 'semi-peripheral' (Santos 1993b), typically European (Magone 1997; Corkill 1999; Syrett 2002; Royo and Manuel 2003), and even 'a country like any other' (Barreto and Pontes 2007). While there may be debate about the relative success of Portugal's convergence with European norms in every social, political and economic domain, there is no doubting the country's singularly rapid transformation over the past fifty years. In this chapter we focus on three policy areas, namely family and gender relations, migration, and the welfare state. We chose these three policy areas for their ability to illustrate the vast but uneven convergence of Portugal with Europe in the past fifty years. First, however, we need to explain the selection of our starting date.

Our analysis starts in 1960, a full twenty-five years before Portugal's formal entry into the European Economic Community. Following Barreto (2003), we argue that 1960 represents the beginning of many of the structural transformations of contemporary Portuguese society. Portugal joined the European Free Trade Association in 1960, ushering in an era of foreign investment, industrialization, and rapid economic growth. Mass tourism, most of it from the wealthier European countries, also developed rapidly in the 1960s, bringing cultural contact in its wake. Similarly, it is in this period that emigration flows from Portugal shifted from the Americas and Africa as the predominant destinations to Europe, further enhancing contact with European norms. Finally, 1961 marked the beginning of the disastrous colonial wars, thus ushering in the end of empire and the fall of the authoritarian regime.

Family structures and gender roles

One of the most reliably predictable outcomes of socio-economic development is the decline in birth and infant mortality rates and the average size of the family, and increases in mean life expectancy (Inglehart and Norris 2003). What is distinctive about the Portuguese story in this regard is the speed with which it developed a more modern demographic profile. In 1950, Portugal had the youngest population in Europe, but today it has one of the fastest aging populations

(Barreto 2003: 163). Figure 5.1 provides a visualization of the speed with which Portugal has developed a more 'European' demographic profile.

This was accomplished by drastically lowering women's birth and fertility rates, maternal and infant mortalities, the size of the average family and increasing the average age at which women opt to start a family (for more details, see: Nunes de Almeida *et al.* 2000). For example, the average number of children per woman aged 15–49 years dropped from 3.2 in 1960 to 1.4 in 1995 and 1.28 in 2012 (Figure 5.2).

This places Portugal among those countries with the lowest fertility rates in the world. As a result of significant investments in health, infant mortality rates dropped precipitously. In 1960 Portugal lost 81 infants per 1,000 born, significantly worse than Spain (44) and Greece's (53) rates, but by 2009 Portugal had surpassed both of those countries, with only three deaths per 1,000 born (Gapminder 2010). That is half the rate of infant mortality of the United States and ranks Portugal among the best performing countries in the world on this development indicator.

These changes were linked to fundamental transformations in women's roles in Portuguese society. In 1960, many women in Portugal still did not have basic citizenship rights. Women were prohibited from the diplomatic service and could not serve as judges (Vicente 1993). Until 1969 they needed written permission to leave the country, and in some parts of rural Portugal, women's positions in society were described as similar to the public roles of women in traditional societies (Cutileiro 1971). However, today women's roles throughout the national territory have converged with European norms, and in some areas, even surpassed them. Take for example Portuguese family structures and the rapid secularization of society. Since 1960, marriage rates have plummeted and the percentage of civil (as opposed to Catholic) marriages surpassed the 50 per cent threshold in 2007 (Figure 5.3). Related to this is the increasing number of children being born out of wedlock and the percentage of unions that involve cohabitation rather than marriage (civil or religious). This is particularly common in Lisbon and the southern half of the country (Nunes de Almeida *et al.* 2000: 42).

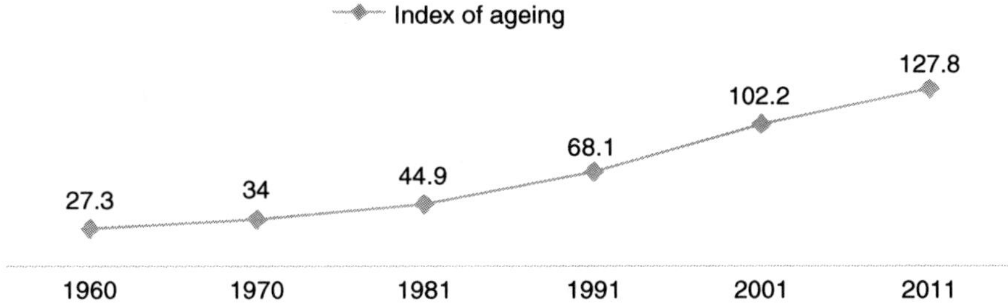

Figure 5.1 Ageing Index, 1960–2011: ratio of those aged 65 and older per 100 youth aged 9–14 (sources: PORDATA (2012) and INE X-XV: General Census of the Population).

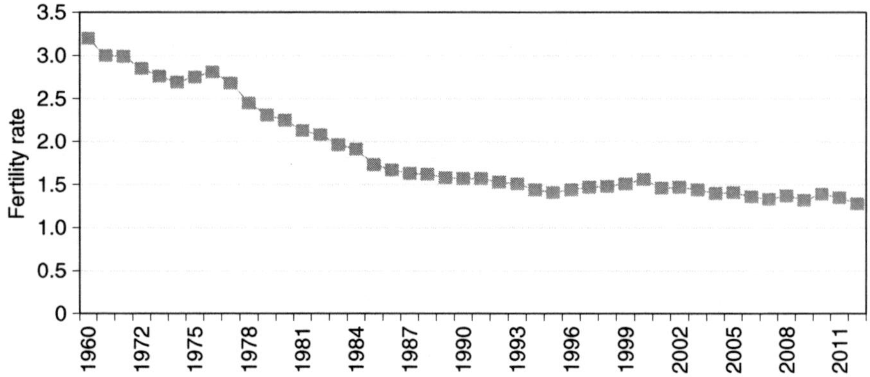

Figure 5.2 Fertility rate, 1960–2012* (women aged 15–49) (source: PORDATA (2013a) and INE).

Note
* Number of live births born that year to women of fertile age.

More recently, abortion up to the tenth week was made legal in 2007 (Freire 2008) and in 2010 gay couples were permitted to marry. Efforts to allow adoption rights for same-sex couples continued through 2012. These were developments that were simply unthinkable before Portugal joined the European Union.

Linked to these transformations in the family and gender roles was the dramatic entrance of women into the paid workforce. In 1960 only 13 per cent of women were in the paid labour force, whereas by 1996 they represented nearly 47 per cent (Nunes de Almeida *et al.* 2000). In terms of activity rates, while women made up only between 20–25 per cent of the labour force in 1960 (Barreto 2003: 167), they now constitute 56 per cent of those who are economically active (Pordata 2010). This profile is atypical for Southern European countries, putting Portugal closer to the rates achieved in Scandinavia and northern Europe. For

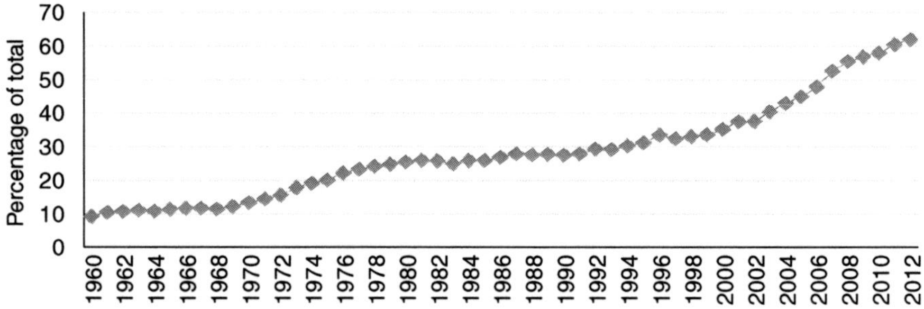

Figure 5.3 Proportion of non-Catholic heterosexual marriages as share of total, 1960–2012 (source: PORDATA (2013b) and INE: Marriage Statistics, various years).

example, in 1995 only Denmark had more young mothers in the active labour force (87 per cent), as compared to Portugal (77 per cent) while, for comparison, Spain's rate was 47 per cent (see Nunes de Almeida *et al.* 2000: 50). As Barreto (2003: 167) argues, while industrialization and 'tertiarization' were partially behind women's integration into the labour force, emigration and the colonial wars were the main factors spurring women to earn cash wages. The low wages of both male and female workers in Portugal have made the traditional 'breadwinner model' difficult there, except for the most well-off families. Moreover, the proximity of families who could be relied upon for daycare and the relative availability of cheap (female) domestic labour are other factors that explain the high rates of female activity (Wall *et al.* 2001). From this perspective, Portugal's dramatic convergence with Europe is primarily a bottom-up process, based upon the micro-motives of individual Portuguese women and families, but that is hardly the whole story.

Such decisions take place in a political and historical context deeply shaped by state action – witness how the colonial wars and the creation of a more export-oriented economy (following EFTA membership in 1959) provided new incentives for women to enter the paid labour force. The same is true for women's education. Education rates for women have improved dramatically, to the point where females are now significantly less likely than males to leave secondary school before completing their compulsory education, and make up 65 per cent of those receiving university diplomas (Barreto 2003: 165). The feminization of university researchers has outpaced most other European countries, such that Eurostat data from 2003 show Portugal in fourth place among the EU25.

Remaining inequalities from what was a traditionally patriarchal society continue to be addressed by the state in response to pressures from both Portuguese civil society actors as well as the diffusion of European best practices. Two examples in the political realm include the creation of a Commission for Equality and the Rights of Women (CIDM), and the government's 2006 passing of a gender quota law mandating that women make up 33 per cent of the candidate lists for European, local, and national parliamentary elections (Baum and Espírito-Santo 2012). Women now make up 27.4 per cent of the national parliament, which places Portugal thirty-third in the world on this indicator of gender parity, well ahead of countries like Greece (seventy-second) or the United States, which is tied for seventy-third place with Turkmenistan (Inter-Parliamentary Union 2010). Evidence of the state's relative progress on the gender equality front is also provided by the United Nation's Gender Empowerment Measure (GEM), which in 2009 ranked Portugal nineteenth in the world, significantly higher than its Human Development Index (HDI) rank of thirty-fourth (United Nations Development Programme 2009a). Even the United Nations' newly created index of gender inequality, called the GII-Gender Inequality Index, ranked Portugal twenty-first in the world in 2010, markedly better than its fortieth-place ranking on the human development index (HDI) for that year (United Nations Development Programme 2010).

On the other hand, we do not wish to present an unrealistic picture of gender equality in Portugal, since the state has clearly been reticent to tackle egregious gender gaps in other critical areas of the economy and society. For example, in a 2006 report issued by the European Professional Women's Network, Portugal was the only country that did not have a single woman on the board of any of its public companies. By 2008 it was still last, with only 2.1 per cent, against a mean of nearly 10 per cent in the seventeen countries reported (European Professional Women's Network 2008: 16). Sociologists have also consistently reported on the relatively unequal division of (household) labour that continues to characterize the typical Portuguese family (Torres 2006: 24). According to that survey, women's 'double duty' is actually about four times greater than men's. Women who work outside the home in Portugal spend nearly four hours per day on household chores while their working male partners only spend 1.3 hours (ibid.).

In this policy area, as in the others we detail below, the convergence story is clearly a mixed one. However, our perspective argues that Portuguese society has been radically altered by the changes that have occurred in the family and gender roles over the past fifty years, even if we have only been able to highlight a few of the most important ones here. We argue that in this policy area, despite uneven progress, the state has effectively promoted policies that have moved the country's gender and family roles to be more in line with European norms, including the implementation of legislation requiring positive efforts to address gender discrimination.

Migration/immigration

Barreto (2003: 164–165) argues convincingly that of all the changes in Portuguese society since 1960, the reversal of Portugal's position as a net exporter of its human capital to one of the fastest growing recipients of foreign immigrants is perhaps the most dramatic. Between 1960 and 1973, before the first oil shock put an end to Europe's *Trentes Glorieuses*, more than 1.5 million Portuguese left their country to find work. No other European country experienced a greater haemorrhage as a share of its population in the 1960s. Barreto (2003: 313) also notes that Portugal occupies the extreme outlier on several other variables of interest here. For example, as a share of the population, the return in the 1970s of the white settler population from Portugal's newly independent ex-colonies in Africa represented the most rapid (and we would argue, the most successful) mass migration back to the country of origin ever in Europe. It reached 7 per cent in just one year. Similarly, in the 1990s and early 2000s, no other European country experienced a faster growth rate of foreign immigrants, despite the fact that their share of the total resident population has never reached greater than 7.2 per cent[1] (United Nations Development Programme 2009b). Figure 5.4, based on annual estimates from Portuguese government departments, SEF/MAI (Borders and Immigration Service/Ministry of Internal Affairs, or Service de Estrangeiros/Fronteiras Ministerio de Administracao Interna) and INE (Instiuto Nacional de Estastica or National Institute of Statistics) illustrates this growth, albeit with significantly lower numbers than those reported by the United Nations.

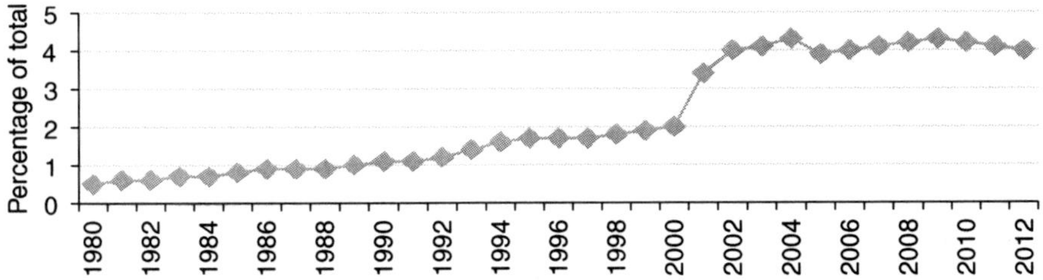

Figure 5.4 Foreigners as share of total population, 1980–2012 (source: PORDATA (2013c); SEF/MAI, INE – annual estimates of resident population).

Whatever their actual share of the resident population, the presence of foreigners, in particular the sharp increase in those without close linguistic or cultural ties to Portugal, has meant that the country's visible identity has become significantly more cosmopolitan, particularly in Lisbon and other coastal cities. Whereas immigration was previously dominated by citizens from the Portuguese-speaking African countries (PALOPs), the profile of immigrants is now much more diversified, with a dramatic increase in the presence of Brazilians. As Figure 5.5 illustrates with Eurostat data from 1998–2009, Brazilians are now the largest group of non-EU27 nationals with a presence in Portugal, followed by the Ukrainians. Cape Verdeans are now only the third largest group of non-EU27 nationals.

While this changeover in Portugal's status as a net 'sender' of its people to a net 'receiver' of other's country's citizens occurred in the 1970s and 1980s, the public perception of immigration as a hot political issue has only recently become more

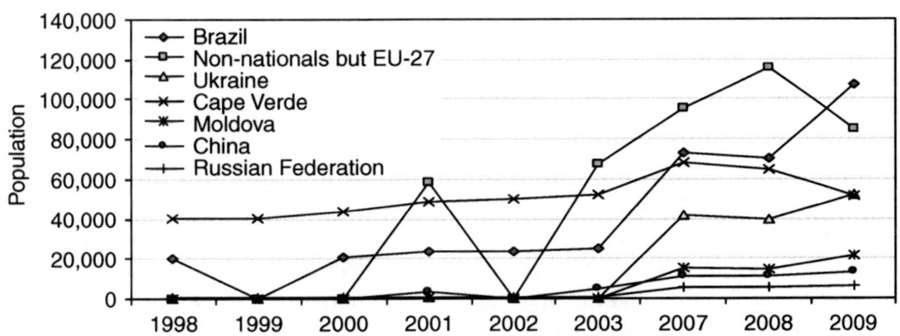

Figure 5.5 Largest groups of foreigners living in Portugal by country/regional group, 1998–2009 (source: European Commission, various years).

Note

Composition of 'usually resident population' by country of citizenship does not include those with 'permits of stay'.

salient. The reasons for this are numerous. First, only recently has the total share of foreigners within the national population begun to reach significant levels. Second, just as immigration has gained visibility as a major social issue in the rest of (Western) Europe, its salience has grown in Portugal, particularly following September 11, 2001 (Ferin *et al.* 2008). Finally, it has also gained visibility as a result of the controversies surrounding the 2008 ratification by the Portuguese parliament of the orthographic accords signed by the Community of Portuguese Language Countries (CPLP in its Portuguese acronym) in 1990 (see Zúqete 2008). Despite this increase, however, we would argue that compared with other EU states, the salience of the immigration issue remains low in Portugal.

As we argue in greater detail below, what is surprising about the rapid influx of foreigners in Portugal is the absence of any significant development of far-right or anti-foreigner political parties. They exist, of course, the most prominent being the *Partido Nacional Renovador* (PNR), but they have never gained enough public support to win any parliamentary or local council seats.[2] However, lest one assume that the Lusotropicalist thesis[3] explains the absence of virulent anti-immigrant or racist feelings in Portugal, or that the country's long history of emigration has somehow served as an empathetic vaccination against foreign immigrants; attitudinal surveys suggest a much more complicated reality.

Jorge Vala *et al.* (2006) have studied racism in Portugal and the different perceptions of threat using 2002 data from the European Social Survey (ESS). Their comparative analysis came to the conclusion that among the four countries they studied closely, the UK, France, Germany and Portugal, Portugal was the country with the highest public expression of opposition to immigration. Even when compared against the full sample average of all EU21 countries included in that module, the Portuguese were the least in favour of admitting 'many or some' people coming from different types of countries – rich European, rich from outside Europe, poor European, poor from outside Europe, and the like (see also Martínez-Herrera and Moualhi 2006). For example, when considering immigrants that originate from European countries that are poorer than the receiving country, the variation between Portugal, the least supportive country, and Sweden, the most supportive, ranged from 39 per cent to 87 respectively (ibid.: 218). Curiously, unemployment rates are a poor predictor of these attitudinal differences, since Portugal had below-average unemployment at the time of the survey, as it had throughout the 1980s and 1990s when immigration growth was booming in Portugal.

Moreover, we may also look at attitudes toward the integration of new migrants, with support for multiculturalism at one end of the spectrum versus support for assimilation at the other pole. Assimilation in this sense is defined as 'the expectation that minorities adapt completely to the host society and its political system through a process of individual change, in which immigrants give up their different cultural backgrounds in order to adopt the hegemonic group culture' (Martínez-Herrera and Moualhi 2006: 222). Here again, Portuguese attitudes stand out as Europe's most *assimilationist* (Martínez-Herrera and Moualhi 2006: 222–223).

The complicated nature of Portuguese attitudes toward immigrants is even more clearly underlined if we look at levels of support (in theory) for immigrants having equal rights with nationals. Two-thirds of Europeans (66 per cent) agreed with the statement that 'people who have come to live to their country ought to have the same rights as nationals'. The rate is 80 per cent in Portugal, the second highest of all the countries surveyed. However, almost half of the Europeans (47 per cent) also agreed with the sentiment that when immigrants experience a long period of unemployment, they should be expelled from the country. The citizens with the greatest support for expulsion were surprisingly the Portuguese (58 per cent agree), as compared to the Spanish (24 per cent) or the Swedes, where only 11 per cent agreed with that sentiment (ibid.: 225).

Now it could just be that the Portuguese are the least politically correct survey respondents in Europe and thus have no qualms about expressing less 'politically correct' sentiments in public surveys, but this fails to explain the inconsistencies we find in the Portuguese data as it relates to attitudes toward immigrants. Maritínez-Herrera and Moualhi (2006) suggest instead that it is more probably related to Portuguese respondents' lack of a thought-out or coherent opinion on the themes of the study. We agree with their suggestion that the limitations of sophisticated public debate on immigration issues in countries with comparatively recent experience of immigration may well be what is behind the inconsistent attitudes. We should also keep in mind the low average levels of education and high levels of poverty in Portugal, which are also presumably related to incoherent opinions on this and other complex policy issues (Freire and Baum 2003; Baum and Espírito-Santo 2012). These ambiguities in public opinion suggest that the state can play an especially influential role in shaping policy in this area.

By institutionalizing in 1996 a new government Commission on Immigrants and Ethnic Minorities (*Alto Commissariado para a Imigração e Minorias Étnicas* – ACIME) and using it to undertake outreach efforts and to commission studies, and propose policy and legislative action, the state has recognized the need to pay attention to the issue of the rising diversity and multiculturalism in Portugal. Pedro Zúqete (2007: 193) for example, has argued that ACIME 'displays a strong cultural and educational activism aimed at both enforcing a "positive" public view of immigration and inoculating it against the message of the extreme right'. To this he also adds the influence of the Catholic subculture in Portugal – with an inclusive and ecumenical discourse – such that it also may serve as a brake on any political discourses of exclusion or intolerance on immigration. The Church, for example, has supported immigration reforms that are 'sensitive' to the needs and demands of the immigrants and based on 'solidarity', and rejects any nationalist leanings, because of Portugal's own historical status as a 'country of emigrants' (Zúqete 2007: 193). While it is true that the power of the Church as a social actor has generally declined in Portugal since democratization, it is still a privileged civil society actor that has an impact on the political behaviour of its members and sympathizers, particularly in certain regions of the country (Manuel 2002).[4]

External assessments of Portugal's relative success at integrating migrants have also been quite positive. For example, Peixoto and Sabino (2009: 5) mention the fact that Portugal is ranked second out of 28 European countries in a recent comparative migrant integration policy index (Mipex), which confirms the state's relatively successful policies in this area, at least in the European context. The Mipex overview for Portugal is worth quoting from directly:

> Proposed new immigration and nationality laws have aimed to simplify and facilitate access to family reunion, long-term residence, and nationality for legally-resident third-country-nationals (hereafter 'migrants') and their children born in Portugal. A relatively new country of immigration, Portugal has put in place a legal framework on integration composed of favourable policies and best practice. Portugal does not have far to go to improve labour market access, family reunion, and anti-discrimination which all score 2nd out of the 28 MIPEX countries. Slightly favourable policies on long-term residence rank fourth in the EU-25, while access to nationality policies rank third.
>
> (Mipex 2010)

Moreover, despite the fact that some researchers and public officials consider the immigration process too complex, bureaucratic and ineffective (Peixoto and Sabino 2009: 5), the fact that no significant anti-immigration party has emerged in Portugal despite a dramatic uptick in new immigrants is, in our mind, yet another positive aspect to how the state has handled this challenge to 'national identity'. Of course, we in no way mean to paste over the fact that racism and prejudice are alive and well in Portugal (SOS 2010) or that at times, state representatives and the media have publicly associated criminality with the presence of immigrants (Ferin *et al.* 2008), but thus far a combination of deliberate state policy and a progressive stance on immigration by the Catholic Church have helped to defuse the 'political opportunity structure' afforded by this structural change in Portuguese society. In this domain, we regard the Portuguese state as a relatively progressive policy maker, rather than a passive policy taker at the European level.

The welfare state and inequality

Since 1960, economic growth, social change and the development of the welfare state have led to dramatic transformations in work and income. One of the most striking changes is that the state has become a crucial provider of non-work income. The number of beneficiaries of the social security system rose from a mere 56,000 in 1960 to 800,000 by 1975, 2 million by 1985 and 2.5 million by 2000. Starting in the late 1960s during the Caetano years, the rapid rise in the 1970s and 1980s reflected decisions to extend the pension system to previously unprotected segments of the population, such as rural workers and domestic servants. As a result of the non-contributory pension scheme, Portugal provides universal access to old-age pensions. Through old-age and widowed persons' pensions, the elderly represent by far the largest group receiving cash transfers from the state, although the unemployed, the disabled, the sick, families and the very poor are also eligible for transfers.

From a human development perspective, this decision had tremendously positive implications (see earlier section on demography and development). However, the cost of providing these benefits is large. From 1995 to 2008, social transfers increased from 11.2 per cent of GDP to 15.6 per cent (Banco de Portugal 2009: 350). By contrast, the weight of social transfers in the Euro Area 12 declined during this period from 16.9 to 16.1 per cent of GDP.[5] Portugal, the poorest country in the Euro Area 12, devotes a comparable share of its wealth to social transfers. The role of the state in income support – either directly through government employment or through social transfers – thus amounted to 28.5 per cent of GDP in 2008. By contrast, the Euro Area 12 average was 26.2 per cent. Portugal has exceeded many of its European counterparts in the degree to which personal income is provided through the state.

The growth in cash transfers was mirrored in the education and health sectors, the two principal services of the welfare state, and can again be seen through the lens of government accounts. In the EU15 in 2008, public spending on health and education (including salaries) consumed 11.7 per cent of GDP. In Portugal, this share was over 13.8 per cent (calculated from Banco de Portugal 2009). Again in this case, government effort in the provision of health and education services, at least as measured in expenditure data, exceeds many of its European counterparts.

It is thus fair to say that in these three areas of access to income – pensions, education, and health – the immense social structural transformations in Portuguese society are deeply influenced by profound changes in the role of the state. This very large government effort has had mixed results. Improvements in health have been dramatic but income inequality and poverty, though reduced, remain high. Although educational access has expanded greatly, serious concerns over quality and attainment remain (Soares 2010: 329–333).

Despite significant state effort in income support, high employment rates and low levels of unemployment through the mid-2000s, Portugal has had high rates of poverty and levels of inequality by Western European standards. In 2007, with an 80/20 income quintile ratio of 6.5 in Portugal, only Romania and Bulgaria had worse levels of income inequality (Eurostat 2009: 34). In the late 2000s, however, it made progress in this area, in part by reducing poverty. By 2009 Portugal's at-risk-of-poverty rate (defined as below 60 per cent of median income) after social transfers was 17.9 per cent compared with a Euro area average of 15.9 per cent (Eurostat 2013a). Portugal ranked better than Spain, Greece and Italy on this measure having improved since 2000, when 19.1 per cent of the Portuguese population lived in poverty (Rodrigues 2007).

The complex financial and sovereign debt problems known as the Euro crisis led Portugal in 2011 to accept a 78 billion Euro bailout from the troika composed of the European Commission, the European Central Bank and the International

Monetary Fund. The deep austerity measures that are a condition of the bailout have exacerbated a severe recession that has lasted, at the time of writing, close to two years. Unemployment rose from 8.5 per cent in 2008 to 15.9 per cent in August 2012 with an under-25 unemployment rate of 38.5 per cent (Eurostat 2013b). From 2008 to 2012, the average gross wage fell by 8.3 per cent (Correia and Santos 2013). Controlling for inflation and increased income taxes, average take-home pay in 2013 is expected to have fallen by over 20 per cent below the level of 2008.

Although the government had some room for manoeuvre in determining the ratio of tax increases to spending cuts, contraction on social spending per beneficiary in the three core welfare state areas of transfers, health and education was largely inevitable given the depth of the agreed-to austerity targets. Particular programs such as unemployment insurance have seen major increases in spending, though a majority of the unemployed fail to qualify for the program due to insufficient work histories or because they have remained unemployed for too long. Substantial increases in utilities costs, public transportation costs and VAT have further reduced the purchasing power of transfers for those who do receive them.

As median incomes have fallen so has the poverty threshold. As a result, increases in the poverty rate appear relatively low, but this is somewhat of a statistical artefact as Farinha Rodrigues has argued. From 2009 to 2010, for example, the poverty rate increased from 17.9 to 18 per cent. However, if the 2009 poverty line (434 Euros a month) is used and anchored for inflation, an additional 160,000 people joined the ranks of the 1.8 million poor in 2010, an increase of 8.8 per cent. By this measure, the poverty rate would have jumped to 19.6 per cent (Rodrigues, in Teixeira 2012). Nonetheless, Portugal's poverty rates, while above the Euro area average, have risen less than those in Spain, Greece and Italy, reflecting both the different depths and effects of the crisis and the different scales and distributive impacts of the austerity measures.

Several factors explain the apparent paradox of convergence to European norms in terms of substantial welfare state effort and a high level of direct state employment, but continued high poverty rates. The first set of factors has to do with the labour market, and with the problem of low wages and high wage inequality. The distribution of income is very unequal and correlates closely with the high inequality in educational attainment. Income among agricultural workers is also low, contributing to significant regional differences in income and poverty rates. This can be seen in the high poverty rates of 50.4 per cent for people working in agriculture and of 48.3 per cent for people with less than the full four years of primary education (Rodrigues 2007).

There is debate about the degree to which the Portuguese tax system reduces income inequality. Many analysts argue that evasion, tax shifting, deductions, reductions in the number of tax brackets and the differential treatment of wage income from capital gains reduce the progressivity of the Portuguese tax system (Lopes 2005; OECD 2001, 2003). Writing in 2001, the OECD found that Portuguese 'income taxation achieves little in the way of income redistribution'

(OECD 2001: 77). Two years later, the OECD had become more pessimistic, writing, 'the fiscal system probably exacerbates the inequality of income distribution' (OECD 2003: 90). The Portuguese welfare state, like many of the welfare states in Southern Europe, privileges pension spending. Although a social pension scheme covers individuals who did not contribute enough during their working lives to qualify for the regular state pension system, the bulk of spending occurs in the latter system and this system is Bismarckian, replicating differences in earned income.[6]

However, other analysts find that state taxes and targeted transfers are indeed redistributive and became substantially more so during the 1990s (Rodrigues 2007). Improvements in tax collection and the development of substantial anti-poverty programmes, such as the *Rendimento Mínimo Garantido* [Minimum Guaranteed Income] were effective in compensating for widening market inequalities of income. It is this greater redistributive effort of the state, countervailing ever-wider wage inequality, which accounts for the relative stability, and at times moderate improvement, in the Gini index.

Because the Portuguese welfare state is pension-heavy, it under-provides community social services such as day centres and long-term care for the elderly, the disabled and the chronically ill (Bronchi 2003). In response, the Portuguese state has developed tax incentives for charitable giving to social service non-profit-making bodies and has contracted with these groups to provide services (Glatzer in progress). The relative paucity of services in this area led some analysts to argue that Portugal was not a welfare state, but a welfare society (Santos 1993a). In the absence of state provision, society – either through the extended family or through the community – met needs. This concept has been challenged by findings that supportive social networks are richer and more prevalent at the higher end of the socio-economic and educational distribution. As a result, informally provided welfare seems to 'reinforce existing social inequalities and to offer less support for those who most need support' (Wall *et al.* 2001: 230). Nonetheless, rates of volunteering and charitable giving have been increasing and the number of nonprofit social service organizations, many of them designed to meet new social needs, continues to grow (Sousa *et al.* 2013). Because the welfare state is increasingly intermeshed with civil society organizations, and because the institutional structure and policy apparatus of the welfare state remains in place, recent cuts to social spending, though severe, do not represent a whole scale dismantling of the Portuguese welfare state.

Conclusion

Given space limitations, our analysis of Portugal's experience with Europeanization can only be partial. We examined three main policy areas as a way of sampling the extent to which Portugal has converged with EU norms since its accession to the community in 1986. The policy areas we assess include family structures and gender roles, migration/immigration, and welfare state developments and their attendant impact on inequality. Since Europe-induced change starts well before countries formally adhere to the EU, we make the case for examining Portugal's change in these policy areas primarily from 1960 on.

Our definition of Europeanization is based upon the work of scholars such as Anderson (2002), Cowles *et al.* (2001), or Goetz and Hix (2001), who see it as an independent variable with uneven but far-reaching effects on the policies and institutions of the member states. We further view the process as having both top-down and bottom-up forces driving the change, due to pressures coming from the EU- and national state-levels, as well as individual and family-level decision-making. Our goal was not only to describe some of the tremendous shifts that have occurred in Portuguese society and economy over the past fifty years, but also to assess the extent to which processes of social transformation have been shaped, encouraged or resisted by the Portuguese state and its public policies.

Previous research on Portugal has at times stressed the uneven distribution of the benefits of Europeanization (Santos 1993b; Magone 1997; Corkill 1999; Syrett 2002), with some studies focusing more on inequalities that are regional/spatial or economy/sectoral in nature, while others evaluate specific public policy areas (Soares 2010). Our analysis follows the latter approach and finds that while progress has been dramatic on several fronts – at least in terms of defining 'progress' as convergence toward EU norms – progress has indeed been uneven, partial, and unequal.

Arguably, the most successful convergence has occurred in the area of family structures and human/gender development indicators. Since 1960, Portugal has gone from a position well behind the other late industrializers of Southern Europe to one of leadership, not only in Europe but at a global level. We specifically cited the progress made on basic health indicators such as infant life expectancy, birth rates and maternal mortality, and other gendered measures of human development, including women's labour activity rates, women's representation in parliament, and the feminization of higher education. In these areas we found strong evidence of a complementary relationship between state-level policies and the micro-level decisions of Portuguese women and their families.

Similarly, we are impressed by the relative ease with which the Portuguese state has introduced progressive social legislation, for example in terms of such potentially divisive issues as gay marriage, abortion, gender quotas to increase women's political representation, and policies promoting the social inclusion of new migrants. It has done so in an attitudinal environment that is not particularly progressive (see the section on Portuguese attitudes toward migrants), and without spawning the kind of counter-attack from more conservative voices that one has seen both in recent Portuguese history, for example during Portugal's First Republic, or elsewhere in contemporary Europe. As a result, Portuguese legislative achievement in this area (courts have played a relatively minor role) make it an important contemporary example of the ways in which the state, as an actor in its own right, can be a promoter of social change (Evans *et al.* 1985). Whether this is due to fortuitous policy designs by Portuguese politicians or the residual weaknesses of Portuguese civil society is a debate better left further research (Baum and Glatzer in progress).

In social policy, the Portuguese state has invested tremendous resources in education, health and income support. Yet, with the notable exception of health and the partial exception of poverty, greatly increased spending has had disappointing results. Educational gaps remain severe and poverty and income inequality remain high. The growth of public sector employment masked an anaemic performance in the private sector and unemployment – which during the 1980s and 1990s was low – is now high (15.9 per cent in 2012) and substantially above the Euro Area average of 11.4 per cent (Eurostat 2013b). Since 2000, Portugal's relative gap with the EU average on important measures such as growth rates and GDP/capita has widened. Increases in state spending outstripped very substantial increases in taxation and one-off revenue measures. More recently, the Euro crisis, along with poor future prospects for economic growth, has led investors to become increasingly skittish about Portuguese debt and deficit spending, forcing the government to accept a bailout that imposes severe austerity and has resulted in a long-lasting deep recession with high unemployment.

Nonetheless, problems such as economic growth and job creation, budget deficits and welfare state reform, population aging and the continued incorporation of immigrants, are issues that confront not just Portugal but many if not most of its European counterparts. Responses to these issues will come from innovation at the national level, policy learning from other states and, crucially, developments at the EU level. In this sense at least, Portugal is now fully European.

Notes

1 There are discrepancies in the reporting of immigrants as a share of the total population. Peixoto and Sabino (2009), for example, cite a figure of only 4 per cent of the total population, based on official Portuguese government figures stating the total number of legal resident foreigners in 2007 as roughly 436,000. The 2009 UNDP study cites a figure of 764,000 resident foreigners in 2005, which equals 7.2 per cent of the total resident population. Jorge Vala *et al.* (2006) cite a figure of 5 per cent, but no date is given.

2 Although see Zúqete (2007), who argues that the recent structural changes in Portuguese society: the sharp increase in immigration, a situation of economic crisis, above-average unemployment rates and divergence from EU living standards, calls for the radical restructuring of the welfare state, and so on, all provide a ripe 'political opportunity structure' for the development of radical right discourse by new political entrepreneurs. To date, this has yet to materialize, but the opportunity for growth remains great.

3 The notion first advanced by the Brazilian sociologist/anthropologist Gilberto Freyre that purports to explain the multi-racial makeup of Brazil as a result of the supposedly unique characteristics of Portuguese colonialism. Specifically, that 'due to a series of interrelated climatological, geographical, historical, cultural, and genetic factors, the Portuguese have been more inclined to racially intermix with peoples of the tropics' (Arenas 2005).

4 Nowadays, Portuguese levels of religiosity, as measured by frequency of church attendance, are quite close to the European average (*Economist* 2010).

5 The Euro Area 12 consists of Austria, Belgium, Finland, France, Germany, Greece, Ireland, Italy, Luxembourg, the Netherlands, Portugal, and Spain.

6 Named after Otto von Bismarck, the German chancellor at the end of the nineteenth century who first developed the welfare state, Bismarckian social insurance systems feature tight links between an individual's wages and pension. This stands in contrast to other systems that redistribute across incomes, where variation in the value of pensions is lower than in wages. A system of flat, universal pensions of equal amount is thus the opposite of a Bismarckian system.

Bibliography

Anderson, Jeffrey J. (2002) 'Europeanization and the Transformation of the Democratic Polity, 1945-2000', *Journal of Common Market Studies*, 40(5): 793–822.

Arenas, F. (2005) '(Post)Colonialism, Globalization and Lusofonia or the 'Time-Space' of the Portuguese-Speaking World', *Institute of European Studies Working Paper Series*, Available: http://escholarship.org/uc/item/0vh0f7t9 (accessed 7 May 2010).

Banco De Portugal (2009) *The Portuguese Economy in the Context of Economic, Financial and Monetary Integration*, Lisbon: Banco de Portugal-Economics and Research Department.

Barreto, A. (2003) 'Social Change in Portugal: 1960–2000', in A. C. Pinto (ed.) *Contemporary Portugal: politics, society and culture*. Boulder, CO: Social Science Monographs.

Barreto, A. and Pontes, J. (2007) *Portugal, Um Retrato Social 07: Um País Como Os Outros*, DVD documentary + book. Directed by A. Barreto and J. Pontes, Lisbon: RTP and *Público* Newspaper.

Baum, M. and Espírito-Santo, A. (2012) 'The Causes of the Adoption of a Gender Quota Law in Portugal', *West European Politics*, 35(2): 319–342.

Baum, M. and Glatzer, M. (eds) (in progress) *Civil Society after Democratization: Reflections on the Quality of Portuguese Democracy*: unpublished manuscript.

Bronchi, C. (2003) 'The Effectiveness of Public Expenditure in Portugal', *OECD Working Paper No. 198/2003*, Available: www-3.unipv.it/websiep/wp/198.pdf (accessed 1 October 2010).

Corkill, D. (1999) *The Development of the Portuguese Economy: a case of Europeanization*, London; New York: Routledge.

Correia A. and P. Santos (2013) 'Salários encolhem ... e muito', *Visão* no. 1039: 44–49.

Cowles, M. G., Caporaso, J. A. and Risse-Kappen, T. (eds) (2001) *Transforming Europe: Europeanization and domestic change*, Ithaca, NY: Cornell University Press.

Cutileiro, J. (1971) *A Portuguese Rural Society*, Oxford: Clarendon Press.

Economist, The (2010) 'Europe's irreligious', *The Economist*, 9 August, Available: www.economist.com/node/16767758 (accessed 18 August 2010).

European Commission (various years) Statistics by theme. Available: http://epp.eurostat.ec.europa.eu/portal/page/portal/statistics/themes (accessed 8 April 2010).

European Professional Women's Network (2008) '3rd EuropeanPWN BoardWomen Monitor 2008'. Available: www.europeanpwn.net/files/presentation_bwm_2008.pdf (accessed 30 September 2013).

Eurostat (2009) *The Social Situation in the European Union: 2007*: European Union. Available: http://epp.eurostat.ec.europa.eu/cache/ity_offpub/ke-ag-08–001/en/ke-ag-08–001-en.pdf (accessed 18 July 2010).

Eurostat (2013a). 'Income distribution statistics'. Available: http://epp.eurostat.ec.europa.eu/statistics_explained/index.php/Income_distribution_statistics (accessed 11 July 2013).

Eurostat (2013b) 'Unemployment statistics'. Available: http://epp.eurostat.ec.europa.eu/statistics_explained/index.php/Unemployment_statistics (accessed 14 October 2013).

Evans, P., Rueschemeyer, D. and Skocpol, T. (eds) (1985) *Bringing the State Back In*, Cambridge: Cambridge University Press.

Ferin, I., Almeida Santos, C., Filho, W. and Fortes, I. (2008) 'Media, Imigração e Minorias Étnicas – 2005–2006', Alto-Comissariado Para a Imigração E Diálogo Intercultural. Available: www.oi.acidi.gov.pt/docs/Col_EstudosOI/OI_28.pdf (accessed 1 October 2013).

Freire, A. (2008) *Sociedade Civil, Democracia Participativa e Poder Político. O Caso do Referendo do Aborto 2007*, Lisbon: Friedrich Ebert Stiftung.

Freire, A. and Baum, M. (2003) '1998 Portuguese referendums: explaining the results and speculating on the future of direct democracy in Portugal', *Portuguese Journal of Social Science*, 2(1 September): 5–19.

Gapminder (2010) 'Gapminder World Database', Available: www.gapminder.org/ (accessed 1 September 2010).

Glatzer, M. (in progress) 'The Portuguese Welfare State and the Role of NGOs', in M. Baum and M. Glatzer (eds) *Civil Society after Democratization: Reflections on the Quality of Portuguese Democracy*: unpublished manuscript.

Goetz, Klaus H., and Hix, Simon (2001) *Europeanised Politics?: European integration and national political systems*. London and Portland, OR: Frank Cass.

Inglehart, R. and Norris, P. (2003) *Rising Tide: Gender Equality & Cultural Change around the World*, New York: Cambridge University Press.

Inter-Parliamentary Union, IPU (2010) 'Women in National Parliaments Database', Available: www.ipu.org/wmn-e/classif.htm (accessed 8 May 2010).

Lopes, J. D. S. (2005) 'Financas Publicas', in P. Lains and A. Ferreira Da Silva (eds) *História Económica de Portugal, Sec. XX*. Lisbon: Imprensa de Ciencias Sociais.

Machado, F. L. and Costa, A. F. D. (2000) 'An Incomplete Modernity: Structural Change and Social Mobility', in J. M. L. Viegas and A. F. D. Costa (eds) *Crossroads to Modernity: Contemporary Portuguese Society*. Oeiras: Celta.

Magone, J. (1997) *European Portugal*, New York: St. Martin's Press.

Manuel, P. C. (2002) 'Religion and Politics in Iberia: Clericalism, Anticlericalism, and Democratization in Portugal and Spain', in T. G. Jelen and C. Wilcox (eds) *Religion and Politics in Comparative Perspective: the one, the few, and the many*. New York: Cambridge University Press.

Martínez-Herrera, E. and Moualhi, D. (2006) 'Predispositions to discriminatory immigration policies in western Europe: An exploration of political causes', *Portuguese Journal of Social Science*, 5(3): 215–233.

Mipex (Migrant Immigration Policy Index) (2010) 'Portugal Overview', Integration Index. Available: www.integrationindex.eu/integrationindex/2509.html (accessed 8 May 2010).

Nunes De Almeida, A., Guerreiro, M. D. D., Lobo, C., Torres, A. and Wall, K. (2000) 'Family Relations: Change and Diversity', in J. M. L. Viegas and A. F. Da Costa (eds) *Crossroads to Modernity*. Oeiras: Celta.

OECD (2001) *Economic Survey: Portugal*, Paris: OECD.

OECD (2003) *Economic Survey: Portugal*, Paris: OECD.

Peixoto, J. and Sabino, C. (2009) 'Immigration, Emigration and Policy Developments in Portugal', *ARI-Real Instituto Elcano*, 1171–7.

Pinto, A. C. (1998) *Modern Portugal*, Palo Alto: Society for the Promotion of Science and Scholarship, SPOSS.

Pordata (2010) 'PORDATA – Base de Dados Portugal Contemporânea', Available: www.pordata.pt/azap_runtime/ (accessed 29 July 2010).

PORDATA (2012) 'Ageing indicators, according to Census in Portugal', available at www.pordata.pt/en/Portugal/Indicadores+de+envelhecimento+segundo+os+Censos-525 (accessed 14 October 2013).
PORDATA (2013a) 'Fertility indicators: total fertility rate and gross reproduction rate', available at www.pordata.pt/en/Portugal/Indicadores+de+fecundidade+Indice+sintetico+de+fecundidade+e+taxa+bruta+de+reproducao-416 (accessed 14 October 2013).
PORDATA (2013b) 'Marriages between people of the opposite sex: total and by type of ceremony', available at www.pordata.pt/en/Portugal/Casamentos+entre+pessoas+do+sexo+oposto+total+e+por+forma+de+celebracao-1933 (accessed 14 October 2013).
Portadata (2013c) 'Foreign population with regular residence as a % of the resident population: total and by sex', available at www.pordata.pt/en/Portugal/Foreign+population+with+regular+residence+as+a+percentage+of+the+resident+population+total+and+by+sex-533 (accessed 14 October 2013).
Rodrigues, C. F. (2007) *Distribuicao do Rendimento, Desigualdade e Pobreza: Portugal nos Anos 90*, Coimbra: Almedina.
Royo, S. and Manuel, P. C. (eds) (2003) *Spain and Portugal in the European Union: The First Fifteen Years*, London: Frank Cass.
Santos, B. D. S. (1993a) 'O Estado, as relações salariais e o bem-estar social na semi-periferia: o caso português', in B. D. S. Santos (ed.) *Portugal. Um Retrato Singular*. Porto: Edições Afrontamento.
Santos, B. D. S. (1993b) *Portugal. Um Retrato Singular*, Porto: Edições Afrontamento.
Soares, A. G. (2010) 'The Europeanization of Portugal', *European Societies*, 12(3): 317–337.
SOS (2010) *SOS Racismo: Notícias sobre imigração, xenofobia e discriminação racial*. SOS Racismo Blog. Available: http://sosracismo.blogspot.com/ (accessed 1 October 2010).
Sousa, S. *et al.* (2013) *As Instituições Particulares de Solidariedade Social Num Contexto de Crise Económica*. Confederação Nacional das Instituições de Solidariedade.
Syrett, S. (ed.) (2002) *Contemporary Portugal: Dimensions of Economic and Political Change*, Burlington, VT: Ashgate.
Teixeira, C. (2012) 'Economia Entrevista: Carlos Farinha Rodrigues', *Visão* N. 1029: 66–68.
Torres, A. (2006) 'Work and family in Portugal', in G. Rossi (ed.) *Reconciling Family and Work: New Challenges for Social Policies in Europe*. Milan: Franco Agneli.
United Nations Development Programme (2009a) *2009 Human Development Report*, New York: UN.
United Nations Development Programme (2009b) 'Human movement: snapshots and trends', *2009 Human Development Report*. New York: UN.
United Nations Development Programme (2010) 'Gender Inequality Index, GII', in UNDP (ed.) *2010 Human Development Report*. New York: UN.
Vala, J., Pereira, C. and Ramos, A. (2006) 'Racial prejudice, threat perception and opposition to immigration: A comparative analysis', *Portuguese Journal of Social Science*, 5(2): 119–140.
Vicente, A. (1993) 'A Brief Look at Women in Portuguese History', *Ditos e Escritos*, No. 4.
Wall, K., Aboim, S., Cunha, V. and Vasconcelos, P. (2001) 'Families and Informal Support Networks in Portugal: The Reproduction of Inequality', *Journal of European Social Policy*, 11(3): 213–233.
Zúqete, J. P. (2007) 'Portugal: A New Look at the Extreme Right', *Representation*, 43(3 September): 179–198.
Zúqete, J. P. (2008) 'Beyond Reform: The Orthographic Accord and the Future of the Portuguese Language', *South European Society and Politics*, 13(4) (December): 495–506.

Part II

The adjustment in policy areas

6 Portugal and the Common Agricultural Policy

Miguel Rocha de Sousa

Introduction

Portugal applied to join the EEC in 1977 and, following completion of the conditionality procedures, its membership took effect on 1 January 1986 at the same time as that of Spain. One of the concerns both for the Portuguese and European authorities was the weakness found in the primary sector (Varela, 1991: 11), including the agriculture, livestock, forestry, and fishing sub-sectors. This chapter is focused on the Common Agricultural Policy (CAP), and its impact on and interaction between the Portuguese and European authorities.

The analysis of the adoption of the CAP in Portugal gives rise to some questions that we shall address. Was the CAP adopted in a passive, reactive, or proactive way in Portugal? What were the conditionalities of its performance in Portugal? What kinds of lessons can be drawn from the Portuguese experience for newcomers, if any? Was it a success or a failure? How do we compare Portugal's performance with its peers?

First we must begin with a very short definition of two objects of study, the CAP in general and the Portuguese conditionalities at the very start. The CAP was first established in the provisions of the Treaty of Rome of 1958 (arts 38 to 47), but it did not specify the forms of price support to be adopted for each product. The reason for the emergence of CAP and its main objective was that of establishing a free market for agricultural goods, which implied the removal of all agricultural trade barriers. One should note that in 1958, the six EEC countries (the Six) had approximately 15 million people employed in farming, which amounted to around 20 per cent of the total working population of the community (Swan, 1995: 247). This was one of the main reasons why the Six adopted a Common Agricultural Policy and why European Free Trade Area (EFTA) did not. As is well known, before joining the EEC in 1986 Portugal was a member of EFTA, a kind of British-led response to the EEC, which was only a Free Trade Area (FTA) and not a Customs Union (CU), thus one could adopt freely an external tariff regarding third parties in EFTA, which allowed Portugal to protect its agricultural sector. Nevertheless, Portugal even benefited from a special EFTA treaty derogation, the so-called Annex G, which allowed for a much swifter transition. Portugal, even after entering the EEC, was still receiving the last parcel of funds from EFTA. This obviously had costs. The swift transition had the cost of making the necessary adjustments in the productive sectors, and the yields per area (hectares) always remained low.

From its inception the CAP was based upon certain principles, according to the Treaty of Rome, which were defined at the Stresa conference of 3–12 July 1958 (Varela, 1996: 23). First, agriculture was an integrated part of economic activity. Second, trade was needed but so too was protection from unfair competition. Third, the pricing policy should avoid over-production but also try to assure protection for less developed regions. Fourth, the improvement in infrastructure should yield returns to European agriculture that were comparable to other economic activities. Fifth, everything would be done in order to assure the competitiveness of smallholdings. Finally, re-orientation of labour and an industrialisation process should resolve the problem of reallocating inefficient factors of production and agrarian enterprises that were not viable in the long run.

Moreover, three principal ideas stand out as the basis for the general CAP (Varela, 1996: 24). First was the idea of a preferential community arrangement, which was meant simply to protect European farmers from unfair foreign competition. Second, market unification was implemented, which meant that all goods had to have the same price in the EEC zone. Third, at this Stresa conference what became to be known in the CAP jargon as its 'original sin' (Varela, 1996: 25), was the idea of levelling up prices upwards – this would later put a huge burden on the EU budget.

One of the main challenges that Portuguese authorities had to cope with was that of adopting the CAP as a kind of modernising and reforming tool for changing the structure of the agricultural sector. Instead of entering into details[1] regarding mechanisms for different price supports that are not easily accessible to the layman, one must understand that CAP had the objective of helping and maintaining farmers' income.

There is nevertheless a prior theoretical consideration regarding the CAP framework, that, as an economist, one must immediately criticise. If the problem is one of farmers' income, the intervention should be done at the income and not at the price level – this is in line with what Lipsey and Lancaster (1956–7) defend in the theory of the second best. If we have two or more distortions, removing one of the distortions might leave us not better off but instead worse. With this in mind we can proceed to a more thorough and detailed analysis of the Portuguese CAP case.

The early years and the broader CAP framework

The CAP was, from its inception, designed to support prices for large major European producers: France, Germany and, after its accession, the UK. Thus, the four new members of 1986, Portugal, Spain, Ireland, and Greece, had severe troubles, starting from a very backward position, in coping with different needs and agricultural structures. The case for Ireland was not so severe because of its soil and climatic similarities with the UK, a major player in European agri-business. On the other hand, Spain, Portugal and Greece have a Mediterranean system of agriculture, and Portugal for instance has almost 80 per cent of world cork production due to large oak forests, and bases itself on wine production and olive oil extraction. Thus, one can immediately see that Portuguese needs were not considered in the CAP's original design.

Jovanovic (1997: 98) stresses the role of the European Agricultural Guidance and Guarantee Fund (EAGFF) as the financing scheme for CAP, because he clearly states that this fund has dominated the CAP since its inception. The largest element of the CAP funding scheme within the EAGFF was the Guarantee component, which always amounted to more than 75 per cent of the funds (Varela, 1996: 93) – the EAGFF percentages of the EEC's total budget were, respectively, 79.2 per cent, in 1978 and 69.4 per cent in 1984. Moreover, of the EAGFF, the Guarantee part amounted to 76 per cent and 67 per cent respectively in 1978 and 1984 (Varela, 1996: 93). This was because it aimed to attain the production and price level maintenance objectives for European farmers. Later on, after many CAP reforms, EAGFF subsidies changed their nature, owing to a stronger need for rural development and thus, currently, the largest financing scheme for the EAGFF goes to the Guidance component. This aims at integrating the farmer as a sustainable 'green' producer, and not just as a European 'subsidy-dependent' worker.

The Portuguese agricultural framework inherited from the past included the Alentejo, in the South, with its large land holdings with extensive cereal production and cork oak (*Quercus suber*) and holm oak (*Quercus ilex*) livestock–forestry systems. Second was the Algarve and the region northwest of Lisbon, which specialised in fruit and horticulture. Finally came the North, dominated by small parcels of land producing excellent wine grape varieties, including Dão, Douro and Oporto wines.

The political and institutional framework should also be taken into account. After the Carnation revolution on 25 April 1974, and what was then called the 'hot summer' of 1975, the country turned to the extreme left and agrarian reform took place. While landowners blame the invasions of estates and nationalisations for destroying the productive sector, on the other side we have former uneducated workers turned into farmer-managers. Obviously this could only lead to disastrous results. The south of Portugal is still paying the price for this misguided policy, because, for instance, generations of genetically improved herds were used for beef consumption on the argument of feeding the poor.

Branco (1988: 150) concluded that the Portuguese agrarian reform, though politically violent, and a sensitive matter, nevertheless allowed in the short run an increase in agricultural production, and, moreover for the period 1975–6, even an increase in productivity, in the Alentejo. This is highly controversial, especially because of the political engagement between different the views of different authors on the subject.

For instance, Barreto (1987: 17) coordinated a series of research studies with different views on the impact of this Agrarian Reform and describes the negative economic impact of this policy. He is clearly one of the most proficient and prolific scholars on this subject, and besides having conducted a serious research project on the topic, he was quite familiar with what occurred afterwards in the hot summer, as he became Minister of Agriculture in the 1980s, and passed a Land Bill culminating in this Agrarian Reform. His views confirm the failure of almost all the agrarian reforms around the globe (Rocha de Sousa, 2008: 321).

Additionally, Rocha de Sousa (2008: 213) conducted a theoretical explanation of Agrarian reforms, making use of a new concept: 'market led' land reform. He applied economic growth models, which suggested that if, after land reforms take place, the unskilled wage rates increase, which is quite common in almost all these processes, the net welfare result is an irrecoverable loss. Moreover, he concluded that in dynamic economic terms, the loss of human capital involved in the eviction of landlords would never be recovered by the entry of uneducated farmers. He also tested his theory in Brazil, in a World Bank project, and in light of this, the result still seemed to be bourne out. So one can state that this policy of agrarian reform clearly curtailed the growth path for the agricultural South in Portugal, and thus undermined the way for the CAP's implementation after Portugal's entry into the EEC.

The initial accession negotiations from 1977 onwards (Varela, 1991: 17, 39, 71, 103) are scrutinised and, furthermore we can observe the stress of the EEC on the importance of trying to integrate Portugal and Spain into the broader European economic market, as stated by Varela (1996: 59–65). One should keep in mind that Varela was present in all the accession meetings from 1979 to 1986 as he was General Director of the Portuguese Division of Agriculture for European Integration, with wide responsibilities involving different ministries, and after accession he participated in several councils and meetings with European Ministers of Agriculture.

Avillez *et al.* (2004: 71, 88, 96) detail, respectively, the current structure of the agricultural economy of Portugal, stating that Portugal still remains one of the least productive in Europe, with low levels of human capital; they also describe the lower intensity of land use in the South of Portugal, and greater land use intensity in the North. In addition, they present the average working tools and machinery data, which show that Portugal cannot compete with France, the UK or the Netherlands. One of the structural deficits is the lack of physical and human capital. The CAP since its inception has tried to deal with this deficiency, and to foster Portuguese economic integration.

Pinto (2000: 153) has done an assessment of the whole CAP up until 2000, and his conclusion is clearly one of a lost opportunity. Once again we face the vision of a scholar who also was familiar with all the files regarding Portuguese agricultural integration, as he was director of the European Commission Division of Agriculture and also a Portuguese Minister of Agriculture. Again, he is sceptical about Portuguese agricultural integration.

Perhaps the most serious research effort assessing the impact of the CAP on Portuguese agriculture was done by Girão (2000: 1). He made a serious effort to understand whether the different targeted objectives of the CAP in Portugal had any real impact on farm yields. His first research was carried out using a short time series. He then resorted to long run time series analysis available from the Bank of Portugal, in order to check whether there were trends, either deterministic or stochastic, in those series. The absence of any trend, whether deterministic or stochastic, would show an absence of innovation or farm yield increases, thus the perpetuation of the *status quo*.

Nevertheless Girão (2000: 1) starts by stating that CAP had in general achieved two primordial aims, namely, to improve yields and productivity and to achieve food self-sufficiency. Unfortunately, as Girão (2000: 13–14) concluded, the Portuguese CAP case is one of dismal results. The only agricultural sector that had shown some positive dynamics (that is, was generating aggregate agricultural gains) was that of livestock. As to vegetable production the author found no associated growth trend. Nevertheless, a disaggregated analysis of animal husbandry concluded that cattle, sheep and goat production showed no econometric growth trend (what is commonly described as a stationary process by economists), and thus did not foster the development of the primary sector. He also concluded that until 2000, Portuguese agriculture was proceeding with no human capital, no strategy and, it could be added, no clear escape clause from a poverty trap either.

Let us now evaluate the development of the CAP following changes as Portugal proceeded along the way of European integration. We shall firstly analyse the CAP reform of 1992, then the reforms of 2000, the interim reform of 2003 and finally the current concerns regarding the Portuguese CAP stance and why it is stated by several scholars that this was a lost opportunity for the agrarian development of Portugal.

The CAP reforms of 1992

The CAP reforms of 1992 came to be known as the MacSharry Reforms, named after the European Commissioner for Agriculture of those days, Ray MacSharry. The Commission introduced two principal topics, a sustained decrease of agricultural prices in Europe in order to increase European internal and world competitiveness; and income compensation schemes to make good farmers' loss of profit (Pinheiro and Carvalho, 2003a: 267).

We can sum up CAP reform in 1992 as one in which the farmer was seen as a guardian of the rural space, in the sense that in addition he contributed to rural development and landscape organisation and management. The CAP finally introduced farmers' income compensation, direct subventions or subsidies, and it created the CAP's second pillar – rural development – recognising the farmers' dual role as both producers and agents of sustainable environmental development (Pinheiro and Carvalho, 2003a: 267).

Cunha (2004: 29) describes in detail the political discussion the EU leaders were engaged in over the 1992 CAP reforms. Cunha knew the process very well, as he was Portuguese Minister of Agriculture, in the first (rotating) Portuguese Presidency of the EU, in the first half of 1992. The agreement was reached after almost two years of debate involving European Commission proposals, European

Parliament consultation and a major debate on agriculture in the European Council of Ministers. He led the process and the agreement was reached at ten minutes past midnight, the clocks having been stopped at midnight. Thus the process was finished by the Portuguese European Presidency, and was not due to the incoming British Presidency, which started at midnight. The Portuguese Presidency during its time produced a document each month, and paid special attention to German support, which was essential in order to reach a favourable agreement. In Cunha's words (Cunha, 2004: 38): 'Germany was the greatest enthusiast of the new direct compensation to income.'

The political process at stake was delicate, and Cunha (2004: 39) once again records that when the Portuguese presidency acceded to British requests in the spirit of the EC (due to the increase of sheep premium eligibility from 750 to 1,000 head), the German Minister of Agriculture abandoned talks in February, and 'the most important locomotive of the negotiations was lost'.

Then came Italy, which was striving for milk quotas, and France, which was not satisfied with the income support that came to be negotiated. But, as Cunha again documents, France finally understood that the global talks that were set in motion at the GATT stage would become inevitable. Thus, the best way to protect French farmers' income was clearly to engage in CAP reforms in order to have an asset for negotiation, and to anticipate GATT global talks.

Let us evaluate how Portuguese interests were managed in the 1992 CAP reforms. For cereals the price support was reduced by 45 ECUs/ton, rather than 55 ECUs/ton, as the EC proposed, thus a much better outcome was achieved: a reduction in the cereal price of only 29 per cent instead of 35 per cent. The 'set-aside' area for cereal, of which 15 per cent was mandatory, became eligible for full funding. Moreover, Portugal, with a 'side letter',[2] signed only by the European Commissioner for Agriculture in order not to disrupt the other negotiations, allowed the specificity of Portuguese agriculture to be taken into account due to its low productivity, allowing an increase in support for cereal productivity from 1.6 ton/ha to 2.9 ton/ha – Cunha (2004: 44). In addition, this recognition of the enhancement of historical productivities allowed the modernisation of agriculture. It was recognised that Portugal was still in transition to a full market economy. So, some cereal crop areas were converted into pasture, still keeping income and price supports, and corn silage became eligible for direct subventions. The cattle sector saw the milking cows' premium increase from 75 to 120 ECUs, the number of eligible sheep premium was also increased from 350 to 500 and from 750 to 1,000 units, respectively in normal regions and in disadvantaged regions, and in the dairy sector, the price reduction was to 5 per cent for butter over two years, and the 2 per cent automatic quota reductions were waived to be negotiable each year by the Council (Cunha, 2004: 46).

A general critical assessment of the 1992 CAP Reforms is in order. On the positive side we can list the following (Cunha, 2004: 47). First, was the quest to enhance the redistributive capacity of the CAP. This favoured the least productive and deficient agricultures, as it introduced direct subsidies based upon cultivated area and effective livestock. The reform penalised the most intensive and surplus agricultures, as the quotas and fines became more binding. It decreased the distorting effects of the price support mechanisms as it introduced direct income compensation schemes. In addition, it allowed the stabilisation of farmers' income, which became less prone to the whims of weather and stochastic variability. Furthermore, it made the CAP more globally competitive and it brought greater transparency in the rules and procedures for farmers' support, thus bringing about better governance. Finally, the income policies were accompanied by adequate financial resources, and not exclusively with price caps and regulations.

On the negative side we could list the rigidity of the production rights. Moreover there was an increase in bureaucracy owing to the perceived risk of corruption associated with production quotas and the set-aside policy. However, an evaluation by the Court of Auditors regarding these matters concluded that in fact corruption did not increase. But the greater dependency and vulnerability of farmers' income to political struggles were evident as they became more determined by the EU budget.

Cunha (2004: 68) claims that the 1992 reform of the CAP was a major success for Portugal, mainly due to the fact that Gross Value Added at market prices (GVAmp) was 10.5 per cent and 17 per cent for employment in the agricultural sector in Portugal's case. Furthermore, agricultural labour productivity, as measured by Gross Value Added factor costs (GVAfc) divided by Annual Work Unit (AWU, or number of workers by year) started from 26 per cent of the EEC average in 1990 rising to 28 per cent and 31 per cent at the end of the decade. Cunha sees this as a success, but it could be seen as a lost opportunity, because Portugal did not consolidate and did not converge faster.

On a final balance one could state that in fact this 1992 reform in general seems to have been highly successful. Nevertheless, one cannot analyse CAP's 1992 reform without putting it into the framework of the Second Phase of transition to the EMU and the Single Market. But when we take this into account, we must recall that in 1988 at the very start of the transition, Portugal negotiated the PEDAP (i.e. *Programa Específico da Agricultura Portuguesa*), the Specific Portuguese Agricultural Programme, which recognised the weak state of agrarian development, and the need for a swift transition to a market economy.

Portuguese negotiators struck a deal in 1988, which foresaw two phases of agricultural transition. In the first phase from 1986 to 1990 Portugal would not be subject to EEC agricultural rules, but would not be eligible either for EAGGF-G (European Agricultural Guidance and Guarantee Fund). The second phase began in 1991, after the difficult negotiations regarding price harmonisations, frontier protection regulations and milk quotas, and allowed immediate access to EAGGF.

The 2000 reforms of the CAP and the interim reform of 2003

One must recognise that the Single Market and the Single Currency brought both stability and competition to the agricultural sector. Incomes and prices immediately became disclosed and available, which represented simultaneously an increase in competition, and a lever for innovation and investment, as it allowed farmers to finance themselves at lower interest rates. Corkill (Chapter 3 in this volume) and Rocha de Sousa (2010: 37) assess the Portuguese politico-economic transition to the euro, which also describes the trajectory in Portuguese interest rates during the escudo transition to the euro.

Another major challenge for the EU and Portugal was the enlargement to the East. Thus the Agenda 2000 budget treaty provisions had to be reformed once again. This was because globally the CAP had always represented the largest part of the EU budget (see Porto, 1998: 26, for a general assessment of Portuguese cost/benefit analysis of Agenda 2000). Girão (2000: 2) suggested that this challenge could once again become a lost opportunity and eventually aggravate the dismal laggardness of Portugal's agricultural development. The Eastern enlargement, which involved ten more countries, all of them from the so-called cohesion range, most of them inheriting a Soviet style of agriculture, became direct competitors for cohesion funds and in European and world agricultural markets.

The EC (2009: 1) assesses the evaluation of Agenda 2000 ex-post; Baltas (1997: 1) gives a general setting of what was at stake with enlargement, as also do several other studies such as Henke and Storti (2004: 1), Jensen and Frensen (2003: 1), and Josling and Walkenworst (1998: 1), all of which tend to stress that the enlargement would hurt the countries from the southern periphery, such as Portugal, owing to more competition for funds from new incoming members.

The reforms of Agenda 2000 were negotiated from 1997 to 1999 and three main aspects were at stake, as Cunha (2004: 85) states. These included the adequacy of competitiveness in world markets and the pressing demand of GATT to become the World Trade Organization (WTO). The dysfunctions of CAP 1992, which did not reduce inequities or desertification, were still present. Finally there was the need to decentralise and prepare for the admission of ten new members. Germany was quite discontent with the way CAP was heading, since it contributed 28 per cent and only received 14 per cent of the budget (Cunha, 2004: 97). Nevertheless, one must also stress again the divergence of Portugal from the rest of the EU. It had a productivity/income that was less than €5,000 (GVAfc/AWU) and it only received €2,000 in support funds per worker (EAGGF/AWU), while the Irish and the Danish received around €14,000 (Cunha, 2004: 113).

So one must obviously conclude that the most productive were getting more support (whether in prices or in income support), and thus the distance between Portugal and the average European country widened. The obvious conclusion is that, with enlargement, Portugal lost its ability to fight for new funds.

The 2003 CAP reform was required as an interim reform on the setting of Agenda 2000, which had disclosed the financial perspectives for 2000–6, but two main aspects led to an emerging need for CAP reform. The first idea, as Cunha (2004: 133) states, is that the European Council should not limit the extent and needs of reform and support required by the agricultural sector, which, in addition, had to be ready for the changes posed in the enlargement. On this second aspect one must stress that the producers' decisions should be taken in line with what markets expect, and not subsidies. The CAP should work more like a public service, thus as a corrective to externalities, so being justifiable to EU citizens. The CAP should ease trade talks at the heart of the WTO and really solve the problems due to enlargement. Blandford and Hill (2005: 1) evaluate the changes in the structure of EU agriculture due to these reforms in more detail.

The Minister of Agriculture, at the time Armando Sevinate Pinto, former director of DG IV, the Agriculture division, was familiar with the files, and he recognised that Portugal had the most backward agriculture in the EU – it had the lowest level of food self-sufficiency and the lowest level of financial support. The minister again tried to play the card of the Portuguese 'special case', namely because the Azores archipelago milk quota had been exceeded, an earlier fine was due, and no further increases would be tolerated. The problem was delicate with elections forthcoming in the Azores, and the fact that milk amounts to 50 per cent of the Azores' GDP. Even though the Minister managed to gain a lot of the shopping list demands from his peers, this led to Portugal voting against and being isolated from the decisions of 2003 CAP reform.

Final balance: the need for a National Agricultural Policy

When it joined EFTA Portugal had an agricultural derogation (Annex G) from 1960 until 1986. When it joined the EEC the weak state of Portuguese agriculture was noted and a two-phase deal was struck recognising the need for a PEDAP. Further in 1992, a 'side letter' to the Commission was required in order to present the Portuguese special case. One question immediately comes to mind: Were all these derogations really necessary? Were the derogations only a political mechanism for capturing votes? In trying to achieve a much swifter transition, were the deals much less effective because they insulated Portugal from strong competition in Europe and the world?

A word of advice to Portuguese negotiators might be appropriate on this issue. Why were Portuguese farmers treated as inefficient instead of being categorised as small business entrepreneurs? This is in line with what economists usually discuss in relation to the speed of reforms adjustment: debating the use of endless derogations or shock therapy. It is important to be flexible about the speed of adjustment, rather than prescribing a specific rate, or adopting a sudden, once-and-for-all change to meet reform requirements. The Commission and all the other European partners eventually came to recognise that Portugal has made a special case for its agriculture ever since the 1960s. However, this case was not made on the basis of its Mediterranean and Southern approach to agriculture, but rather because of its backwardness. Portugal does in fact need a Portuguese and Mediterranean model of agriculture, and a National Agriculture Policy that defends strategic aims in relation to the CAP.

The European Commission (2010a: 1, 2010b: 1, 2010c: 1) gives a preview of what the future CAP would be, but nevertheless one must also note that Portuguese people, namely farmers, did not participate actively in its design. And they could have done so, as the Germans or French did.

Thus, the principal conclusion is that the Portuguese CAP has not managed to bridge the gap between Portugal's agricultural sector and the European one. From 1986 until the enlargement to the East in the 2000s we do not blame the Portuguese authorities for the lack of, or excessive competition for, funds. There were funds that were sometimes quite inappropriate because they endorsed activities in which Portugal had no competitive advantage and, ultimately, they were not used well, or even worse they were not used at all (sometimes funds were allocated that had to be repaid by the government to the EU, because they were not used). Of course here our criticism is twofold: were the funds appropriate or not? And if appropriate why were they not all spent?

These are more than rhetorical questions as they address the true nature of the CAP, its adequacy in relation to Mediterranean cultures and crops and the weak nature of Portuguese agrarian development. A thorough study would imply a whole book, ranking efficiency between alternative crops and production and respective yields – in line with what Jamila Curtiss (2002: 15) did for the Czech Republic. Nevertheless, this immediately leads to a provocative conclusion. If the funds were appropriate and were not spent, this indicates inefficiency and bad governance policies in the agricultural sector or, even worse, if the funds were not spent because they were inappropriate this reveals the lack of political bargaining power of the Portuguese authorities. Thus, the dismal conclusion is that if there is a lesson to be learnt from the Portuguese role in the CAP it is that the Portuguese stance was weak and passive, and not even reactive or pro-active.

Moreover, in order to create a reformist agricultural policy, a truly national agricultural policy that fosters an adequate Common Agricultural Policy is required. What we mean is that a clear strategy for Portuguese rural development in the framework of Mediterranean conditionalities must be coupled with a true bargaining spirit and political capacity on the part of Portuguese agricultural authorities in Brussels – taking into account what Spain has accomplished, for example. There is a true national agricultural policy in Spain, and thus the Spanish strive within their capacities to reform the CAP with their strategic aims and long run policies – which is in line with Pinheiro and Carvalho's proposals (2003b: 305–7).

We can sum up our own proposals in order to increase efficiency and equity in the Portuguese CAP stance. First, increase the political bargaining capacity in Brussels in order to develop a fully sustainable 'green' agrarian strategy that can cope with the Portuguese Mediterranean special case concerning, for instance, the cultivation of trees for olive oil, and of cork oak and holm oak within the CAP framework. Second, develop a clear marketing strategy for wine grape varieties, trying to attain better economic value added, and thus playing the special case by economic differentiation with improved quality. Third, end loose loopholes and cross subsidies that foster corruption and bad practices, subsidising only what is vital for a sustainable green economy in the world and European framework, without losing its focus on Portuguese competitive advantage. Fourth, increase human and physical capital in Portuguese agriculture, trying to foster it as leverage for industrial development, for instance, by dealing with the problem of ageing farmers, increasing programmes for youth agrarian employment, and innovation for growth. Fifth, promote an active engagement of agrarian research as a tool to spur agrarian Portuguese growth. Finally, last but not least, focus on agrarian activities as a profit- and market-driven entrepreneurial activity in the green economy.

Thus, the CAP has come to stay, but it should have been taken much more seriously as an opportunity than it has been by Portuguese authorities and today's farmers. One should take as an example what Spain has achieved, defining clear agrarian priorities and even investing in intensive olive exploitation across the border in Portugal.

One of the most difficult aspects to change is the way agriculture is perceived in Portugal – as a decaying heritage of lost fields and farms. Such obstacles are made even more pressing, as policy makers have held a strong belief that investing in agriculture would not lead to economic development.

The CAP should have been taken more as an opportunity for conversion to enable Portuguese integration into European and world agrarian markets, and not merely as subsidies to pacify the real and still strong class struggles in agriculture. Agriculture is, like any other activity, an economic activity, and thus its future is contingent on its historical past, but also on its various forthcoming opportunities.

This is not intended as a personal criticism of any given political actor responsible for the Portuguese CAP stance; one should always blame the nation as a whole, which has created the national governance structure. This leads to a more serious and recent dilemma. All integration effort at the time of writing seems to be at stake, with a caretaker government negotiating a major public bailout, in the turmoil of the Eurozone crises. Agriculture has already been lagging, with these forecasts and austerity measures one can only cope with fortitude.

Notes

1 For detailed technical policy explanations regarding price supports, see Varela (1987: 45), and for different structural policies, see Varela (1988: 43).

2 A 'side letter' means simply that this was a closed deal, kept apart from the European-wide negotiation table and thus one that only the European Agriculture Commissioner and the Portuguese Agriculture Minister were familiar with and were kept updated on, in order not to disrupt the EU negotiations.

Bibliography

Avillez, F., Jorge, M., Trindade, C., Pereira, N., Serrano, P. and Ribeiro, I. (2004), *Rendimento e Competitividade Agrícolas em Portugal*, Almedina, Coimbra.

Baltas, N. (1997), 'The restructured CAP and the periphery of the EU', paper presented to the *4th Biennial International Conference, European Community Studies Association*, South Carolina, recovered on 13 February 2011 at: http://aei.pitt.edu/7302/01/002973_1.pdf.

Barreto, A. (1987), *Anatomia de uma revolução. A reforma agrária em Portugal 1974–76*, Europa-América, Lisbon.

Blandford, D. and Hill, B. (2005), 'Structural change and public policies in EU agriculture: An Overview', paper presented to the XIth Congress of The EAAE, 'The future of Europe in the global Agri-Food System', Copenhagen, recovered on 13 February 2011 at: http://dblandford.aers.psu.edu/PDF/Papers/EAAE_Copenhagen__Blandford_Hill.pdf.

Branco, M. (1988), *La Transformation de Structures Agraires et le Développement: La Réforme Agraire au Portugal*, EHESS, Unpublished PhD Thesis, Paris.

Corkill, D. (2014), 'The Portuguese economy: the impact of European Monetary Union membership' (Chapter 3, this volume).

Cunha, A. (2004), *A Política Agrícola Comum na era da Globalização*, Almedina, Coimbra.

Curtiss, J. (2002), *Efficiency and Structural Changes in Transition. A Stochastic Frontier Analysis of Czech Production*, Shaker Verlag, Aachen, Germany.

European Commission (2009), 'Agenda 2000: A CAP for the future', recovered on 13 February 2011, at: http://ec.europa.eu/agriculture/publi/review99/08_09_en.pdf.

European Commission (2010a), 'The common agricultural policy after 2013. Your ideas matter. Summary report', recovered on 13 February 2011, at: http://ec.europa.eu/agriculture/cap-post-2013/debate/report/summary-report_en.pdf.

European Commission (2010b), 'The common agricultural policy after 2013. Your ideas matter. Executive report', recovered on 13 February 2011, at: http://ec.europa.eu/agriculture/cap-post-2013/debate/report/executive-summary_en.pdf.

European Commission (2010c), 'The CAP explained', recovered on 13 February 2011, at: http://ec.europa.eu/agriculture/publi/capexplained/cap_en.pdf.

Girão, J. A. (2000), 'A agricultura portuguesa: Em passeio aleatório ou em regime estacionário?', *Faculdade de Economia da Universidade Nova de Lisboa (FEUNL), Working Paper* no. 391, Lisbon, recovered on 5 April 2011 at: http://fesrvsd.fe.unl.pt/WPFEUNL/WP2000/wp391.pdf.

Henke, R. and Storti, D. (2004), 'CAP Reform and EU Enlargement: Effects on the Second Pillar Endowments', paper presented to the *87th Seminar of the European Association of Agricultural Economists*, Vienna, *Assessing Rural Development Policies of the CAP*, recovered on 13 February 2011 at: www1.inea.it/ops/pubblica/workingpaper/Paper%20Henke%20Storti%2087%20EAAE.pdf.

Jensen, H. and Frensen, J. (2003), 'Impacts of the Eastern European Accession and the 2003 – CAP reform. Consequences for individual countries', *Danish Research Institute of Food Economics, Working Paper* 11/2003, recovered on 13 February 2011 at: www.foi.life.ku.dk/English/Publications/~/media/migration%20folder/upload/foi/docs/publikationer/working%20papers/2003/11.pdf.ashx.

Josling, T. and Walkenhorst, P. (1998), 'Can the CAP survive enlargement to the East?', paper presented to the 4th Biennial International Conference, European Community Studies Association, South Carolina, recovered on 13 February 2011 at: http://aei.pitt.edu/7331/01/003026_1.pdf.

Jovanovic, M. (1997), 'Common Agricultural Policy', in *European Economic Integration*, Routledge, London.

Lipsey, R. and Lancaster, K. (1956–7), 'The general theory of the second best', *Review of Economic Studies*, 24(1), 11–32.

Pinheiro, A. and Carvalho, M. L. S. (2003a), 'A Política Agrícola Comum', Chapter 13 in *Economia e Política Agrícolas*, Edições Sílabo, Lisbon.

Pinheiro, A. and Carvalho, M. L. S. (2003b), 'A Política Agrícola Portuguesa e a Adesão à CEE', Chapter 14 in *Economia e Política Agrícolas*, Edições Sílabo, Lisbon.

Pinto, A. S. (2000), 'European Integration of Portuguese Agriculture', in (eds) Vasconcelos, A. and Seabra, M. J., *Portugal A European Story*, Instituto de Estudos Estratégicos Internacionais, Principia, Lisbon.

Porto, M. (1998), *Portugal e a Agenda 2000*, Almedina, Coimbra.

Rocha de Sousa, M. (2008), *Análise Económica de Reforma Agrária em Contexto Dinâmico*, Unpublished PhD Thesis, Évora, Portugal.

Rocha de Sousa, M. (2010), 'Lessons from the Political Economic Transition to the euro (1986–1999)', *Perspectivas Portuguese Journal of Political Science and International Relations*, #4, pp. 37–55, Braga, Portugal, English version recovered 1 October 2013 at http://ideas.repec.org/p/evo/wpecon/11_2009.html.

Swan, D. (1995), *The Economics of the Common Market. Integration into the EU*, 8th edition, Penguin, London.

Varela, J. S. (1987), *A Política Agrícola Comum e a agricultura portuguesa. A política de preços e mercados*, 1st edition, D. Quixote, Lisbon.

Varela, J. S. (1988), *A Política Agrícola Comum e a sua aplicação à agricultura portuguesa. Política de estruturas e reformas*, 1st edition, D. Quixote, Lisbon.

Varela, J. S. (1991), *As negociações com a C.E.E. e a agricultura portuguesa*, 1st edition, D. Quixote, Lisbon.

Varela, J. S. (1996), *A Política Agrícola Comum. Os Princípios, as Reformas Actuais, a Futura Europa Verde*, 1st edition, D. Quixote, Lisbon.

7 Portuguese trade diplomacy

Projecting national interests into EU trade policy

Maria Helena Guimarães

EU trade policy was established by the Treaty of Rome and is one of the original common policies of the EU. It is, moreover, one of the major areas of exclusive Community competency. The EU exclusive competencies on trade policy are established by Article 133 TEC, now Article 207 of the Treaty on the Functioning of the European Union. It states that the common commercial policy is based on uniform principles regarding changes in tariffs, trade agreements, the achievement of uniformity in measures of liberalization, export policy and trade defence measures. In complying with these common principles, EU Members States do not have autonomous capacity to take decisions on the use of the main trade policy instruments towards third countries (i.e. non-EU Members) – trade regimes and tariffs.[1] Consequently, Portuguese trade policy is, by definition, developed in the strict framework of EU trade policy.

EU trade policy has to bring together the community interests and aims of the EU with the national policy objectives of the Member States. In this regard, EU trade policy is not impermeable to national perspectives and interests. Furthermore, the EU trade policy process does allow for Member States to feed in their views.

In the early years of Portugal's integration in the EU, Portugal had to absorb and implement the EU *acquis*. This influence of EU law was especially profound in two of its common policies – not only in agricultural policy but also in trade policy. The underlying policy flow was mainly from Europe into Portugal, while the country took in the trade *acquis*. As a result of this implementation process of EU trade policy, Portuguese trade with third countries became more open, and the Portuguese economy more internationalized. Nowadays there is more of a two-way relationship between Europe and Portugal in trade policy formation. In addition to the implementation of trade policies, Portugal is presently also fully involved in the negotiation processes of EU trade policy and able to insert the country's interests, priorities and concerns into the EU trade policy decision-making process.

Defining Portuguese external trade interests is the responsibility of the Ministry of Foreign Affairs (MNE), and in particular of the Department of European Affairs. To define its final positions, there is a consultation process, led by the MNE, where the relevant ministries provide their input. The Ministry for

Economy and the Ministry for Agriculture have, of course, a special role, as many of the trade subjects fall under their technical competences. The Permanent Representation of Portugal to the European Union (REPER), in Brussels, conveys Portuguese interests into the EU decision-making process, and has a specific staff group with expertise in trade issues and in EU trade policy, in particular.

To assess the ability of Portugal to protect its interests in the design of EU trade policy it is indispensable to analyse its role in the Article 133 Committee. The Committee, whose name became the Trade Policy Committee during the Swedish Presidency in 2009, assists the Commission in trade policy negotiations and is composed of Senior Officials from all Member States. It is the key *forum* for collecting information from the capitals and on each Member State's interests, and also to put forward common negotiation positions, forge alliances and build coalitions in order to get national interests accommodated in the Commission's final deliberations. The Article 133 Committee has been the core mechanism for Portugal to feed its interests into the EU policy process. Since its accession to the EU, Portugal has gained a solid position in the Committee and is considered a serious and credible partner. Portugal has a considerable record of interventions in the Committee and has followed objective-driven, open and balanced negotiation strategies.

Presidencies: a key platform to project national interests

The Council Presidency is a source of power for EU Member States, but especially for small EU countries. In fact, one of the main instruments for a small country to exercise influence and to have a stronger role in the EU policy-making process is the Presidency. The Presidency places the country in a privileged negotiation position, and even small country Presidencies can have significant leverage in the EU. Tallberg (2008: 697) concludes from an empirical study on the European Council that small and medium EU Member States perceive the Presidency as their most important source of power.

To hold the Presidency is a unique opportunity to influence the policy process because of its distinctive power resources. First, the Presidency has the opportunity to influence the negotiation agenda (its structure, the relative importance of the items in the agenda, the introduction of topics of Presidency interest). Second, the Presidency has privileged information: besides the information that the Commission is necessarily obliged to share with the Member State that holds the Presidency and the inside knowledge it gains from bilateral meetings with the other Member States' governments, third countries and other interlocutors, it benefits from the valuable technical support of the Council General Secretariat. Third, the Presidency decides the frequency and the format of the meetings, conducts them, and drafts the conclusions. All these power resources put the Presidency in a privileged bargaining position to reach agreements on issues of its interest.

Portugal has held, since its accession, three EU Presidencies – in 1992, 2000 and 2007. For all three Presidencies, Portugal established trade policy objectives.

The objectives of the Portuguese Presidencies, compared to the results the country actually achieved during them, are a yardstick against which to evaluate Portugal's ability to influence EU trade policy decisions. Objectives and outcomes are indicators of the efforts of the Portuguese government in trade policy issues and of their impact in the design of EU trade policy.

Portuguese perspectives on EU trade policy issues are long established. In its three Presidencies, Portugal has focused sustained attention in several geographical regions: Africa, Latin America and Brazil/MERCOSUR, and the Mediterranean. Transatlantic relations were also always included in Portugal's EU trade agenda.

EU trade policy towards different geographical regions has always been embedded in a political context: on the one side, the political interests and priorities of EU Member States, and on the other, and increasingly so, the links the EU establishes between trade policy and its wider foreign policy goals. Hence, when analysing EU trade policy and the role of the member countries in its design, one has to look into the broader political context of the trade initiatives. As the Treaty of Lisbon reiterates (article 207), '[t]he common commercial policy shall be conducted in the context of the principles and objectives of the Union's external action'.

For an evaluation of the role of the Portuguese Presidencies, it is revealing to focus on the most recent Presidency, in 2007. As stated in a report of the Portuguese Parliament (Assembleia da República, 2007: 3) the 'specific priorities' of the Portuguese Presidency were structured in four chapters, one of them being 'Europe and the world'. Within its external priorities, Portugal emphasized the areas with more relevance for the country and in which the Portuguese Presidency could have an effective added value due to Portugal's particular positioning, particularly the summits with Brazil and Africa.

The Programme for the 2007 Presidency of the Portuguese Government (Programme for the Portuguese Presidency, 2007: 11), states that '[t]he Portuguese Presidency will develop a specific political dialogue with Brazil. We shall be organizing the first EU–Brazil Summit. It will be the launching point for the establishment of a strategic dialogue that reflects the international influence of both sides.' In fact, during the 2007 Presidency, Portugal promoted the first EU–Brazil Summit, which was actually still held in the very same Presidency (Lisbon, 4 July). This can be considered a success story of the uploading of Portuguese interests into the EU policy process, including trade policy interests. Portugal believed Brazil was an important partner for the EU in Latin America, and acted in order to grant it a role of privileged interlocutor in the region. As the Ministry for Foreign Affairs assesses in a report on Portugal in the EU (Ministério dos Negócios Estrangeiros, 2007: 14), the Summit contributed to set the dialogue between the European Union and Brazil at the highest level, establishing a strategic partnership between the EU and Latin America. The Summit was the result of Portugal's active promotion of closer ties between the two regions (Programme for the Portuguese Presidency, 2007: 11).

Although some say that Brazil never recognized the role of Portugal in bringing Brazil closer to the EU, the momentum for this partnership was indeed created by Portugal. The fact is that it was during the Portuguese Presidency that the first ever EU–Brazil Summit was held. And merely one-and-a-half years later the second EU–Brazil Summit was held in Rio de Janeiro (December 2008), and the third less than a year after that (October 2009) in Stockholm.

The Portuguese Presidency had another principal focus regarding EU external relations: Africa. In the priorities notebook (Programme for the Portuguese Presidency, 2007: 10) the Portuguese Government clearly states that the Portuguese Presidency places an emphasis on the holding of the Lisbon Summit between the EU and Africa, identifying it as one of its major priorities. The second EU–Africa Summit, held in Lisbon, on 8 and 9 December 2007, may also be considered an important achievement for Portugal. In fact, the previous and only other EU–Africa Summit was held during the previous Portuguese Presidency in 2000, and its renewal had been successively postponed since 2003. These two Summits, both under the Portuguese Presidency, corroborate the assertion that Africa has always been a priority of Portuguese diplomacy in Brussels.

African, Caribbean and Pacific (ACP) countries have consistently been on top of the Portuguese Presidencies' agenda, as well. For the 2007 Presidency, Portugal stated it 'will continue to pursue the goal of integrating ACP countries into the world economy' (Programme for the Portuguese Presidency, 2007: 11). Although the EU priority regarding ACP countries is mainly political and trade issues are not the primary objective, trade relations with ACP countries have been a key part of the EU agenda. Portugal supported the reinforcement of the continuing negotiations of the Economic Partnership Agreements (EPAs) – planned in the Cotonou Agreement and aimed at replacing its commercial chapters – with the goal of finishing the negotiation process in December 2007, as necessary in order to fulfil World Trade Organization (WTO) commitments. In spite of the difficulties of the negotiations, which went on for years, Portuguese diplomacy did commit itself to pushing these agreements forward. Actually, one complete EPA and twenty Intermediate EPAs, with an emphasis in trade issues, were signed at the very end of the Portuguese Presidency. These agreements were an achievement that Portugal likes to emphasize, but also an accomplishment for the Commission.

An effective trade diplomacy in informal networks

Networks are informal structures composed of experts with recognized knowledge and skills in a specific subject area. These epistemic communities (Haas, 1992) have a strong potential for inducing cooperative and joint problem-solving negotiation strategies and have significant influence on negotiation outcomes. Informal networks are very useful for articulating interests and building common positions among groups of EU countries.

In the initial phases of the EU negotiation processes, networks play a central role. At this phase the negotiations are characterized by information asymmetries, insufficient knowledge of the interests and priorities of the other

Member States and by a significant level of uncertainty on the impact of the various policy choices. At this early stage, in these informal networks, Member States perceive the importance of exchanging information and of finding together the costs and benefits of the various possible negotiation outcomes. There is a mutual learning environment that induces cooperation and integrative solutions. Consequently, negotiations tend to be less politicised, as decisions do not have to be taken, and value-creating (Raiffa, 1982) strategies tend to prevail over value-claiming (Lax and Sebenius, 1985) strategies.

EU trade policy networks include a large set of public and private actors who promote informal contacts to exchange information on trade issues. They are dense and quite informal networks, two essential conditions for reaching cooperative solutions (Elgström and Jönsson, 2000), and are considered very effective in feeding their views into the decision-making process. At this level, small countries are more likely to voice their interests and to be heard than at higher levels of the EU negotiation process.

For a small country, informal networks are the key to promoting national priorities and interests and to ensuring that a Member State's interests enter the equation of EU policy formation. As Panke (2010: 7) states, while large states' interests tend to be accommodated at the end of negotiations small states, on the other hand, 'cannot wait until the end of negotiations to make their voices heard', as by this time it will be too late.

This is true for any EU policy, and it is even more so for a common policy like trade policy. These networks are fundamental for small EU countries like Portugal to express their views, perceptions and objectives, and have been instrumental for the uploading of Portuguese trade priorities. Portugal has clearly benefited from the characteristics and advantages of this lower level of the negotiation process.

The focus: trade defence policy

The EU Commission tends to support market opening and trade liberalization. As a consequence it gives strong support to a rule-based system, which ensures legal certainty and transparency to all economic operators. Trade defence rules and actions therefore have their place in the Trade Policy legal framework and this in spite of some claims of the risk of these measures being perceived as protectionist. Although WTO-based, the EU has more stringent rules on trade defence. Hence, for the economic operators involved and for the EU Commission as well, it is not particularly easy to prove that certain trade defence measures are definitely justified. In addition, a proposal by the European Commission to apply such measures needs to get the necessary support of the Member States at the Council level. Therefore, Member States need to be proactive in order to move their specific interests forward regarding trade defence measures.

Informal networks on trade defence issues are instrumental for small countries, like Portugal, to ensure a level playing field for the economic operators facing unfair trade practices. They allow Member States to voice their concerns, to convey their trade defence perceptions and to substantiate better their cases. Informal trade networks do have an influence on the EU's trade defence policy. Portugal, as an industrial country reliant on EU markets for its exports, has strong interests in offsetting the effects of unfair practices (such as dumping and subsidization) and in granting fair competitive conditions. It has, therefore, a record of being quite effective in its positions on trade defence issues.

Portugal is particularly involved in the Anti-Dumping Committee and, as already mentioned, is keen on exchanging views informally with other Member States. These contacts are particularly helpful between Member States sharing similar concerns – for example, Member States that produce textiles and footwear – given the importance of traditional industries and sensitive sectors for the Portuguese economy, such as the automobile industry. Common and sounder positions around shared interests are often forged within these networks, and the alliances and coalitions that they facilitate have been quite effective in conveying Portuguese interests. One important reason is that in these informal networks the resulting positions gather all the arguments and proof collected by each Member State and by several national industries' representatives. Actually, the industries' representatives have been vital in building Portugal's positions and in allowing Portuguese interests to be presented properly, which can then be passed on more effectively to higher levels of the EU negotiation and decision-making process. In addition, the European federations of industries, in particular, have been playing a very important role in helping to define Portuguese positions, and in defending them. Euratext, the European representative of the textile industry, is a pertinent example for Portugal in this respect, as Portugal traditionally takes very committed positions to defend the interests of the textile industry.

Portugal has also been defending the adoption of measures to avoid the EU unilateral weakening of anti-dumping instruments. It has given particular attention to defending the fair trade expectations of specific Portuguese industries other than textiles and footwear, such the manufacturing of bicycles, chemicals and steel products. Portugal has, whenever necessary, confronted the Commission's views on the EU's anti-dumping policy and has made significant efforts to convince it to maintain the status quo of its trade defence system (Ministério dos Negócios Estrangeiros, 2007: 260), which Portugal considers to be rigorous and balanced.

In brief, by means of informal networks, Portugal has been able to voice more perceptibly its interests in trade defence matters to the Commission and other Member States, and has succeeded in incorporating them, at least in the formal results of negotiations.

Trade policy towards Korea appropriately illustrates the attention that the Portuguese representatives in Brussels give to an EU rule-based and balanced trade defence system. The negotiations of the EU–Korea Free Trade Agreement (FTA), initiated in 2007, have been followed very closely by Portugal, particularly regarding the rules of origin and duty drawback issues. Under the Agreement, Korean exports to the EU are in direct competition with Portuguese traditional industries, and Portugal has been very vocal in defending a level playing field for them. It is undisputed that Portugal has taken a stronger role than other countries of a similar size. The outcome of the negotiation process has been quite positive for Portugal – it has secured whatever it could take advantage of, and when costs have had to be incurred Portugal has tried not to be at a disproportionate disadvantage. According to a source from the Trade Committee of the European Parliament, Portuguese trade diplomacy in Brussels has been active, it has evaluated the economic impact for Portuguese industry of the various possible negotiation outcomes, and it has asked for an adequate means of response in case of unfair practices. Given Portugal's negotiating resources, the general perception has been that Portugal has succeeded in protecting the interests of its traditional industries.

In the automotive sector, in turn, Portugal adopted an assertive defensive position in the negotiation of the EU–Korean FTA. Portugal has worked in close cooperation with Member States with similar interests, impeding an agreement that would completely put in jeopardy the European automotive industry and would open a precedent in future FTA negotiations.

In carrying out its trade defensive and offensive (i.e. market opening) objectives Portugal has been counting on the support of a group of natural allies. For small EU countries, any successful trade initiative must be taken collectively. Indeed, for a small EU country like Portugal, coordination of positions is central for integrating national interests into EU trade policy. Alliances in trade policy issues are of variable geometry, because positions will vary from one topic to another. However it is possible to categorize Member States as either liberal or 'defensive liberal' allies. The liberals are an informal group that includes the EU Northern countries, the United Kingdom, the Netherlands, Slovenia, Germany and Ireland. The 'defensive liberals' comprise mainly Southern and Eastern Europe Member States. The countries in this group constitute Portugal's natural allies. The alliance includes France, Spain, Italy, Greece, as well as Malta, Cyprus and Romania. This natural alliance focuses mostly on trade defence instruments, trade barriers, labour-intensive industries and market opening issues affecting various other industries, and on agriculture. Portuguese interests often coincide with these countries' positions, hence coalitions with the EU southern countries and often with France are frequent in Portuguese trade diplomacy.

Two intervening variables: resources and the share of extra-EU trade

If one looks back at the twenty-five years of Portuguese trade diplomacy in Brussels, a positive evaluation is apparent. But to assess it accurately two factors have to be accounted for – the country's limited negotiation resources and the small share of extra-EU trade in Portugal's total trade.

Regarding negotiation capabilities, it is consensual that Portugal has qualified top-level civil servants, recognized by their peers in the various EU institutions, and has been reaching important negotiating outcomes in issues sensitive for the country. However, compared to other EU Member States, Portugal has substantially fewer negotiating resources and does not count on para-diplomatic actors (Guimarães and Antunes, 2003), such as regional governments, that may intervene indirectly in the negotiations, pushing forward regional interests through the national government. Taking as an example the Mandarin oranges case, in 2004, a request for protection due to a significant surge in imports from China was brought forward by Spain (the only EU producer) in the name of the regional interests of Valencia. This para-diplomacy is not yet very perceptible in the case of Portugal, which does not have regional bodies acting in Brussels in these areas.

The second intervening variable in assessing Portugal's trade diplomacy in Brussels is the importance of intra-EU trade compared to extra-EU trade – the object of the EU Common Trade Policy. Portugal trades mainly with EU countries – its trade with other EU Member States accounts for more than 70 per cent of its total trade. This must be factored in to explain the pattern of Portuguese trade diplomacy in Brussels. The free movement of goods in the internal market is therefore of greater importance for Portuguese economic operators. And although Portugal is in general open to offensive trade policies (for accessing new markets in third countries), such as the signing of new free trade agreements, it is the intra-EU free movement of goods that matters most. As a consequence, regarding external trade policy, notably in the framework of free trade agreement negotiations, Portugal is especially concerned with creating balanced and reciprocal conditions that do not harm the competitiveness of its more vulnerable, labour-intensive industries; hence the emphasis of Portuguese trade diplomacy in Brussels in maintaining the current EU trade defence policy system.

A scholarly case

The literature in various fields often emphasizes the advantages of Portugal being an EU member. In trade issues one indisputable advantage is that membership does discourage third country unilateral protectionism directed individually against Portugal. However, as Portugal has to comply with EU decisions on trade policy, sometimes membership may have costs. In such cases the EU may provide ways to offset part of those costs. A scholarly case (Bayne and Woolcock, 2007) that illustrates the ability of Portuguese trade diplomacy in Brussels in ensuring compensation for the costs incurred by a Member State as a consequence of a common trade policy is the side-payment made by the EU to Portugal at the end of the Uruguay Round trade negotiations, when the Textiles and Clothing Agreement was signed. The EU recognized the need to adapt Portuguese industry to face the increase in fierce competition, as a consequence of the new Agreement and the resultant opening of the EU market to Chinese exports. To help the adjustment process of the Portuguese textile and clothing industries to trade liberalization – after more than thirty years of trade protection under the Multi-fibre Arrangement – Portugal was compensated within the EU structural funds framework. In 1995 the European Council adopted a special measure[2] that involved a contribution of 400 million Euros of financial assistance to implement a specific modernization programme for the Portuguese textile and clothing industry (Iniciativa de Modernização da Indústria Portuguesa – IMIT). The EU Commission in turn, gained Portugal's support for signing the multilateral agreement. This scholarly case of the use of side-payments in international trade negotiations is also an illustration of the effectiveness of Portuguese trade diplomacy within the framework of the EU Common Trade Policy.

Negotiating trade interests in the economic and financial crisis

The financial crisis of 2007 and 2008 and the current economic slowdown have decreased global demand, raised unemployment levels and toughened international competition. In this context, protectionist pressures have expanded worldwide. Even EU governments are tempted to introduce trade restrictions, which impact on small states' viability to adjust to the changing economic conditions and financial constraints by resorting to export-led growth strategies.

In the face of potentially fracturing trade interests of EU member states in the present economic environment, and given their consequences to EU trade relations with the rest of the world, small countries like Portugal must pay added attention to the negotiation of EU trade policy.

Portugal's sovereign debt crisis and the pressures from financial markets make an increase in Portuguese exports ever more crucial to face the country's economic and financial problems. Hence the opening of foreign markets should be at the top of the Portuguese trade agenda in Brussels. This objective emerges as an imperative for Portuguese negotiators, as the economy is in recession and Portugal has been experiencing, concomitantly, a serious decrease in its export competitiveness.

Given the relatively small size of Portugal as an EU member state, and its limited negotiating resources and bargaining leverage, continued active engagement in trade negotiations and involvement in the relevant trade networks is key in order to ensure that the country's voice is heard and its interests accommodated. In the face of the present external challenges, the diverging interests of member states, and the country's own internal constraints, Portugal must rely on network governance to compensate for the disadvantages of being a small country. Today, more than in good economic times, the chances of influencing trade negotiation outcomes, of successfully projecting national trade preferences and influencing the design of EU trade policy lie within informal networks, not at the higher, more politicized levels of the EU decision making process.

Looking into the future

With the Treaty on the Functioning of the European Union a new dynamic is conferred to EU trade policy. On the one hand, more competences are transferred from Member States to the Commission, mainly in the areas of services and investment. On the other hand the Commission is more limited in its initiative powers, by the new role of the European Parliament. For the Commission, times ahead will be harder, as the Parliament will have the same information as the Member States on trade policy, and information asymmetry may not be used by the Commission to push policies forward as easily. But the EU Commission will have time to adapt to the new dynamic while the European Parliament accumulates know-how. The Member States, in turn, will have to adapt to the inputs of the Parliament as a more active actor in trade policy. That is a new challenge for a small country like Portugal, given its limited, though motivated and qualified, human resources in Brussels.

The Global Europe Strategy, of October 2006, is a strategy for opening markets in third countries, focusing on concrete problems that EU businesses face in these markets. The Strategy may allow for greater participation of Member States in EU trade policy, as it initiated a novel decentralized partnership between the Commission, Member States and business, intended to identify and overcome trade barriers abroad. Therefore, the Global Europe Strategy may open new channels for Portugal to reinforce its trade interests in third markets. The informal character of the Market Access teams, and the fact they are focused on defensive trade policy, suggests that Portugal may benefit from this Strategy particularly well. Portugal has been quite effective in integrating its interests in informal networks, and can capitalize on its past experience in future EU trade policy negotiations.

Notes

1 Within the framework of the EU Common Trade Policy, Member States do keep some room for initiative, for example in trade promotion or in taking action to further specific bilateral economic relations with third countries. Portugal for example, has given a particular endorsement to trade initiatives with lusophone countries.

2 EC Regulation 852/95 (10 April 1995).

References

Assembleia da República (2007) 'Apreciação Parlamentar do Relatório do Governo relativo à Participação de Portugal na União Europeia' Lisbon: Comissão de Assuntos Europeus.

Bayne, N. and Woolcock, S. (eds) (2007) *The New Economic Diplomacy. Decision-Making and Negotiation in International Economic Relations*, Aldershot: Ashgate.

Elgström, O. and Jönsson, C. (2000) 'Negotiation in the European Union: bargaining or problem-solving?' *Journal of European Public Policy*, 7 (5): 684–704.

Guimarães, M.H. and Antunes, S. (2003) 'France – Portugal: La Diplomatie Commerciale des Régions' *Pouvoirs Locaux*, 56 (1): 125–30.

Haas, P.M. (1992) 'Introduction: Epistemic communities and international policy coordination', *International Organization*, 46 (1): 1–35.

Lax, D.A. and Sebenius, J.K. (1986) *The Manager as Negotiator. Bargaining for Cooperation and Competitive Gain*, New York and London: The Free Press.

Ministério dos Negócios Estrangeiros (2007) 'Portugal na União Europeia'. Lisbon: Direcção-Geral dos Assuntos Europeus.

Panke, D. (2010) *Small States in the European Union. Coping With Structural Disadvantages*. London: Ashgate.

Programme for the Portuguese Presidency (2007) 'A Stronger Union for a Better World'. Lisbon: Ministério dos Negócios Estrangeiros.

Raiffa, H. (1982) *The Art and Science of Negotiation*, Cambridge, MA and London: Harvard University Press.

Tallberg, J. (2008) 'Bargaining Power in the European Council', *Journal of Common Market Studies*, 46 (3): 685–708.

8 EU structural funds in Portugal

A mixed picture

Alfredo Marques

Introduction

Since 1989 regional policy has become a central part of the EU's effort to take economic integration forward. The aim of this policy is the reduction of disparities in levels of economic development between regions and member states, assuming that the lack of cohesion that they represent can be a threat to the integration process. As a consequence the Union has a role to play, in addition to national efforts. Structural funds (SF) are the main instrument to achieve that goal.

The purpose of this chapter is to make a contribution to the evaluation of structural funds intervention in Portugal, which is one of their main beneficiaries due to the low level of development of its regions in comparison to the Community average.

Considering that the need for such a policy is a controversial issue among economists, we will start by a brief discussion of theoretical foundations of regional policy. This is the subject of the first section.

The second section explains the method of evaluation applied, before carrying out, in the subsequent sections, an empirical analysis.

Rationale for structural funds

The question whether integration contributes towards more or less disparity is not easy to answer. Economic theory shows that there are some mechanisms which determine convergence while others generate divergence.[1] As Pelkmans (2006: 339) underlines, one empirical reason to discuss the arguments in favour and against regional policy is that decades of monitoring European economic integration have yielded a mixed picture, with both convergence and divergence occurring.

Convergence

The Heckscher–Ohlin–Samuelson (HOS) model predicts that factor returns, in all regions of an integrated area like the EU (where there is a customs union and a common market), tend to converge. This outcome requires perfect competition and identical production technologies in all regions (where there are initially different factor endowments) as well as an unlimited flow of factors. As the first conditions are supposed to be fulfilled, the role of public authorities in such a context is only to eliminate the obstacles to free movement of goods, services, labour and capital (negative integration according to Tinbergen, 1965: 76–82).

The standard neo-classical growth model (Solow) employs capital decreasing returns, which means that output grows proportionally less than the stock of capital. As rich countries/regions have a larger capital stock than poor ones, the latter will tend to grow faster and gradually converge. In the long run the rate of economic growth, as measured by the growth rate of output per person, depends on the growth rate of total factor productivity, which is determined in turn by the rate of technological progress. This theory assumes the rate of technological progress to be determined by a scientific process that is separate from, and independent of, economic forces. Economists can take the long-run growth rate as given exogenously from outside the economic system. However, technological progress is assumed to spread between countries without barriers.

The model based on the life cycle of the product (Vernon) may also lead to convergence, as it assumes the gradual absorption of know-how in areas benefiting from foreign direct investment to develop production at the middle stages of a product's life cycle. This permits them gradually to develop their own innovation capacity and to upgrade the quality of production.

Divergence

New trade theory, in contrast with the HOS model, assuming an initial advantage of a country/region based on innovation (Posner) within an imperfect competition framework characterized by the existence of scale economies (Krugman), suggests that the countries or regions that take the initial advantage are likely to gain more from integration. They start by benefiting from a monopoly that may persist due to economies of scale.

Endogenous growth theory (Romer, Lucas, Aghion and Howitt), in opposition to the standard neo-classical growth model, is based on increased returns of capital, which may explain divergence. The notion of capital is here widened to include human capital and knowledge (innovation capacity). As this capacity is higher in the most advanced areas, development disparities will remain or increase. Growth does not slow as capital accumulates. Innovation can result from experience (learning by doing) as well as from R&D expenditures undertaken by profit-seeking firms. Technical progress is therefore endogenous to the economic system. Economic policies with respect to trade, competition, education, taxes and intellectual property can influence the rate of innovation by affecting the private costs and benefits of carrying out R&D.

Agglomeration theory (Marshall, Perroux, Myrdal) and the Clusters approach (Porter) lead to the conclusion that firms should benefit from increasing returns resulting from a trinity of agglomeration economies: a local pool of skilled labour, local supplier linkages, and local knowledge spillovers. New economic geography (Krugman) adds two other factors to explain the preference of firms for locating in places where economic activity is already concentrated – economies of scale and transport costs. These different and complementary forces will generate divergence.

Among the different arguments explaining divergence, agglomeration effects and endogenous growth are probably the most influential in shaping European regional policy. Investments in infrastructure and human capital, for example, are seen as adequate measures to attract firms (and thus to generate employment and to increase production) by creating the basic conditions for economic activity. Subsidies to firms (directed to productive investment or to R&D) are also used for the same purpose. They can be justified on economic grounds by the existence of market failures (Chang, 1996) and are authorized by EU competition rules, for this reason (EC, 2001a), in backward regions for different types of investment and in every region for particular types of investment (mainly R&D and SMEs).

The welfare costs of such a policy have however to be weighed against the welfare gains. In the first two types of measures (infrastructures and human capital) there are opportunity costs (financial resources applied in these investments are no longer available for similar action in core regions). In the third case (regional incentives) in addition to opportunity costs (money can be applied in another type of action) there are also efficiency costs (distortions of the market mechanism caused by intervention). It is not certain in any of these cases that the marginal utility of production factors in lagging regions is sufficient to generate a positive net welfare effect.

Method of evaluation applied

Evaluating a public policy is a difficult task because of the counterfactual problem. We cannot know exactly what would have happened if the policy that we want to analyse had not been in place. In principle, the evaluation should answer three key questions related to the policy under analysis, namely appropriateness, effectiveness and efficiency.

The aim of structural funds (SF) is not to solve short-term problems, but to improve structural (long-term) conditions that determine disparities. So, to be appropriate, or relevant, SF intervention must concentrate on the growth potential of backward countries and regions. In other words, it must try to remove the deficiencies in the supply side of the economy. Therefore this is the point of view that will be favoured in our analysis of appropriateness.

An important issue that arises regarding this question is the relationship between cohesion and competitiveness. As we are dealing with regional/national economies that are exposed to international competition, it is obvious that convergence implies the enhancement of competitiveness. This can be defined as 'the ability of companies, industries, regions, nations and supra-national regions to generate relatively high income and employment levels while being exposed to international competition' (OECD, 1996).

Cohesion, according to Molle (2007: 5), means the degree to which disparities in social and economic welfare between the different regions and groups within the EU are politically and socially tolerable. Comparing the two concepts, it is clear that competitiveness is a necessary condition for cohesion, which implies that measures to improve the latter must be combined with actions to enhance the former. However, as we will see in the empirical analysis, the way SFs have been shaped and applied over a long time-period does not reflect this combination.

As for the second evaluation question, SF intervention can be considered effective if *ex post* results match *ex ante* expected effects. This is not however easy to establish, because we need to distinguish between the internal objectives of SF programmes and the contribution of these programmes to the reduction of disparities. The former can be comfortably achieved if they are carefully defined, while the latter faces the counterfactual problem mentioned above. Moreover, there are no quantified objectives in SF for reducing disparities, which is the key problem of regional policy. Effectiveness is therefore a controversial issue (Molle, 2007: 229–230).

Finally, efficiency implies that the policy results were attained using as few resources as possible. An example of an efficiency indicator is the cost of creating a certain number of jobs. The problem of evaluating efficiency lies both in the quantification of objectives and in isolating the contribution of the policy for their achievement. As the main objective (the reduction of disparities) is not quantified and as evaluating the specific contribution of SFs for the observed results concerning this objective is problematic, evaluating efficiency (for a programme or a policy, not necessarily for a project) is even more complex than the two previous tasks.

Taking into account the above considerations and the limited scope of this chapter, the evaluation of the EU structural funds intervention in Portugal that follows concentrates on appropriateness and effectiveness. We will carry out this evaluation for the different intervention periods of SF. In view of the relatively small space for this contribution, the analysis is necessarily made only in general terms.

The first two intervention periods (1989–1993 and 1994–1999)

During the first two SF intervention periods (1989–1993 and 1994–1999) there was no causal link between cohesion and competitiveness under the guidelines of EU regional policy. Both were seen as desirable for backward regions, but they were supposed to occur separately. This dissociation is clearly reflected in the Portuguese operational programmes applied in Objective 1 Regions (all the regions of the country in these two periods). Within this framework the highest priority was given to cohesion, seen as the endowment of the territory with basic (physical) infrastructure: for example, roads, water supplies, sanitation, education, culture, sports, health services. At the same time, for companies, the priority was to replace old (or very old) equipment.

When Portugal joined the EC in 1986, one of the main impediments to the development process was indeed the lack of all kinds of infrastructure in the country as a whole. We have in Table 8.1 an illustration of the situation for roads (motorways), in comparison with countries such as Belgium or the Netherlands, or even Spain, which joined the EC at the same time as Portugal. Table 8.2 shows a similar situation for healthcare, while in Table 8.3 we can see that after a decade of SF intervention the country is still in a very bad situation in terms of sanitation.

As for companies, according to an enquiry into industry made by Godinho and Sousa (2000), in 1996 (i.e. many years after the beginning of SF intervention), the average age of equipment was still more than 10 years in about 17 per cent of companies and was between 6 and 10 years in more than 56 per cent of them.

Taking into account that the results of investments in these domains only appear some years later, concentration of funding in infrastructures of collective use and, more generally, in physical assets, can be seen as justified during these two periods. In fact, this kind of policy, even if its first purpose from the EU and the Portuguese authorities' viewpoints was the improvement of cohesion in the sense explained above, leads to the creation of basic conditions for growth. That is why such a policy benefits from a large consensus among economists.

Table 8.1 Motorway network

	Year	*Km per inhabitant*
Portugal	1990	0.03
	2000	0.14
	2006	0.24
Greece	1990	0.02
	1992	0.03
	–	–
Ireland	1990	0.01
	2000	0.03
	2005	0.06
Spain	1990	0.12
	2000	0.22
	2005	0.26
Belgium	1990	0.17
	2000	0.17
	2006	0.17
Netherlands	1990	0.14
	2000	0.14
	2004	0.14

Source: Eurostat database.

Table 8.2 Healthcare

	Year	*Hospital beds (per 1,000 inhabitants)*
Portugal	1991	4.3
	1995	3.9
	2004	3.7
Greece	1991	5.0
	1995	5.2
	–	–
Ireland	1991	6.2
	1995	7
	2005	5.6
Spain	1987	4.4
	1995	3.9
	2005	3.4
Belgium	1989	11.9
	1995	7.4
	2005	7.4
Netherlands	1991	11.4
	1995	5.3
	2005	4.4

Source: Eurostat database.

Table 8.5 shows, for the whole Objective 1 (backward) Regions of the Union, that funds applied in infrastructures, over the period 1989–2006, represent more than one-third of total SFs and that the same applies to productive activity.[2] We can see in Table 8.6 that in Greece, Spain and Portugal, in particular, the weight of investments in these two groups of investments reached the same level (two-thirds for both groups) during the period 1994–2006 and represented more than 70 per cent in the sub-period 1994–1999.

Before SF, Portugal had no real structural policy since infrastructure and other long-term projects were few and were only carried out on a case-by-case basis.

Table 8.3 Sanitation and water supply, share population coverage

	Portugal (%)		*Greece (%)*		*Ireland (%)*		*Belgium (%)*		*Netherlands (%)*	
Year	*1998*	*2006*	*2000*	*2006*	*2002*	*2007*	*1998*	*2006*	*1998*	*2006*
Sanitation	42	72	56*	85	66**	84***	38	56	98	99
Water supply	85.0	91.3	85.0	92.0	90.0	85.0	94.3	98.8	99.9	99.9

Source: Eurostat database.

Notes

* 1997, ** 1999, *** 2005.

Table 8.4 Education, share of population by highest level

	Year	*Lower secondary (%)*	*Upper second and post-second. Non-tertiary (%)*	*Tertiary (%)*
Portugal	1992	81.3	10.7	7.9
	2000	81.1	12.0	6.9
	2008	73.3	15.1	11.6
Greece	1992	64.3	26.0	9.7
	2000	53.2	34.1	12.7
	2008	44.9	36.9	19.3
Ireland	1992	59.4	26.4	13.9
	2000	41.9	34.1	17.0
	2008	34.5	34.6	27.6
Spain	1992	74.4	15.3	10.3
	2000	62.2	17.5	18.7
	2008	53.0	21.1	24.6
UE-15	1995	45.0	15.3	13.5
	2000	40.4	17.5	16.6
	2008	36.7	21.1	21.4
UE-27	2000	38.9	40.4	15.3
	2008	34.4	44.4	20.0

Source: Eurostat database.

With the financial package of SF and the high funding rate of projects (up to 75 per cent of the total cost in the case of public investments[3] and the same ceiling applied to companies in the period 1989–1999 in backward regions), we can assume a significant additional effect of SF, even if it is difficult to calculate it precisely.[4]

Thus, the concentration of SF in infrastructure of collective use has profoundly changed the former situation in this domain in both absolute and relative terms. This can be seen in particular in Tables 8.1 and 8.3. It has also consequently improved the basic conditions for growth and life conditions. At the same time, there were many incentives provided to companies for the acquisition of physical assets and the construction of facilities. For the whole economy the weight of SF in total investment was significantly high (about 13 per cent over the period 1989–1999 and 11 per cent in the period 2000–2006[5]).

However, as we can see in Table 8.4 the initial needs in Portugal in terms of human resources qualifications were also very high. Table 8.6 shows that the percentage of SFs allocated to this domain in the period 1994–1999 was only 27 per cent, against 36 per cent in Ireland, and remained practically unchanged in the period 2000–2006. This can be considered as a failure of SF in Portugal as human capital is a crucial factor of development by increasing productivity[6] and by contributing to raising the employment rate.[7]

Taking into account the above figures and considerations, the policy options made in Portugal for the allocation of SF in the periods under analysis seem to have been generally appropriate, although not completely so. There was a preference for investments that were more strictly related to cohesion (in the sense mentioned earlier) and with more immediate and more visible results to the detriment of those more directly linked to competitiveness and with less visibility in the short run (intangible investment). In other words, the choices made suggest the lack of a long-term strategy.

As for effectiveness, the test can be seen as positive if we take into consideration the direct results for physical factors. However, the opposite applies to human capital. Probably for this reason, and also because there was no preference for other intangible growth factors (in particular R&D and innovation), the results in terms of GDP per capita (which appear only some years later) confirm, as we will see later, the lack of (or the insufficient) effectiveness of cohesion policy in these two periods.

The third period (2000–2006)

As we can see in Figure 8.1, SF intervention in Portugal in the first two periods was not sufficient to ensure a sustainable convergence process. The figure shows that there was a slow convergence during the 1990s but that this process had

Table 8.5 Breakdown of SF by intervention domain in Objective 1 regions (share of total)

	Infrastructure (%)	*Human resources (%)*	*Productive activity (%)*	*Other (%)*
1989–1993	35.2	29.6	33.6	1.6
1994–1999	29.8	24.5	41.0	4.7
2000–2006	41.3	23.1	33.8	1.8

Sources: EC (2001b: Part III, Table 14); EC (2004 – Statistical Annex of Part 4, Table A4.4).

Table 8.6 Breakdown of SF by intervention domain in the four 'cohesion countries' (share of total)

	Time period	*Infrastructure (%)*	*Human resources (%)*	*Productive activity (%)*
Greece	1994–1999	45.8	23.5	30.2
	2000–2006	38.1	24.0	34.3
Ireland	1994–1999	17.3	35.7	39.9
	2000–2006	20.1	33.3	44.0
Spain	1994–1999	37.2	24.4	30
	2000–2006	21.6	46.6	30.9
Portugal	1994–1999	29.5	26.6	39.6
	2000–2006	27.7	27.8	42.2

Sources: EC (2001b: Statistical Annex, Table A.36); EC (2004: Part 4 – Statistical Annex, Table A4.9).

stopped before the end of that decade (when the full effects of the previous intervention were supposed to appear). Between 1999 and 2004 there was divergence, and more recently the trend is uncertain.

When assessing this evolution on the basis of the employment rate and productivity, we can see in Table 8.7 that it does not result from the former because Portugal performs well above the EU average. Figure 8.2 demonstrates that the problem lies in labour productivity, in which the country performs very poorly. At the same time the disparities between regions inside the country have increased (Figure 8.3), which confirms the lack of effectiveness of cohesion policy in terms of output, considering that the poorest regions have received more funding than the rest.

In view of this situation, the third Community Support Framework (CSF) (2000–2006) was supposed to give rise to a profound change in priorities for implementing SF in the country. An additional reason for this was that the new period began when the European Council launched the Lisbon Agenda in March 2000. This represented a strategic objective for the EU as a whole, which was aimed at making the European Union 'the most competitive and dynamic knowledge-based economy in the world, capable of sustainable economic growth with more and better jobs and greater social cohesion'. This strategy became a framework for the various areas of both Community and national policies. Moreover, it was accompanied by the definition of several specific and, in some cases, quantified targets in areas such as R&D, innovation, ICT, education, economic reform, employment and cohesion.

A problem of inconsistency appeared however between SF and the Lisbon Strategy, as the former basically maintained the guidelines of the two first periods. At the same time as the latter had a very limited implementation until the middle of the decade, in 2005 the Commission presented the Communication 'Working together for growth and jobs – A new start for the Lisbon Strategy' (EC, 2005a), which led to its reorientation towards the following objectives:

Table 8.7 Employment rate (share)

Year	*EU–27 (%)*	*Euro area (%)*	*Portugal (%)*
1996	–	58.0	64.1
1997	60.7	58.5	65.7
1998	61.2	59.3	66.8
1999	61.8	60.5	67.4
2000	62.2	61.5	68.4
2001	62.5	62.2	69.0
2002	62.3	62.4	68.8
2003	62.5	62.6	68.1
2004	62.9	63.0	67.8
2005	63.4	63.7	67.5
2006	64.4	64.6	67.9

Source: Eurostat database.

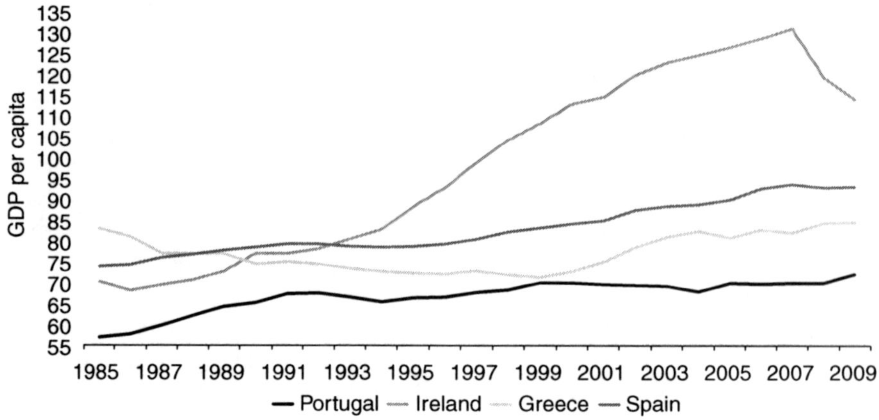

Figure 8.1 GDP per capita index in PPS* (EU 15 = 100) (source: OECD database).

Note
* PPS = Purchasing Power Standard.

(increasing) knowledge and innovation; (making the EU) an attractive place to invest and work; and (generating) growth and jobs for social cohesion.

No changes occurred, however, in SF guidelines in spite of the fact that there was a mid-term review in 2003, as dictated by the SF Regulations. This immobility remained in place until the end of the third CSF, although the European Council of March 2005 established a connection between the Lisbon Strategy and cohesion policy, with the following wording:

> Europe must renew the basis of its competitiveness, increase its growth

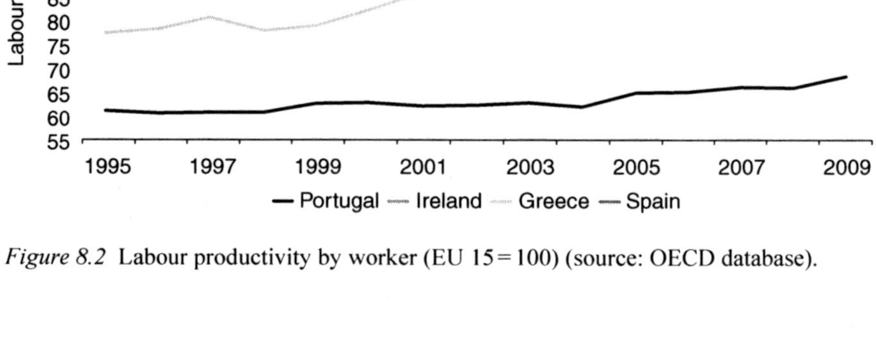

Figure 8.2 Labour productivity by worker (EU 15 = 100) (source: OECD database).

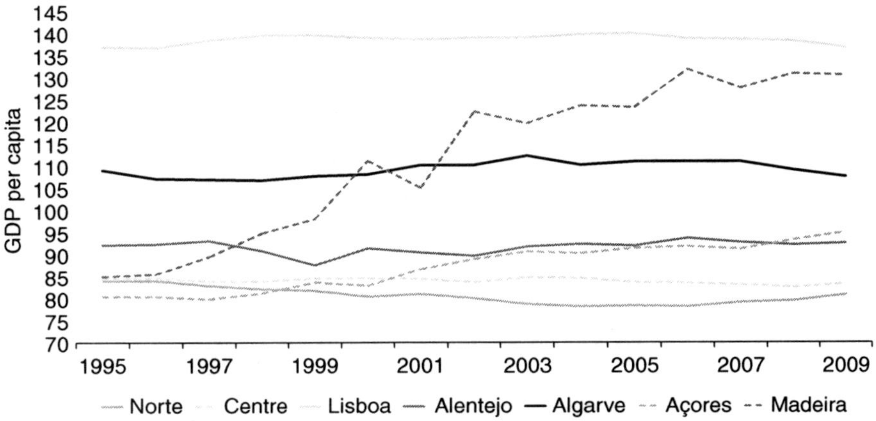

Figure 8.3 GDP per capita index at current prices (PT = 100) (source: Instituto Nacional de Estatística database).

> potential and its productivity and strengthen social cohesion, placing the main emphasis on knowledge, innovation and the optimization of human capital. To achieve these objectives, the Union must mobilize to a greater degree all appropriate national and Community resources – including the Cohesion Policy[.][8]

It is not therefore surprising to see in Table 8.6 that Portugal (which has always remained very passive in face of the room for manoeuvre allowed by SF rules) shows more or less the same percentages for the different intervention domains as before. We can take the intervention in the domain of productive activity, which presents the highest percentage of fund allocation, as a good example of the dissociation between SF and Lisbon Strategy for reasons that we are going to see.

This intervention was basically concentrated in the Operational Programme (OP) 'Economy', which aimed to provide incentives to companies and entities belonging to the National Innovation System (NIS). According to the evaluation report of this programme made by independent experts (PRIME, 2006: Chapter 5), there were many incentives for companies to make productive investments with innovation content. However, this was effectively an inaccurate notion of innovation, as old equipment was being replaced by new machines to produce the same products as before and in many cases on the basis of the same or similar production processes.

A second conclusion is that there was a bias in favour of scientific and technological infrastructure (universities, R&D centres and so on) to the detriment of R&D projects in companies, with the following features. Up until 2005, there were many projects supported by the programme for the former (about 170 for a total number of these entities which was very limited in the country), while for companies (whose number was much larger) there were only 230.

According to the final execution report of this programme (PRIME, 2010), covering the whole period 2000–2006, support for R&D projects of companies represented only 6.9 per cent of the total number of projects funded by the programme, 3.5 per cent of the total supported investment and 4.4 per cent of the total aid provided by the programme. Such a result represents undoubtedly a failure of incentives aimed at the generation of knowledge directly involving companies and immediately applied in the introduction of new processes or new products.

A second aspect of this distortion is a lack of focus in NIS projects, illustrated, for example, by the fact that there were very few projects in partnership between companies and those entities. In other terms, the aim of most NIS projects was research that was not directly linked to innovation.

Finally, a mistake in the form (and in the intensity) of aid was made. While for NIS projects there were subsidies without reimbursement and with high intensity (aid as a percentage of costs), from 2003 support for companies took the form of reimbursable grants (with a lower intensity). Companies then stopped applying for incentives for R&D. Such a result is not surprising as R&D activity generates spill-overs to other firms that did not bear the costs of this investment. That is why there is a consensus among economists that public support is necessary to stimulate firms to make the maximum level of R&D. Without incentives with a sufficient intensity firms can cease R&D activity or reduce the level of investment in this field.

A third conclusion is that, in spite of the fact that there was an aid scheme for small projects (rather than for small companies), it did not include incentives aimed directly at the promotion of entrepreneurship. This is another aspect of the erroneous orientation of this policy, as experience demonstrates in the most advanced OECD countries that SMEs and self-employment can play a major role in economic growth and employment creation (OECD, 2010).

Therefore, in regions that are lagging behind, incentives to companies that seem capable of producing significant positive effects when they are shaped properly (IFO, 1989), in order to outweigh their competitive disadvantage resulting from the lack of positive externalities, do not seem have played their potential role in Portugal. We must recall that these incentives were closely dependent upon SF, as such a policy did not exist in the country before SF support arrived.

A more detailed analysis would show that, as in the two previous periods, SF intervention under the third CSF also produced some positive results. However, the breakdown of SF by domain and the example of the OP 'Economy' suggest that this period represented a lost opportunity for getting Portuguese structural policy in line with the recommendations coming from the EU as far as the Lisbon Strategy was concerned.

The present period (2007–2013)

In contrast with the previous period, the priorities for the present one (2007–2013) are in line with the Lisbon Strategy, complete with the Gothenburg Agenda, which represents its environmental dimension. SF guidelines defined at the EU level are now also connected to that strategy (EC, 2005b; EC, 2006). Portuguese priorities also take into account the results of cohesion policy in the previous periods, which were analysed in detail in a study made by a team of independent experts (Mateus, 2005). The general conclusion of this study was that up to that time SF had produced much more positive results in Portugal in terms of cohesion (in the sense mentioned above) than in terms of competitiveness.

The reflection of this new orientation in the breakdown of funds by domain can be observed in Table 8.8. There was a large increase in funds for economic activity and innovation as well as for human resources, and a decrease for infrastructure. Human resources represent 37 per cent of the total EU funds allocated to Portugal in this period, which means a rise of more than nine percentage points. This means that in terms of appropriateness, cohesion policy for 2007–2013 was defined more accurately than for the previous periods.

At the operational level, one of the particularities of the present period is the diversity of status of the different NUTS II Regions (Convergence Regions, Competitiveness and Employment Regions, Phasing Out and Phasing In), compared with the homogeneity in the previous periods (only the Lisbon Region had a particular status in the third period). The four Regions (Norte, Centro, Alentejo and Açores), which make up the Convergence Group, are now the main beneficiaries of SF. However, their priorities are the same as for the others (Lisbon, Algarve and Madeira): cohesion linked to competitiveness. This may be regarded as a second positive sign of appropriateness.

A third sign can be found in the domain of incentives to companies (which represents a very large part of funds allocated to economic activity). The purposes of aid schemes are now the promotion of R&D in firms (with an autonomous and significant budget), the qualification and internationalization of SME (exclusive to this size of companies), innovation (through tangible and intangible assets) in existing companies and the promotion of entrepreneurship.

Table 8.8 Breakdown of SF by intervention domain in Portugal, 2007–2013

Domain	*EU fund*	*Variation (%) constant prices*	*Variation (%) current prices*
Infrastructures of collective use	ERDF	–40.9	–33.4
Human resources qualification	ESF	+25.0	+40.9
Economic activity and innovation	ERDF + Cohesion Fund	+47.2	+65.8

Source: Rodrigues, 2013.

Another feature of these new aid schemes is the reduction in the number of eligible sectors and, for the first time in the country, the option for a particular focus in certain clusters in parallel with horizontal incentives. At the same time, the criteria for evaluating the quality of projects to be supported has become more selective, especially as far as the concept of innovation is concerned.

Finally, all the projects supported by SF must comply with the principle of sustainability. This applies not only to companies (which are more directly exposed to international competition), but also to public investments at the different territorial levels (national, regional and local).

As for effectiveness, a conclusive evaluation only may be made at the end of the programme (after 2013). We can however make a first test of the effects of the above changes, once more taking incentives to companies as an example. In the first three years of implementation of the three aid schemes (2008–2010), incentives to R&D projects of companies represented 21 per cent of the total number of projects funded by these aid schemes (against 6.9 per cent in the period 2000–2006), 11 per cent of the total supported investment (against 3.5 per cent in the previous period) and 15.5 per cent of the total aid (against 4.4 per cent before).[9]

This example suggests that the above reorientation of SF seem to be effective, as far as their direct effect on inputs or production factors is concerned. This is, of course, only a partial and very provisional picture. Moreover, the most important results, which are the definite test for convergence and cohesion, will be seen later in GDP/per capita rate of growth.

Conclusion

The intervention of EU structural funds in Portugal, since 1989, shows both positive effects that would not have occurred without this financial support, and some failures and lost opportunities. In the first case, we can mention their contribution to investments in physical assets (collective use infrastructure and equipment for productive investment in companies), which were clearly lacking in the country as basic conditions for growth.

However, in the period 2000–2006, instead of being redirected to the priorities of the Lisbon Strategy (knowledge, innovation, competitiveness) and the Gothenburg Agenda (sustainable development), SF remained mainly addressed to the former objectives. This immobility represents a lost opportunity for the country at a crucial time.

In order to put SF intervention in the present period (2007–2013) in line with the above priorities, funds allocated to the qualification of human resources and innovation have substantially increased, while those directed to infrastructure have fallen. At the same time, cohesion is no longer regarded as an objective independent of competitiveness, but as being closely linked to the latter.

This means that in terms of appropriateness, cohesion policy for 2007–2013 was defined more accurately than for the previous periods. As far as effectiveness is concerned, a first test made here, although partial and provisional, seems to show also a positive evolution. It is however necessary to wait for the end of the period to make a more precise and complete evaluation. In addition to common factors that may affect negatively the implementation and the results of a policy of this nature, the financial and economic crisis that has emerged since 2008/2009, as well as the Economic Adjustment Programme applied in the period mid-2011 to mid-2014, have introduced additional troubling elements.

Notes

1 Brief overviews of convergence and divergence theories can be found in all handbooks on the economics of European integration, including our own handbook (Marques, 2006). For a more detailed survey, see Martin (1998).
2 This means essentially, in this case, investments in physical assets.
3 This percentage has increased to 85 per cent in the present period, 2007–2013.
4 The European Commission applies a proxy for determining the additionally of SF (based on national spending in the prior period), which can give a general idea of this effect, but does not provide precise results. Moreover, as far as public spending is concerned, the restrictions imposed on national fiscal policies by the Growth and Stability Pact make this method more problematic.
5 EC (2001b: Part III, Table 9).
6 Paul Romer and Robert Lucas, 'fathers' of endogenous growth theory (after Kenneth Arrow), show that human capital is the engine of growth, as human capital accumulation raises the productivity of both labour and physical capital. See also OECD (2003).
7 In addition to productivity, the employment rate is also a growth factor
8 This can be seen as the first attempt to establish a link between cohesion and competitiveness. However, this attempt had no practical consequences.
9 Figures collected from the database of the *Rede de Incentivos QREN* (National Incentives Network).

Bibliography

Chang, H.-J. (1996), *The Political Economy of Industrial Policy*, MacMillan Press: London.

EC (European Commission) (2001a), Ninth Report on state aid in the European Union: Brussels.

EC (2001b), *Second Report on Economic and Social Cohesion*: Brussels.

EC (2004), *Third Report on Economic and Social Cohesion*: Brussels.

EC (2005a), Communication to the European Council, 'Working together for growth and jobs – A new start for the Lisbon Strategy': Brussels.

EC (2005b), *Cohesion Policy in Support of Growth and Jobs – Community Strategic Guidelines, 2007–2013*: Brussels.

EC (2006), 'The Growth and Jobs Strategy and the Reform of European Cohesion Policy', *Fourth Progress Report on Cohesion*: Brussels.

Godinho, M. M. and Sousa, C. (2000), 'Panorama Tecnológico da Indústria Portuguesa', in Lança, I. S. (Org.) *A Indústria Portuguesa – Especialização, Internacionalização e Competitividade*, Celta: Oeiras: 86.

IFO (Institut Für Wirtschaftsforschung) (1989), 'An Empirical Assessment of Factors Shaping Regional Competitiveness in Problem Regions': Munich.

Marques, A. (2006), *Economia da União Europeia*, Almedina: Coimbra.

Martin, R. (1998), *Regional Policy in the EU: Economic Foundations and Reality*, CEPS, Brussels.

Mateus, A. (2005), *Competitividade Territorial e Coesão Económica e Social*, Estudos, Observatório do QCA III, Lisbon.
Molle, W. (2007), *European Cohesion Policy*, Routledge, London.
OECD (1996), *Industrial Competitiveness*: Paris.
OECD (2003), *The Sources of Economic Growth in OECD Countries*: Paris.
OECD (2010), *SMEs, Entrepreneurship and Innovation*: Paris.
Pelkmans, J. (2006), *European Integration: Methods and Economic Analysis*, 3rd edition, Prentice Hall, London.
PRIME (Programa de Incentivos à Modernização da Economia) (2006), 'Actualização da Avaliação Intercalar – Relatório Final': Lisbon.
PRIME (Programa de Incentivos à Modernização da Economia) (2010), 'Relatório Final de Execução': Lisbon.
Rodrigues, D. (2013), *Portuguese NSRF 2007–2013*, Observatório do QREN: Lisbon.
Tinbergen, J. (1965), *International Economic Integration*, 2nd edition, Elsevier: Amsterdam.

9 Portugal and the Lisbon strategy

Arminda Neves, Carlos Zorrinho and Manuel Laranja

Since the mid-1990s, and in response to a rapidly changing global context, Portuguese governments have embraced wider and more ambitious economic and social development policies. Parallel to these changes, in 2000 the European Union launched a series of important political initiatives, framed within the ‘umbrella’ of the Lisbon Strategy – a vision of a more competitive Europe, through wider qualification, knowledge and innovation, with social cohesion and sustainability (economic, social and environmental). These initiatives, at national and European levels, represent a renewed multi-level policy approach motivated by the need to improve competitiveness and economic growth. Notwithstanding these new policy efforts, it is still unclear to what extent European-level initiatives have been able to influence the dynamics and nature of Portuguese policies and goals. Our objective in this chapter is to examine whether the overall dynamics of European Policies, as framed by the Lisbon Strategy, have helped to (re)shape domestic policies and, if so, in what domains this influence has been stronger. After reviewing the literature on the global dynamics of trade, investment and knowledge, interpreting globalization and the strategic reactions to it, we will look at three cycles of the implementation of the Lisbon Strategy in Europe and in Portugal:

1 The global dynamics of trade, investment and knowledge. Why reactions to globalization are region specific.

In the last two or three decades, it is fair to say that worldwide economic growth has been increasingly associated with the wide spread of information, communication and transportation technologies. While this has opened up new possibilities for investment outsourcing from high-wage to lower-wage economies, the growing industrial capabilities of new developing countries (especially China, India and countries of South East Asia) have also increasingly given rise to vast new consumer markets and an increase in exports from lower-wage countries to high-wage societies.

Along with trade and investment, knowledge is also becoming increasingly global. Scholars of technology and economic change define knowledge as both a public and a private good, but because private knowledge has a strongly tacit character its accumulation and diffusion tend to be geographically bounded, in that it is not freely available anywhere in the world. Public knowledge, however, travels freely and it is easily available anywhere in the world. Increasing international flows of trade, finance, investment and knowledge is what we would normally call an acceleration of the globalization process started many years ago (Berger, 2006; Gros, 2005), but following the fall of the Berlin Wall it has been accelerating further and entering a new stage.

Although scholars have a general idea of what constitutes globalization, there is little or no agreement about its political consequences for Europe, for countries individually and for the international balance of power. For example, some believe that the world is without borders (Friedman, 2005; Ohmae, 1990; *Economist*, 1995), and therefore, in the long run, there will be only one single global market, fuelled by technology (Castells, 1996; Tapscott, 2008), by financial liberalization and deregulation and by interests and neo-liberal ideologies.

Others appear to accept that the impacts of globalization are asymmetric and therefore, depending on their historical context, nations/regions have a range of political choices in reacting to the consequences of globalization. Much the same way, and taking the notion of 'agency' (Braun, 2003), we argue that nations/regions react differently to normative pressures from international organizations and strategies on how to deal with globalization trends. However, inevitably the differences are associated not just with local historical and institutional contexts – or even with varieties of capitalism (Albert, 1993), but also with local mediation processes in which a variety of local interests, political parties, ideologies, business strategies and contingencies and leadership, play a major role.

The Lisbon Strategy 2000–2004: rationale and promises

The launch of the Lisbon project in 2000 was possibly a collective European level response to the effects of globalization. On the one hand, the economic literature was calling attention to the European productivity and innovation gap compared with the US (Begg, 2008), this was interpreted as the result of economic and social rigidities (Padoan and Mariani, 2006), and also as related to the high degree of public regulation, the dominant role of protected oligopolies and the rigidity of the labour market (Gruner, 2002). On the other hand, in parallel with the economic literature, political scientists proposed a rather normative foundation of the strategy based on reconciling external pressures for productivity and competitiveness with the European social model (social and environmental dimensions) and with specific political and institutional dynamics (Borrás and Jacobsson, 2004; Zeitlin and Pochet, 2005).

Whatever the precise rationale, Europe set itself the Lisbon Strategy in 2000 as a new vision, defined as making Europe 'the most competitive and dynamic knowledge economy in the world, capable of durable economic growth, higher employment levels and jobs of a better quality and of improved social cohesion'.[1]

This collective reaction to global trends would have to be based on a society in which knowledge would be the main source of opportunities for value and employment creation and for sustaining the European social model (Sapir, 2004; Rodrigues, 2002). This vision was considered as utopian by many, not just because of its ambitions, but also because it attempted to reconcile competitiveness with social cohesion and environmental sustainability. Nevertheless, others saw it as a promising step, not only to improve socio-economic performance but also, and perhaps mainly, to legitimize further European integration (Natali, 2009). As argued by Rodrigues (2002) – one of the architects of the Lisbon agenda – the emphasis on this new EU strategy was more political than economic. Europe needed a more 'forward-looking' approach to socio-economic development based on sustaining EU citizens' living conditions, making Europe a key player in globalization and improving the legitimacy of EU institutions.

Moreover, to achieve the ambitious objective of becoming the most competitive knowledge-based economy in the world, Europeans also recognized the need to introduce new 'participatory' governance mechanisms – the so-called Open Method of Coordination. Again this may be justified in terms of the need for more economic coordination to deal with inter-regional interdependencies, spill-overs and complementarities (e.g. product market and employment policies), or alternatively, looking at other streams of literature from political science, to stimulate policy learning and mutual adjustment across Europe in a multi-level setting (Pisani-Ferry and Sapir, 2006; Dyson, 2000).

How have all these developments influenced policies and governance in Portugal at the initial stages of the Lisbon Strategy? If we focus on implementation, rather than on conception or political discourse the Lisbon Strategy in Portugal started in 2001 with the creation of the 'Integrated Innovation Support Programme' (PROINOV). This was a rather programmatic approach focusing on innovation and knowledge but attempting to combine different policy domains such as science, education, skills, the information society and employment, represented by the corresponding Ministries. Economic and social partners were also represented in the PROINOV governance structure together with invited experts from different fields.

Perhaps the most visible effect of this initiative was to call the attention of Portuguese policy makers to the need to focus overall economic and social development around endogenous sources of knowledge and innovation with an explicit association to questions relating to training, qualifications and skills. One could also argue that PROINOV set important methodological bases for the development of industrial clusters and for the prospective diagnosis of training needs in line with the growth of the economic base.[2] It is at this initial stage that we can identify a first attempt to mount a horizontal coordination mechanism involving several policy domains. The whole PROINOV experience, however, lasted for only a year, ending shortly after the election of a new government in 2002 and therefore producing little visible effect. Nevertheless, as we will see further, this first attempt to create a new governance structure, clearly induced by the Lisbon strategy, would be re-established in 2005.

The Lisbon Strategy, 2005–2008: a new start for Europe and for Portugal

In 2004, in face of an unfavourable economic climate, the Council and the European Commission asked the Prime Minister of the Netherlands, Wim Kok, to lead an expert group that could review the Lisbon process. In November of that year, the group completed the so-called 'Wim Kok Report' (Kok, 2004), which concluded that little progress had been made during the initial years of the Agenda's implementation, and recommended 'refocusing the Strategy on the objectives of growth and employment'. The Wim Kok report also highlighted the need for 'real ownership' of the reform agenda by Member States through greater appropriation and commitment to implementation at a national level.

On the basis of this report, at the spring 2005 European Council the Heads of State and Heads of Government of the Member States decided to relaunch the Lisbon Strategy for Growth and Jobs. This relaunch called for greater articulation of European and National policy levels, the former supported by the 'Community Lisbon Programme' and the latter by National Reform Programmes (NRPs), more fully appropriated by local governments, social partners and civil society. Each country also had to nominate a National Coordinator for the Lisbon Strategy and align its National Reform Programme, 2005–2008 (NRP), with 24 'Integrated Guidelines', which formed the basis for the preparation of both national and European-level policies, focusing on macroeconomic and microeconomic policies and on employment.

These changes had an almost immediate impact in Portugal. Following the spring 2005 European Council, and coinciding with the coming of a new parliament with a change of governing party, the new Portuguese Government appointed a National Coordinator for the Lisbon Strategy reporting to the Prime Minister. Following the early experience with the horizontal articulation of different domains of policy, initiated in 2001 with PROINOV, the Coordinator of the Lisbon Strategy was supported by a Coordination Network comprising representatives of all the Ministries. The Lisbon Strategy National Coordination Network was given the task of designing the National Reform Programme for the period 2005/2008 (Coordenação Nacional da Estratégia de Lisboa, 2005). From the outset this network form of governance was sought as a semi-formal system of coordination of 'focal points' for related measures in different policy domains, complemented by a rather more formal system for policy monitoring associated with indicator-driven targets, impacts and country-rankings.

The stronger impact of the Lisbon strategy in Portugal at this stage may perhaps be seen in the much higher visibility given to the domain of knowledge and innovation policies, namely with the so-called Technological Plan defined as a 'policy agenda for mobilization that envisions to promote a decentralized but articulated implementation of a wide set of measures for science, technology and innovation' (PT, 2006). Although the Technological Plan originated during the 2005 election campaign, shortly after its launch by the Ministry of the Economy, and in view of its cross-cutting nature, it was transferred to the Coordinator of the Lisbon Strategy and its support network, then renamed the National Coordination Network of the Lisbon Strategy and the Technological Plan (CNEL_PT).

In this new cycle (2005–2008), in essence, the problems and policies now 'packed' in the NRP, with a renewed and widened focus on technology and innovation, were not new, relative to the short experience with PROINOV in 2001. The main novelties induced by European practices were the adoption of a network governance mechanism organized in policy domains and the use of international rankings, indicators and quantified objectives, in line with practices of New Public Management.[3] In the scope of the Technological Plan interministerial measures such as the launch of Technology and Competitiveness Poles and Clusters and ambitious initiatives in the recognition of informal skills such as 'Novas Oportunidades', as well as a more explicit linkage to lifelong learning and social inclusion, can also be taken as the positive influences of the Lisbon strategy on domestic policy.

Reactions to the crisis and beyond: the Lisbon Strategy after 2008

The crisis is assumed to have been the result of a double failure, namely the regulation of the global financial market and excessive financial liquidity due to historically low interest rates (Quaglia, 2010). Starting in mid 2007 with the drying up of liquidity in financial markets, the crisis took a turn for the worse following the collapse of Lehman Brothers in 2008. This was followed by a broad economic recession that hit Europe in 2009. The last stage was exemplified by the Greek budgetary crisis and consequent tensions in the EU.

While governments and the EC promptly introduced emergency measures to prevent the collapse of the financial system, as far as the Lisbon Strategy is concerned, they have been largely criticized for the weakness of their approach to regulating financial markets and to other areas, such as competition and standards.

Moreover the budgetary tensions resulting from the much-needed short-term stimulus packages gave rise to further criticism of the agenda proposed by the Lisbon strategy and its governance. Overall it has become obvious that budgetary surveillance and broad economic policy guidelines as the basis of the Stability and Growth Pact were greatly insufficient mechanisms for preventing instability, since by and large instability originates in the private sector.

Therefore, it should not come as a surprise that responses to the crisis were individual rather than European, and taken outside the frame of the Lisbon strategy that is, outside the Stability and Growth Pact, in most cases using budgetary stimulus and Keynesian policies to deal with the downturn (Pisani-Ferry *et al.*, 2008).

This 2008–2010 cycle appears therefore to have exposed not only inherent limitations in the Lisbon Strategy political economy framework but also fundamental contradictions and tensions between budgetary stability and structural reforms. On the one hand, macro stability (or austerity) was expected to contribute to the structural reforms of social and employment policies (Rodrigues, 2002) and favour the conditions for structural changes in productivity and competitiveness. However, on the other hand, macro budgetary stability held back, rather than assisted, in paving the way for structural reforms, by not providing adequate political and budgetary conditions to compensate the segments of society most affected by the reforms.

Portugal was no exception to the European pattern of responses to the crisis. The National Reform Programme (NRP) for the New Cycle (2008–2010) (Coordenação Nacional da Estratégia de Lisboa, 2008), aimed for greater rationality and focus on reform measures in six priority areas, but overall responses to the crisis were prepared outside the framework and governance structure of the NRP. Nevertheless, the new NRP emphasized consolidation of older and more recent reforms, namely the reform of public administration, social security, the education and training system, the S&T and innovation system, particularly through the establishment of competitiveness and technology and other clusters,[4] and of logistics platforms. At this stage one can also identify a much stronger role played by energy and climate policies, with the introduction in Portugal of an ambitious programme of renewable energies based on wind, solar and hydric sources.

The first report of this 2008–2010 cycle, presented in October 2009, included an evaluation of the Portuguese response to the economic crisis and its articulation with the reform measures of the Lisbon Strategy as well as a first contribution to the post-2010 period, in terms of a forward-looking review to ensure continuity with the renewal of existing policies.[5]

Discussion

As we move through the 2010s in the framework of the new EU2020 initiative, it is important to reflect on whether the Lisbon strategy initiative improved or more generally influenced domestic policies in Portugal. Our account is mixed. Over the past decade the European vision and policies positively influenced a number of domains, but fell short of expectations in others.

It results from our analysis above that the Lisbon Strategy had a strong positive influence in focusing overall socio-economic development in knowledge and innovation policies. This started in 2001 with PROINOV and, in particular after 2005 with the launch of Technology Plan Portugal, which adopted a broader approach to innovation policy, focused on progress measured by the European Innovation Scoreboard. Another area where the Lisbon strategy appears to have had a most positive influence in Portugal is in reinforcing policies towards education (at all levels), qualifications and skills as the core of the concept of a knowledge-based economy brought about by the Lisbon Strategy, particularly with regards to the official recognition of informal skills, lifelong learning and on-the-job learning. In much the same way, the Lisbon Strategy helped to raise the importance of national social policy issues in Portugal such as activation, prevention, gender and social inclusion. The Lisbon Strategy in

Portugal also played a major role, particularly in pushing renewable energies and climate issues as central priorities in the economic growth strategy.

To a certain extent, from 2005 onwards, we can argue that the governance network established for the coordination of the NRPs was instrumental in helping to break with traditional vertical cleavages between different Ministries – for example between the Ministry of Science and the Ministry of Economy, and in 2008 between economic and environmental policies with respect to the need to push Portuguese energy policy higher up the list of national priorities. Moreover, bridging measures such as the Technology and Competitiveness Poles and clusters, induced the Ministries of Economy, Science and Territorial Planning to collaborate, helping to introduce specific issues of horizontal coordination and avoiding the duplication of efforts.

However, our interpretation of the influence of the Lisbon strategy in Portuguese policy includes also a number of less successful issues that need to be discussed. Perhaps the most important concern is that the participation of local stakeholders in the policy process has proved to be limited and somewhat uneven. Particularly in the first five years of implementation, participation in the Lisbon Strategy was deemed problematic. However even after 2005, the fact is that policy makers and stakeholders in Portugal and perhaps also in other European countries, although adopting and understanding the logic and the governance structure behind the Lisbon strategy (for example, the strategic guidelines, the existence of a formal national coordinator, and the like), see it as exogenous to the local political system. The result is that a truly participatory mode of governance emphasizing learning, mutual adjustment and democratic experimentalism in the context of the multi-level European system has not been truly achieved. Clearly the notion of 'agency' (Braun, 2003) explains much of what has happened in Portugal and possibly in other European countries.

Another important governance issue to be discussed relates to the coordination network created in 2005. As we all know network governance is not a panacea for all multi-domain policy problems (Laranja, 2012). A weak point of network governance is that it is often less efficient, unrepresentative, and has less political legitimacy and little or no direct intervention capacity (Berner *et al.*, 2004). Furthermore, network forms of governance usually face the well-known problem of collective accountability – the politics of blame avoidance. We see this as a major limitation of the coordination network created in 2005.

A related aspect is that of the policy mix. At the core of the Lisbon strategy, in its implementation stance, we see the idea of inducing change from a multi-domain policy portfolio created by the summation of discrete policies and instruments in different domains (employment, social cohesion, knowledge, competitiveness, and the like), into a dynamic, interactive policy mix agenda (Flanagan *et al.*, 2011). This would be a most needed step forward, deemed necessary for effectively counteracting previous policy silos and forcing more radical institutional reforms. However, the PROINOV example early in 2001 and later the NRP 2005–2008 and 2008–2010, functioned as joined-up policies and policy instruments, rather than truly integrated programmes where the mix of policies accounts for combined effects, interdependencies, and so on. To a large extent this explains why, at least in some cases, objectives and measures in such NRPs are oriented to maintaining or improving the current institutional set-up, rather than inducing more or less profound institutional reforms. Finally, a common issue in need of further discussion is that the resources for implementing the policy actions directly associated with the Lisbon strategy were often scarce or were controlled by key actors responding to vertical Ministerial structures, not always aligned with the same objectives and in many cases not directly involved at the conception stage.

With regard to future challenges in the framework of the EU2020, and although the Lisbon agenda has represented in many respects a decisive step in the EU approach to social and economic development, a number of substantive and analytical questions remain to be dealt with to shed light on how best to articulate European and national-level policies. The recent financial and economic crisis has contributed to bringing these questions to the forefront of the scientific and political debate. There are new open tensions (or trade-offs) that EU policy makers (and scholars) will have to face in the near future.

An initial question to be addressed is that of the political and economic foundation of the EU project and the reform of the European social model in the global economy. The Lisbon project represented a first attempt to find a compromise through a broad strategy. The limitations of the Lisbon approach to adjust social cohesion and economic competitiveness with environmental policy, productive growth, fiscal stability and structural reforms are now more or less evident. To a certain extent the Lisbon strategy appears as a mechanistic addition of different aims and goals rather than a truly integrated solution to interdependencies and trade-offs. The specific issue here, which has now become clearer, is the need to go further with a broad political agenda can solve the tensions between budgetary policies and economic, employment and welfare reforms, and at the same time focus more on social and labour market policies.

Perhaps a fundamental second question, more directly illustrated by the Portuguese case study presented in this chapter, is that the multi-level governance introduced through the Lisbon strategy is still in need of improvements. Even if improvements in facilitating new forms of meaningful participation of different sectors of government (different policy domains) and of civil society at the domestic level have been discerned, relative to the Lisbon strategy, the EU2020 needs to improve democratic legitimacy, deliberation processes, participation and transparency at both national and European levels.

Notes

1 Conclusions of the Spring Council, March 2000.
2 See 'Para uma Política de Inovação em Portugal', Rodrigues *et al.*, 2003.
3 See annual reports at www.estrategiadelisboa.pt.
4 Competitiveness and Technology Poles and Clusters (Pólos e Clusters de Competitividade e Tecnologia) is an inter-ministerial measure involving the Ministry of Economy and the Ministry of Science and Higher Education. Regional Coordination Committees

(regional authorities) are also involved in the case of smaller clusters. The measure involves use of ERDF funds to support R&D, innovation and internationalization projects, possibly involving training, proposed by large consortia of actors and envisioning long-term collective development strategies.

5 See Relatório PNR 2008–2010, Outubro 2009 at www.estrategiadelisboa.pt.

Bibliography

Albert, M. (1993) *Capitalism vs Capitalism*, New York: Four Walls Eight Windows.

Begg, I. (2008) Is there a convincing rationale for the Lisbon Strategy? *Journal of Common Market Studies*, 2 (46), 427–435.

Berger, S. (2006) *How We Compete: What Companies around the World are Doing to Make it Today's Global Economy*, New York: Crown Business.

Berner, T., Reinike, W.H. and Witte, J.M. (2004) *Multisectoral Networks in Global Governance: Towards a Pluralistic System of Accountability. Government and Opposition Ltd.*, 191–210, Malden, USA: Blackwell Publishing.

Borrás, S. and Jacobsson, K. (2004) The open method of coordination and new governance patterns in the EU. *Journal of European Public Policy*, 11 (2), 185–208.

Braun, D. (2003) Lasting tensions in research policy-making – a delegation problem. *Science and Public Policy*, Volume 30, Number 5, 1 October, pp. 309–321.

Castells, Manuel (1996) *The Rise of the Network Society*. Oxford: Blackwell.

Coordenação Nacional da Estratégia de Lisboa (2005) Estratégia de Lisboa: Portugal de Novo – Programa Nacional de Acção para o Crescimento e o Emprego (PNACE) 2005–2008, October.

Coordenação Nacional da Estratégia de Lisboa (2008) Estratégia de Lisboa: Novo Ciclo 2008–2010, Consolidar as Reformas, October.

Dyson, K. (2000) *The Politics of the Euro-zone: Stability or Breakdown?*, Oxford: Oxford University Press.

Economist (1995, 7 October) The myth of the powerless state.

Flanagan K., Uyarra, E. and Laranja, M. (2011) Reconceptualising the 'policy mix' for innovation. *Research Policy 2011*, 40 (5), 702–713.

Friedman, T. (2005) *The World is Flat: A Brief History of the Twenty-first Century,* 1st edition. New York: Farrar, Strauss and Giroux.

Gros, D. (2005) Perspectives for the Lisbon Strategy: How to increase the competitiveness of the European economy?. Paper prepared for the international conference, Europe after the Enlargement, organized by CASE – Center for Social and Economic Research in Warsaw on 8–9 April, available at: http://ssrn.com/abstract=1441926 (accessed 1 October 2013).

Gruner, H.P. (2002) Unemployment and Labour market reform: A contract theoretic approach, *Scandinavian Journal of Economics*, 104, 641–656.

Kok, Wim (coordinator) (2004). Facing the challenge. The Lisbon strategy for growth and employment. Report from the High Level Group, EC: Office for Official Publications of the European Communities, November.

Laranja, M. (2012) Networked Governance of Innovation Policies: the Technological Plan in Portugal. *Science and Public Policy* 39: 655–668.

Lemola, T. (2002) Convergence of national science and technology policies. *Research Policy* 33 (3): 1481–1490.

Natali, D. (2009) The Lisbon Strategy ten years on, A critical review of a multi-disciplinary literature, Transfer: *European Review of Labour and Research*, 15 (1): 111–137.

Ohmae, K. (1990) *The Borderless World*. New York: Harper Collins.

Padoan, P. and Mariani, F. (2006) Growth and Finance, European Integration and the Lisbon Strategy, *Journal of Common Market Studies*, 44 (1), 77–112.

PT (Technological Plan) (2006) Technological Plan: A growth strategy based on knowledge, technology and Innovation. Presentation document available at: www.planotecnologico.pt/document/technological_plan_presentation_document.pdf (last accessed December 2010).

Pisani-Ferry, J. and Sapir, A. (2006) Last exit to Lisbon. Bruegel Policy Brief Issue 2006/02 (prepared at the request of the Austrian Presidency). Brussels: Bruegel.

Pisani-Ferry, J., Sapir, A. and Von Weizsacker, J. (2008/09) A European Recovery Programme, Bruegel Policy Brief. Brussels: Bruegel.

Quaglia, L. (2010) The 'Old' and 'New' Politics of Financial Services Regulation in the EU, *OSE Paper Series*, Research Paper No. 2, April, 19 pp.

Rodrigues, M.J. (ed.) (2002) *The New Knowledge Economy in Europe – a Strategy for International Competitiveness and Social Cohesion*. Cheltenham: Edward Elgar.

Rodrigues, M.J., Godinho, M. and Neves, A. (eds) (2003) *Para uma Política de Inovação em Portugal* [For Innovation Policy in Portugal], Lisbon: D. Quixote Publications.

Sapir, A. (coordinator) (2004) *An Agenda for a Growing Europe – The Sapir Report*, Oxford: Oxford University Press.

Tapscott, D. (2008) *Grown Up Digital: How the Net Generation is Changing Your World*, New York: McGraw-Hill.

Zeitlin, J. and Pochet, P. (eds) with Magnusson L. (2005) *The Open Method of Coordination in Action: The European Employment and Social Inclusion Strategies*. Brussels: Peter Lang.

Part III

Redesigning Portuguese foreign policy

10 Portugal and the development of a European foreign and security identity

Shifting to committed Europeanism

Laura C. Ferreira-Pereira

Introduction[1]

The accession of Portugal to the European Community (EC), in January 1986, coincided with the formalization of European Political Cooperation (EPC), conceived to foster development of a common identity in the realm of foreign policy. Since then, but especially after the end of the Cold War, the European political integration process has experienced a critical evolution that has translated itself into both the establishment of the European Foreign and Security Policy (CFSP) and the creation of the European Security and Defence Policy (ESDP), in 1992 and 1999 respectively.

The foundation of ESDP, in particular, represented the beginning of a new chapter in the European venture. This was one characterized by multiple efforts made by the European Union (EU) to acquire an autonomous military capacity, thereby emerging as a provider of stability, not only in its strategic neighbourhood, but also on the world stage. The Union's desiderata to transcend its original regional identity and assume a gobal role on both political and security fronts (Howorth, 2007; Bretherton and Vogler, 2006; Maull, 2005; Ginsberg, 2001; Smith, 2003) was put forward in the European Security Strategy (ESS) approved in December 2003. This conveyed the idea of the inevitability and indispensability of such a global engagement in the promotion of international peace, democracy and respect for human rights. The first European mission carried out in the Balkans, in January 2003 – the European Union Police Mission (EUPM) in Bosnia and Herzegovina – was followed by a period of unprecedented dynamism as reflected in the planning and launching of over 20 missions in different geographical locations such as Africa, the Balkans, and Central and Southeast Asia. This had a major bearing on the external capacity and image of the EU's foreign policy with all this carries with it in terms of gains for the organization's visibility and leverage in international politics (Lucarelli and Fioramonti, 2010; Martin and Kaldor, 2010). More recently, under the aegis of the Lisbon Treaty, the ESDP was renamed the Common Security and Defence Policy (CSDP) and assigned new tasks, tools and mechanisms designed to enable the EU to assert itself as a respected foreign policy player on the international scene.

Given that Portugal has been participating, from the outset, in all the collective efforts towards endowing the EU with an international political *persona*, this chapter aims to examine the country's evolving engagement in the building up of a European foreign and security identity. Furthermore, it seeks to shed light upon Portugal's standpoint regarding the emergence of a 'European Union of Security and Defence', including the underpinning rationale that has informed its contribution to the implementation of the ESDP since 1999. The present chapter points conclusively to a shift in attitude from a strict Atlanticism, which inspired the Portuguese initial reluctance *vis-à-vis* both the EPC and CFSP, to a committed Europeanism as mirrored in the political ambition to position the country in the frontline of the CSDP. The country's participation in all military operations and most of the civilian missions undertaken under the aegis of the CSDP, despite the prevailing lack of material and human resources, stands out as an illustrative signal that such a change of attitude has indeed taken place. To be sure, this was a consequence of an incremental political learning process combined with the conceptual and institutional development of CFSP, which eventually came to match the Portuguese perspective on the nature of the policy in the area – namely eminently intergovernmental, inclusive, complementary to NATO's role in the field of crisis management and supportive of the continued primacy of the Atlantic Alliance in the European security and defence architecture.

1 From EPC to CFSP: early engagement in the building up of a European foreign policy identity

The early years of membership were marked by Portugal's adjustment to procedures governing the EPC, which presented itself as a *fait accompli*. The latter had been enshrined in the Single European Act in whose negotiation national representatives had some voice, but not any voting power given the then status of Portugal as a candidate country. During the difficult negotiations of the EPC dossier that were marked by a fierce conceptual quarrel between the Atlanticists and the Continentalists, Portugal seconded the British concerns, which were eventually accommodated in the framework of the intergovernmental EPC arrangements. Alignment with Britain stemmed from the deeply felt assumption that Atlanticism was one of the most important pillars of the country's independence and assertion in the world (Martins interview, 2005).[2] Hence the acceptance of the EPC by the authorities in Lisbon was altogether unproblematic.

In 1985, governmental authorities were aware that, in the new treaty, the EPC was somehow connected with the goal of forging a common European identity in the foreign policy domain and it seemed to evoke the European political project lying on the horizon since the early 1950s. Be that as it may, at that time, they were too eager about getting their hands on the money coming from Brussels (Mathias interview, 2005)[3] to worry about the eventual implications springing from the codification of a mutual consultation mechanism on foreign policy matters that was of an intergovernmental and voluntary character.

Against the backdrop of such momentous episodes as the falling of the Berlin Wall and the Gulf War, François Mitterrand and Helmut Kohl called an intergovernmental conference on political union with the particular objective of defining and implementing a common foreign and security policy. During that intergovernmental conference, Portugal took a defensive and prudent line in all security and defence-related issues on the agenda. At the negotiation level, the country belonged to the Atlanticist caucus led by Britain, and followed closely the latter's evolving position. Amidst Atlanticists, there was widespread rejection of integration in the foreign and security policy sphere, as it was viewed as detrimental to both transatlantic relations and to the United States' commitment to European security.

The initial reaction of Portuguese foreign policy makers to the emergence of the CFSP was conveyed in a memorandum that circulated amongst the member states' representatives before the beginning of the Intergovernmental Conference (IGC) on Political Union. This document clearly stated that advances towards the establishment of the EU's future second pillar should proceed 'in a gradual manner …, respect the national identities and diversity … and preserve the existing institutional balance' (Pereira, 1993: 34). From that standpoint, it is possible to infer three major concerns of the national negotiators. First, it was important to ensure that the CFSP evolved in an incremental manner, according to the 'petit pas' method and in strict relation to national specificities. Among such specificities the collective defence commitments undertaken in the framework of NATO featured prominently. Hence the Portuguese understanding was that European security should continue to rest on NATO, and there was no credible alternative to it. Second, there was a concern linked to the role of the European Commission in the purview of the CSFP. According to Portuguese foreign policy makers, the new policy area should not be placed under this institution's tutelage since this could pave the way to the communitarization of the CFSP and the subsequent loss of the veto prerogative. Third, there were fears about the bearing of the future CFSP on specific Portuguese interests scattered across the Lusophone world, notably on the country's post-colonial relations in Africa, Brazil and East Timor.

The above-mentioned concerns should be associated with three fundamental pillars that have traditionally conditioned Portuguese foreign and security policy making. These are, first, Portugal's loyalty to and dependence upon NATO, which explains the country's alignment to the Anglo–American side and its support of healthy transatlantic relations; second, its commitment to the promotion of the Community of Portuguese-Speaking Countries (*Comunidade dos Países de Língua Oficial Portuguesa* – CPLP) and Lusophonia, through which the country endeavours to stress its specificity while punching above its weight; and, finally, its relationship with the EU whose centrality in the country's external strategy has grown stronger since 1986. In addition, a major aspect typifying the Portuguese foreign and security policy tradition must be underlined. This is the zeal towards safeguarding the hard core of sovereignty that ascribes to the country the capacity to formulate and implement a national foreign, security and defence policy in an autonomous way. Portugal is indeed a sovereignty-oriented state, this being an historic byproduct of a cohesive national identity and longstanding border stability – two generally recognized characteristics of one of the most genuine and oldest nation-states in Continental Europe.

Unswerving loyalty to NATO and zeal regarding state sovereignty explains the instinctive Portuguese reaction to the developing CFSP project, which was characterized initially by circumspection for the latter being perceived as carrying with it potential seeds for developing into an alternative to NATO. Eventually, however, the final assessment revolved around the idea that despite the underlying risks, there was no immediate incompatibility between the EU acquiring a security role on the one hand, and the maintenance of strong transatlantic ties and a solid Atlantic Alliance on the other hand. Both constructive ambiguity and explicit reference to NATO's collective defence commitments (under the Washington Treaty of 1949) in the CFSP provisions of the Maastricht Treaty (Articles J4.1 and J4.4) concurred to make national engagement in the emerging policy more acceptable. Equally important, the unanimity rule allowed for national representatives to hold back any development that was ultimately likely to give rise to a clash between CFSP and NATO (Pereira, Interview, 2006).

In the post-Maastricht Treaty period, however, concerns with the safeguard of both sovereignty and Atlanticism gradually dwindled, and an enthusiastic engagement in the realm of CFSP started to gain roots. Nevertheless, such engagement was not without 'ifs and buts' (Ferreira-Pereira, March 2007). The following section will explore the major reasons underpinning the change in Portugal's approach towards the CFSP. On the one hand, there were a number of lessons identified and learned that led to a shift in the Portuguese security mindset. On the other hand, there was the incremental progress undergone by the CFSP, which eventually came to match the Portuguese view on the conceptual and institutional design of this policy area.

2 The CFSP as a new challenge for Portuguese foreign and security policy

The implementation of the Maastricht Treaty and, later on, its review exercise leading up to the signing of the Amsterdam Treaty in 1997, occurred at a time when the Portuguese authorities were under pressure. This was due to the prevailing doubts about what the CFSP project held in store and its eventual repercussions at both national and EU level. It was also a phase of increased adaptation of national structures and policies to European requirements (i.e. Europeanization).[4] Furthermore this period saw a deeper socialization of national foreign policy makers with both their European peers and the Union's officials operating in various institutions, with all this implies in terms of internalization of a common *modus faciendi*.

This Europeanization process, coupled with an accumulated knowledge of and experience in CFSP affairs, fostered political acknowledgement of the relevance of a security dimension within the context of the EU. Moreover, the deepening of the CFSP by means of both the conceptualization and institutionalization of the ESDP came to fit into the Portuguese foreign and security thinking about the way the second pillar should be structured. Such thinking was based upon the 'four Is' formula, according to which the CFSP should evolve *I*ncrementally, *I*n harmony with NATO's primacy while retaining its original *I*ntergovernmental and *I*nclusive character (Ferreira-Pereira, May 2007). Incidentally, this was the view that informed the Portuguese stance during the review of the Maastricht Treaty's provisions that took place under the IGC in 1996–1997. At that time, the national authorities subscribed to a partial merger of the Western European Union (WEU) and the EU through the conversion of the WEU's Petersberg tasks (i.e. humanitarian and rescue tasks, peacekeeping tasks, and tasks of combat forces in crisis management, including peacemaking) into missions to be undertaken under the aegis of CFSP. This specific expedient, which was mainly promoted by the Nordic militarily non-allied states (Ferreira-Pereira, April 2005: 23–25) and espoused by Britain, dispelled the perception of the militarization of the EU and did not challenge NATO's prominence on the collective defence front.

Lessons identified and lessons learned

Throughout the 1990s, Portugal drew a number of important lessons from its experience with the handling of CFSP-related issues, which above all made national authorities clearly aware of the limitations inherent to the second pillar. As a result of this, they became convinced about the necessity of the EU's assertion as an autonomous strategic and security actor in the international arena. The learning process was particularly significant during the period that the country was at the Union's helm, that is, during its first European Presidency in 1992. At this time, the Portuguese confronted the need to manage the Union's negative political image caused not only by the marginal role it played during the Gulf War, but also from its inability to present itself as a cohesive and influential bloc in the context of the secession wars in the former Yugoslavia.

Equally important were the lessons derived from the country's direct exposure to the conflicts in the Balkans which, again, increased during the presidential mandate. Traditionally speaking, in the national political psyche, the Balkans have always been considered as a remote region, totally disconnected from immediate strategic interests. However, direct engagement in such a volatile theatre that encompassed the leadership of the European Community Monitor Mission (ECMM) and mediation efforts between the warring camps had an enormous impact upon the elites' mental maps in demonstrating the existing nexus between stability in the Balkans and the EC's internal security. The perception of this nexus became even more pronounced after Portugal's historic participation, with approximately 1,000 troops, in NATO's Implementation Force (IFOR), in Bosnia-Herzegovina.[5]

The Portuguese experience in IFOR and in subsequent missions undertaken by NATO in the region (i.e. the Stabilization Force and the Kosovo Force) bolstered the internalization of the idea that the country was in a condition to be a security provider (Freire, 2007: 89, 90). It also brought about a new concept of border security – one that no longer coincided with the physical border defining conventionally the state's territory (Comissão de Defesa Nacional, 2005: 32–33). In fact, the 'Balkans effect' helped to inaugurate a new security mindset that engendered a reinforced sense of mission when it came to the role that Portugal could play in promoting peace in Europe and the world.

After a decade or so of political setbacks and traumas generated by the European collective inability to manage conflicts in the Balkans, there was a widespread realization among the Portuguese foreign policy makers that the EU should be able to overcome general criticism about its inability to solve conflicts within its own territory. It could not indeed discard the responsibility of shouldering its own share of the international security burden. What is more, considering the indivisibility of security and the growing complexity of threats, which evinced the states' 'unsustainable inability' to tackle them in an isolated way, the Portuguese authorities become persuaded that the Union's interest in having an active role in the promotion of international peace and security should be perceived as part of the national interest.

Finally, attention should also be drawn to the lessons identified and learned throughout the diplomatic campaign carried out by the Portuguese, at the European level, in favour of East Timorese self-determination. The inordinate number of debates and difficulties that accompanied the process leading to the adoption of the first common position regarding East Timor by the Council of Ministers in 1996 contributed to convincing national authorities of the desirability of a common foreign identity. The 'Timor experience' has furthermore revealed the potential of the CFSP as an instrumental platform of multilateralization and amplification of national foreign policy-related matters.

Conceptualization of the CFSP compatible with national goals

Besides the lessons identified and learned, as mentioned above, another reason behind the change in the Portugal's attitude regarding the CFSP was the realization that this policy's design tended to exhibit conceptual, institutional, legal and operational aspects that did not directly challenge national foreign and security policy parameters.

As empirical evidence for this one should point, first of all, to the Joint Declaration on European Defence issued at the Anglo–French Summit in Saint Malo (December 1998), which safeguarded the primacy of NATO in the European security architecture by means of entrusting the Atlantic Alliance the 'right of first refusal'. By the time that France and Britain had agreed upon the necessity of endowing the EU with the capacity to decide and act autonomously to respond to international crises 'where the Alliance as a whole is not engaged',[6] the Portuguese authorities received an important guarantee. This was that the deepening of the CFSP would not undermine NATO's prominence since there was room for the building up of a constructive complementarity as part of a 'positive sum game' between the two organizations. Consequently, unlike other European counterparts such as the militarily non-allied states (i.e. Austria, Finland, Sweden and Ireland), which at least in the beginning nurtured serious mistrust regarding the defence project (Ferreira-Pereira, April 2005), the Portuguese saw efforts towards providing the EU with a military capacity to respond to international crisis in a positive light since their inception. These efforts were inaugurated in the Cologne Summit of June 1999 with the formal launching of the ESDP which sowed the seeds for the incremental development of a common security and defence policy.

Attention should be also drawn to the conclusion of the 'Berlin Plus' agreements (in December 2002), which established conditions for EU–NATO coordination in order to avoid the 'three Ds' errors coined by Madeleine Albright (i.e. 'Decoupling, Duplication, and Discrimination'). This development was strengthened by the signing of the EU–NATO Declaration on ESDP, which welcomed the Union's 'capacity to conduct EU-led crisis management operations, including military operations, where NATO as a whole is not engaged', as well as the idea that 'a stronger European role will help to contribute to the vitality of the Alliance'.[7] Equally important was the European Council Declaration on Transatlantic Relations (December 2003), which asserted that the 'transatlantic relationship is irreplaceable'.[8] Taken together, all these three key political declarations largely maintained the *status quo ante* when it cames to NATO's ascendancy within European security and defence.

Finally, it is worth mentioning that the ESDP-related provisions enshrined in the Constitutional Treaty (2004) and later incorporated into the Lisbon Treaty (2007) corroborated the intergovernmental and NATO-friendly structure of the ESDP.

3 Participation in the common security and defence policy: charting new ground

As a result of a number of lessons learned and an evolution of the CFSP compatible with national goals, the Portuguese authorities came to the conclusion:

> [that] in the specific framework of National Defence ... we are interested in the participation in the so-called Petersberg Missions, and it is in our interest that the European Union is able to have a more effective role in the resolution of conflicts or crises that are of its own concern.[9]

This statement was conveyed in the National Defence Strategic Concept (2003), which acknowledged the unprecedented advances made by the EU in the domain of security and defence, notably the collective commitment towards the development of assets and capabilities for European crisis management operations under the impetus of both the military and civilian Headline Goals. Moreover, it pointed to the incorporation of lessons, experiences and know-how accumulated throughout a decade of participation within the CFSP purview into the conceptualization of the national security and defence strategy.

The same can be said in relation to another national strategic document entitled Specific Missions of the Armed Forces (2004) (*Missões Específicas das Forças*

Armadas – MIFA04), within the framework of which the country took upon itself the responsibility of 'employing military forces and resources to secure the fulfilment of commitments undertaken by Portugal thereby securing a balanced and credible contribution to … the defence structures of the European Union'.[10]

Along the lines articulated in the 2003 National Defence Strategic Concept, the ESDP came gradually to be seen as an instrument of foreign, security and defence policy, through which Portugal should endeavour to boost its leverage at both European and international levels. The relevance ascribed to this instrument became evident in the programmes of the XVII and XVIII Constitutional Governments put forward by José Sócrates in 2005 and 2009, respectively. Both documents highlighted the political resolve to place Portugal '*at the frontline of the Common Security and Defence Policy*, including its participation in military missions under the command of the European Union, as well as its participation in the permanent structured cooperation in defence matters'.[11] In the governmental programme of 2009, the national involvement of the Armed Forces in military missions undertaken under the aegis of the CSDP was considered a priority alongside participation in international military missions carried out by NATO.[12]

The prioritization of the CSDP in official foreign policy strategy, as well as Portugal's ambition to position itself within the group of countries taking the lead in this common policy advancement, can be presented as symptomatic of a change in the country's stance regarding the CFSP. This should not be dissociated from the leading role that national representatives had in the implementation of the ESDP during the first half of 2000 when Portugal took over the EU Presidency. With the aim of fulfilling the mandate assigned by the preceding (Finnish) Presidency of the Council of the EU, the country oversaw the setting up of the ESDP interim politico-military institutional apparatus[13] and the translation of the political ambition underlying the Headline Goal 2003 (HG 2003)[14] into a concrete military reality (Ferreira-Pereira, March 2007, 38). It also took the lead in the process to define the fundamental principles guiding civilian crisis management. This has involved both the identification of priority areas (i.e. police, strengthening of the rule of law, strengthening civilian administration and civil protection) and the establishment of a police HG by means of which member states have agreed to create, by 2003, a force comprising 5,000 police officers aimed at intervening in crisis management missions and conflict prevention.

Portuguese direct engagement in the process of implementing the ESDP was reinforced in 2007, during the EU presidency, when the country took upon itself, for the first time ever, responsibilities in the sphere of security and defence. This applied to both missions and the capability development process within the HG 2010 framework[17] and the European Defence Agency (EDA). More specifically, Portugal oversaw the launching of civilian missions in Afghanistan and the Democratic Republic of Congo, the discussion, at the politico-strategic level, about a future operation in Chad, and the process involving both the conception and approval of the Progress Catalogue, deemed to guide the development of European military capabilities until 2010. Other examples of concrete Portuguese involvement in giving further substance to the ESDP include endeavours to deepen the relationship between EU and Africa on security and defence cooperative matters that led to two major gatherings. One was the co-sponsoring (along with the EU Institute for Security Studies) of the High Level Conference on ESDP, Crisis Prevention and Conflict Resolution in Africa. More important than that, national authorities organized the first informal meeting between the Ministers of Defence of the 27 EU member states and the five Maghreb countries (Algeria, Libya, Morocco, Mauritania and Tunisia). In the latter case, Portugal was able to draw on the experience it had accumulated within the '5+5 Initiative' to improve its relative weight *vis-à-vis* both sides. To these examples one should add that it was under the auspices of the 2007 Portuguese Presidency that the first joint Council of development and defence ministers was held, which launched the first action plan designed to develop the security–development nexus.

The two leadership experiences, that is the 2000 and 2007 EU Presidencies, (Ferreira-Pereira, September 2008) contributed not only to a more substantial familiarization with the CSDP structures, instruments and mechanisms, but also to a greater identification of the Portuguese authorities with the emerging 'Europe of Security and Defence', which was still in a state of flux. In fact, the circumstance of having taken part in the development of ideas, concepts and procedures and, later, in the process of implementing them, gave them a sense of ownership over the ESDP project.

Reactive and proactive engagement within the CSDP purview

Portugal has been actively participating within the CSDP purview not only as a means to avoid marginalization and isolation (Teixeira, 2009: 106), but also as a way to gain appreciation and prestige in the eyes of its European peers. The country has taken part in all military operations carried out to date (i.e. Concordia, Artemis, Althea, EUFOR RDCongo, EUFOR Chad/RCA, AMIS II, EUNAVFOR and EUTM Somalia) although, in general, its contributions have been limited in nature. A study undertaken in 2010 placed Portugal in the top ten contributors to military CSDP operations over the last six years in absolute numbers (Soder, 2010: 7). When it comes to civilian missions, national authorities have opted out in some missions, such as the EUPOL AFEGHANISTAN, the Aceh Monitoring Mission, the EUPAT, in Macedonia, and the EUJUST THEMIS Georgia.

If some member states, like Sweden, can be clearly identified as having championed the civilian component of crisis management (Lee-Ohlsson, 2009), Portugal has stood out as a vocal promoter of the African dimension of the ESDP. The rationale underlying the promotion of this dimension is linked to the political willingness to reinforce the Portuguese presence and influence in Africa with a special emphasis on the Lusophone area. Over the last two decades or so, efforts towards that reinforcement have been carried out under the umbrella of the so-called technical–military cooperation[15] with the member states of the CPLP, in the framework of which Portugal has been investing both human and material resources. Not surprisingly, the country has participated in all EU-led missions and operations conducted on African soil.

In so far as the development of military capabilities is concerned, the Portuguese response has revealed prevailing limitations at the national level, while signalling a readiness to contribute to the strengthening of the ESDP. The national contribution to the HG 2003, as it was officially presented in the context of the Capabilities Commitments Conference (November 2000) amounted to 1,000 military personnel.[16] This contribution was considered appropriate in light of the lack of both military personnel and financial resources. Understandably enough, this was replicated in the context of the HG 2010, conceived to allow for the creation of a rapid reaction force, based upon the concept of 'Battlegroup' (BG), which was deemed to be engaged in peacekeeping missions, peace enforcement and crisis management.[17] The Portuguese commitment was not upgraded between 2000 and 2004, largely because the country was operating at its maximum capacity. This was so because of the engagement of national forces in other international missions (i.e. NATO-led missions), besides the persistent budgetary difficulties.[18]

Portugal has been endeavouring to be and remain inside the process with respect to the formation of the BGs. To this end, the country has already participated in two initiatives – an amphibious BG, having Italy as a Framework Nation, and a land BG led by Spain, in which Portugal participated with a company of marines and an engineering company, respectively (Ferreira-Pereira, March 2007; Pinheiro, 2009).

In the domain of civilian crisis management, the Portuguese contributions for HG 2003 were 350 police officers, three teams for rescue missions, one field hospital, and one supply and logistics team for a refugee camp (Pereira, 2005). In 2004 and 2007, national authorities endorsed the establishment of new Civilian Headline Goals – Civilian Headline Goal 2008 and 2010, respectively. These were directed at improving the Union's capabilities to conduct missions in such new domains as support for the EU Special Representatives, the reform of the security sector and border control, and the combination of civilian and military tools in line with a comprehensive approach.

When it comes to the EDA, after some initial reluctance, Portugal came to acknowledge the key role ascribed to this agency in the development of military capabilities in support of the CSDP, as well as in fostering conditions for the building up of a European defence industry. Hence it has been contributing to the EDA's budget and participating in some of its projects, notably one dedicated to maritime de-mining (Pinheiro, 2009).

Significantly, Portugal also came to participate in important projects launched in 2008 by the French EU Presidency to strengthen European military capabilities, notably the European Air Transport Fleet, the European Carrier Group Interoperability Initiative (ECGII) and the Military Erasmus.

Although, generally speaking, Portuguese participation in the CSDP has been characterized by an eminently reactive nature (Palma, 2009: 5 and 26), a proactive posture could be seen in the leadership of the EUPOL Kinshasa and participation in the 'Military Erasmus'. Portuguese diplomacy was actively engaged in getting the post of Head of the Mission EUPOL Kinshasa, which was eventually assigned to a national police officer originating from the Public Security Police (*Polícia de Segurança Pública* – PSP). Incidentally, when that operation gave way to EUPOL RD Congo, this officer kept the same post. In the case of the Military Erasmus, national authorities showed that they wanted to be involved in this initiative since its inception by making themselves available to organize the first experimental 'ESDP module', which took place in September 2009 at the Military Academy.

In addition to these illustrative examples, attention should also be drawn to the small reform security sector mission in the former Portuguese colony, Guinea Bissau (EUSSR Guinea Bissau), in the launching of which Portuguese diplomacy has invested considerable time and effort. More recently, the Portuguese authorities saw the materialization of a strategic and pioneering idea that they had been pursuing for several years. This was the conversion, on a permanent and structured basis, of the EUROFOR (European Rapid Operational Forces) in the first EUROFOR BG as part of the process of incorporating the European forces in the realm of the CSDP. After taking on the command of the EUROFOR in September 2010 (for a two-year period), Portugal was assigned the important task of acting as the Lead Nation in this first EU EUROFOR BG during the second half of 2011.

Both the reactive and proactive engagement of national authorities aimed at positioning the country at the frontline of the CSDP should be understood in the light of a somewhat multidimensional rationale inspired by a strong perception of diverse benefits and opportunities stemming from this developing policy area. One of the perceived benefits relates to the (exogenous) incentive for the internationalization and modernization of the armed forces as a result of continued exposure to up-dated (doctrinal and technological) information, as well as to a series of synergies and lessons that this entailed. The *Defence White Book* of 2001 asserted that the modernization of armed forces should be carried out according to the 'international commitments undertaken, among which stands out, in short term, the edification of a Rapid Reaction Force of the European Union'(78).[19] Indeed, this was one of the major factors that encouraged the Foreign Minister Luís Amado to sanction Portuguese involvement in the BG process.[20]

On the other hand, an enhanced participation in the CSDP has been considered instrumental in spawning political and economic dividends, which range from gaining a more influential voice within both the EU and other international fora to strengthening the bargaining power of national politico-diplomatic authorities. Thus, the CSDP has been progressively emerging as a medium of empowering the Portuguese politico-diplomatic elite as it attempts to safeguard national interests and pursue specific objectives in vital dossiers (such as the structural funds and Common Agricultural Policy) (Ferreira-Pereira, March 2007: 41). This also includes the goal of securing top ranking positions within the Union's institutions and international operations. The conviction prevails that the alternative to an active engagement in the realm of the CDSP is the country's strategic irrelevance (Teixeira, 2009: 106). Hence Portugal should seize every opportunity to strengthen 'its status as a credible state, a net producer of international security' and to be viewed as a 'useful ally in the promotion of stability and peace in the international system' (ibid.: 125 and 234).

More specifically linked to the CSDP operations being conducted in Africa, two additional considerations account for the weight that has been accorded to national participation. The first aspect relates to conflict resolution dynamics and the subsequent promotion of regional stabilization – equated as outputs of CSDP missions – for all the benefits that this engenders in terms of improving economic and trade links, notably with such emergent powers as Angola. Understood along these lines, CSDP has the potential to function as a stabilizing factor for Lusophone Africa. The second links to the perceived window of opportunity opened up by the ESDP missions for Portugal to further consolidate its role as one of the United States' main interlocutors in Sub-Saharan Africa. In this regard, by means of sustaining a continued presence in the European missions carried out in Africa, Portugal should be able to capitalize further on its regional expertise (i.e. Lusophone Africa) and become a more relevant actor in the eyes of American foreign policy makers who seek to boost the US's influence and prestige in the continent.

4 Looking forward: what is in store for Portugal in the Lisbon Treaty

The Treaty of Lisbon introduced new provisions and arrangements on the basis of which the CSDP gained legal substance. Among these provisions conceived to endow the EU with an international political *persona*, the inclusion of a mutual assistance clause, in case of military aggression (Art. 42.7), and a solidarity clause (Art. 222) stands out. There is also the establishment of two cooperation mechanisms, that is 'reinforced cooperation' and 'permanent structured cooperation' (Arts 42.3 and 46) and an expansion of the original spectrum of Petersberg Missions, in which the EU can employ both civilian and military assets (Art. 43.1), further reflecting the new persona. As was recognized by the Defence Ministerial Directive 2010–2013, all these provisions (except the latter) represent 'important challenges, with implications for Portugal'.[21]

The 'permanent structured cooperation' designed to bolster the development of European military capabilities was viewed as one of the most demanding aspects of the post-Lisbon CSDP, with enormous repercussions for strategic defence planning. (Teixeira, 2009: 60; Pinheiro, 2009). To be sure, the preoccupation with responding to this challenge had already been conveyed implicitly in the governmental programmes of 2005 and 2009, alluded to earlier. Lisbon's authorities felt strongly that, in the name of the national interest, Portuguese participation in this mechanism should be secured *ab initio* as it had been the case with the establishment of Economic Monetary Union and the Schengen Agreement. Only by this means could Portugal claim its place at the 'hard core' of European defence (Teixeira, 2009: 61). It is therefore foreseeable that foreign policy makers will take concrete measures to enable the country to meet access criteria that might include, *inter alia*, the level of national expenditure on defence equipment, the contribution of combat units to BGs, the percentage of national forces made available to the EU and level of participation in the EDA's key activities programmes.[22]

Given the expansion of the Petersberg Missions' spectrum, the introduction of the solidarity-related clauses pointing to new scenarios for the European Union's missions and the Central and Eastern European enlargement (of 2004 and 2007), the likelihood that the EU will envisage a substantial increase in demand for a global interventionism is high. This will not be without major consequences for all member states and, particularly, for small powers like Portugal, which have been struggling with chronic shortages of human and economic resources. Indeed, the multiplication of European engagements in both civilian and military battlefronts will confront Portugal with dilemmas in making strategic choices, considering the national authorities' longstanding concern to maintain a balance between participation in EU and NATO operations.

Conclusion

This chapter has attempted to shed light upon the evolution of the Portuguese stance towards the CFSP from its conception to the implementation of its operational component, that is, the CSDP. This evolution pointed to a shift from a position of strict Atlanticism to committed Europeanism, which can be said to be symptomatic of the putative relevance of the political integration dynamics for safeguarding national interest(s).

In the wake of the 1990s, there was an initial suspicion as to where the CFSP project could lead, which stemmed mainly from a foreign and security tradition informed by concerns with the safeguarding of both sovereignty and Atlanticism. In fact, the eventual impact of the fledging CFSP upon the Atlantic Alliance's status as *primus inter pares* within the post-1989 security architecture was itself problematic, given the key role played by NATO in the country's national defence strategy, its geo-strategic position and security identity. Equally important was the fact that the CFSP emerged as a venture with the potential to hit hard at the heart of national sovereignty.

Portugal has taken comfort from the inclusion in the EU treaties of a provision accommodating the collective defence commitments existing under the Washington Treaty. Nevertheless, latent anxiety as to what the CFSP held in store in military terms produced tension across Portuguese chancelleries on both sides of the Atlantic. This would only be mitigated by the clarification conveyed by the Saint Malo Declaration. Later, it was virtually overcome as the unfolding of the ESDP left little doubt about its inherently intergovernmental and crisis management-oriented nature. In the meantime, a series of lessons learned throughout the 1990s springing from both the Balkans trauma and the East Timor affair led to the CFSP project being seen through a more constructive prism.

Eventually, Portuguese foreign policy makers came to embrace the CSDP and search for a place for the country at the forefront of the new common policy. It is hard to escape from the conclusion that their participation in the foundation of both the CFSP and the ESDP helped to mould these policies throughout two decades or so and seems to have been critical in their identification with the political integration process. The experience of holding the EU Presidency (in 2000 and 2007) in the context of which national representatives oversaw the process of developing concepts, institutions, procedures and mechanisms needed to flesh out the ESDP blueprint that were put forward in the Cologne Summit, only strengthened the feeling of both identification with and belonging to the security and defence project.

Finally, an explanation for the enthusiastic and active engagement of Portugal in the CSDP, besides the need to avoid marginalization, should be found in the perception of the latter as a newly discovered source of opportunities that the country's authorities intend to seize to the maximum extent possible. All in all, they know that it is not enough to claim or aim at a place in the hard core of the CSDP if this is not to translate itself into different forms of tangible engagement in an increasingly complex post-Lisbon Treaty landscape. Hence the Portuguese authorities are expected to sustain the country's participation in major EU military missions as well as in the most emblematic defence projects (such as the European Air Transport Fleet, the ECGI and the Military Erasmus).

Notes

1 The author would like to thank Paulo Vizeu Pinheiro and Colonel Rui Clero for their valuable comments on an earlier draft.
2 Interview with Victor Martins, former Secretary of State of European Affairs (1985–1995), Lisbon, December 2005.
3 Interview with Leonardo Mathias, former Ambassador to the Portuguese Permanent Representation to the European Community, Lisbon, December 2005.
4 According to Reuben Wong, the concept of Europeanization includes three dimensions, namely, 'downloading', 'uploading' and 'crossloading'. When referring explicitly to 'Europeanization', the author intends to stress the first dimension, which involves the adaptation of national policies and political convergence (also known as 'downloading') (Wong, 2008).
5 This constituted the first military intervention in a European theatre since the involvement of Portugal in the First World War.
6 Cf. Joint Declaration issued at the Anglo-French Summit, in Saint Malo, 3–4 December 1998, available at www.fco.gov.uk/resources/en/news/2002/02/joint-declaration-on-eu-new01795, accessed on 28 September 2011.
7 Cf. www.nato.int/docu/pr/2002/p02–142e.htm, accessed on 23 September 2011.
8 This declaration was adopted at the Brussels European Council held on 12 and 13 December 2003, and was annexed to (Italian) Presidency Conclusions. At the time the European Council also adopted the European Security Strategy. Cf. www.consilium.europa.eu/ueDocs/cms_Data/docs/pressData/en/ec/78364.pdf accessed on 24 September 2011.
9 Cf. Council of Ministers, *Conceito Estratégico de Defesa Nacional* [National Defence Strategic Concept], approved by the Council of Minister's Resolution no 6/2003, 20 January 2003.

10 Cf. *Missões Específicas das Forças Armadas – MIFA 04* (Specific Missions of the Armed Forces), issued by the High Council of National Defence on 21 October 2004.
11 Cf. Programme of the XVII Constitutional Government, p. 159 and Programme of the XVIII Constitutional Government, p. 119. Author's translation and emphasis.
12 Cf. www.portugal.gov.pt/pt/GC18/Documentos/Programa_GC18.pdf, p. 120. Accessed on 24 September 2011.
13 As of 2001, these structures became permanent and they were as follows: the Political and Security Committee, the European Union Military Committee, the European Union Military Staff and the Committee for the Civilian Aspects of Crisis Management.
14 The HG 2003, also known as the Helsinki Headline Goal, was established at the December 1999 Helsinki European Council meeting. At the time, the EU Member States set themselves a military capability target to be met by 2013, which required the former to be able to deploy up to 50,000–60,000 troops, within 60 days and sustainable for a year. These military forces were to be used in support of the full range of Petersberg Tasks.
15 The technical–military cooperation encompasses an array of activities directed at the organization, restructuring and training of the Armed Forces and respective military personnel, which takes place in the framework of bilateral agreements signed between Portugal and the Portuguese-speaking countries in Africa (i.e. Angola, Cape Verde, Guinea-Bissau, Mozambique, and São Tomé and Príncipe). One of the principal pillars of the technical–military cooperation is the so-called Programme for the Support of Peace Missions in Africa (*Programa de Apoio às Missões de Paz em África*, or PAMPA) designed to empower the CPLP states to enable them to contribute to peace and security at a regional level.
16 As to forces and capabilities, the Portuguese detailed commitment was the following: two infantry battalions, one artillery group, one support group unity, one reconnaissance company, one military police company, one tank company, one communications company, one engineering company, one special operations group, two observer teams, one frigate, one submarine, one offshore patrol boat, one replacement ship, one survey ship, one Portuguese marine battalion, twelve F-16s, four C-130s, four 3P-3 Orions, twelve C-212 Aviocars, two Tactical Air Control Parties (TACP) and helicopters. Data provided by the Ministry of Defence, July 2005.
17 The Headline Goal 2010, endorsed by the European Council of 17 and 18 June 2004, builds on the Helsinki Headline and capability goals, and was conceived to reflect the EES, the evolution of the strategic environment after 09/11 and lessons learned from the EU-led operations that had been undertaken since January 2003. Broadly based on the BG concept, it conveyed the EU's ambition to develop a rapid response to international crisis. In concrete terms, this entailed the capacity for the EU to launch a BG operation within five days of approval by the Council; and once the decision to launch an operation has been made, troops from a BG should be on the ground implementing their mission within ten days. The development of a European rapid response was deemed to strengthen the EU's ability to respond to possible UN requests and objectives. For more details, see the Headline Goal http://ue.eu.int/uedocs/cmsUpload/2010%20Headline%20Goal.pdf, accessed on 1 October 2013.
18 Interviews in Lisbon, June 2006.
19 Cf. http://antigo.mdn.gov.pt/Publicacoes/livro_branco/Livro_branco.pdf, accessed on 26 April 2010.
20 Interviews at the Ministry of Defence, Lisbon, June 2006.
21 Cf. www.portugal.gov.pt/pt/GC18/Governo/Ministerios/MDN/Documentos/Pages/20100504_MDN_Doc_Directiva_Defesa.aspx, accessed on 10 May 2010.
22 Throughout 2010, the criteria for participation in the 'structured permanent cooperation' remained a thorny political question. As became clear during a seminar organized by the Spanish Presidency on 16 March, there was scepticism on the part of

some member states' representatives as to the timeliness, feasibility and viability regarding an early implementation of the new cooperation mechanism in view of the prevailing economic and financial global crisis. Cf. 'Presidency Report – Seminar on Permanent Structured Cooperation', The Spanish Presidency of the European Union, Ministry of Defence, 16 March 2010. Provided by the Portuguese Ministry of Defence, in May 2010.

Bibliography

Bretherton, Charlotte and Vogler, John (2006) *The European Union as a Global Actor*, London/New York: Routledge.

Comissão de Defesa Nacional (ed.) (2007) *Portugal e as missões de paz*, Lisbon: National Parliament, Volume I.

Council of Ministers (2003) *Conceito Estratégico de Defesa Nacional* [National Defence Strategic Concept], approved by the Council of Minister's resolution no 6/2003, 20 January.

Council of the European Union (30 March 2010) *Consolidated versions of the Treaty on European Union and the Treaty on the Functioning of the European Union* (*Treaty of Lisbon*), Official Journal of the European Union.

Ferreira-Pereira, Laura C. (April 2005) 'The Militarily Non-Allied States in the Foreign and Security Policy of the European Union: Solidarity "Ma Non Troppo" ', *Journal of Contemporary European Studies – Special Issue: Security Policy in the Post-Communist Era*, 13 (1): 21–37.

Ferreira-Pereira, Laura C. (March 2007) 'Portugal and ESDP', in Klaus Brümmer (ed.), *The South and ESDP: Greece, Italy, Portugal and Spain*, Gütersloh, Bertelsmann Stiftung, 32–49. Also available at www.bertelsmann-stiftung.org (accessed 2 October 2013).

Ferreira-Pereira, Laura C. (May 2007) 'Between Scylla and Charybdis: Explaining Portugal's Approach to the European Foreign and Security Policy', *Journal of European Integration* 29 (2): 209–228.

Ferreira-Pereira, Laura C. (September 2008) 'Portugal and the 2007 EU Presidency: A Case of Constructive Bridge-Building', *Journal of Common Market Studies*, 46 (Supplement 1): 61–70.

Freire, Miguel (2007) 'O *Modus Operandi* de Segurança e Defesa de um Pequeno Estado Euro-Atlântico', *Nação e Defesa* (118): 69–105.

Ginsberg, R.H. (2001) *The European Union in International Politics: Baptism by Fire*, Lanham, MD: Rowman and Littlefield.

High Council of National Defence (2004) *Missões Específicas das Forças Armadas MIFA 04 [Specific Missions of Armed Forces]*, Lisbon: Ministry of National Defence, 21 October.

Howorth, Jolyon (2007) *Security and Defence in the European Union*, Basingstoke: Palgrave Macmillan.

Lee-Olsson, Fredrick (2009) 'Sweden and the Development of the European Security and Defence Policy: A Bi-Directional Process of Europeanization', *Cooperation and Conflict*, Vol. (44): 123–142.

Lucarelli, Sonia and Fioramonti, Lorenzo (eds) (2010) *External Perceptions of the European Union as a Global Actor*, London/New York: Routledge.

Martin, Mary and Kaldor, Mary (eds) (2010) *The European Union and Human Security: External Interventions and Missions*, London/New York: Routledge.

Maull, Hans W. (2005) 'Europe and the new balance of global order', *International Affairs*, 81 (4): 775–799.

Palma, Hugo de Melo (2009) *European by Force and by Will: Portugal and the European Security and Defence Policy*, Bruges, College of Europe, EU Papers Diplomacy – 7.

Pereira, Manuel Fernandes (1993) 'A evolução das posições portuguesas nas negociações sobre a PESC', *Política Internacional*, 1 (6): 31–40.

Pereira, Manuel Fernandes (2005) Conference presented at the National Defence Institute to the National Defence Course, Lisbon.

Pereira, Manuel Fernandes (2006) 'Política Externa Portuguesa e Política Externa e de Segurança Comum da União Europeia', *Negócios Estrangeiros*, 9 (1): 134–245.

Pinheiro, Paulo Vizeu (2009) A Política Externa e de Defesa Europeia', Communication presented at *Ciclo de Conferências sobre o Papel da União Europeia no Mundo e o Diálogo Intercultural*, University of Minho (Braga).

Smith, Karen (2003) *European Union Foreign Policy in a Changing World*, Oxford: Blackwells.

Soder, Kirsten (2010) 'EU military crisis management: an assessment of the member state's contributions and positions', paper prepared to the COST meeting held in Brussels, 10 June.

Teixeira, Nuno Severiano (2009) *Contributos para uma Política de Defesa*, Lisbon: Ministry of National Defence.

Wong, Reuben (2008) 'Foreign Policy', in Paolo Graziano and Maarten P. Vink (eds), *Europeanization: New Research Agendas*, Basingstoke: Palgrave Macmillan.

11 From failure to success

Portuguese foreign diplomacy towards East Timor

Rui Alexandre Novais

East Timor had to tread a long road before it achieved the goal of self-determination and independence in May 2002. For a long time, East Timor had been the stage of one of the oldest and most longstanding cases of human rights violations in recent world history. The former Portuguese colony, therefore, had to remain a nation in waiting for years and had to cope with isolation, fear and terror.

While presenting a brief synopsis of the contemporary historical background of the former Portuguese colony, this chapter mainly draws on the vicissitudes of the East Timor affair from the decolonization epoch, passing through the period of Indonesian de facto control and some of the events that led to its independence. Furthermore, it assesses how the simultaneous occurrence of particular political and economic contingencies in the international community in general, and in Indonesia and Portugal in particular, facilitated the change in the territory. Above all, it discusses the extent to which the Portuguese accession to the European Community (EC) in 1986 enhanced its positioning *vis-à-vis* its former colony, which prompted a dramatic change in the affair. East Timor went from being a footnote reference in the government's consecutive programmes to becoming a priority issue in Portuguese foreign policy.

Invasion and takeover in a Cold War scenario

The eastern half of Timor Island, in the vast Indonesian archipelago, was invaded in 1975 and annexed by Jakarta a year later as its twenty-seventh province in complete defiance of international law and UN resolutions, which granted this island the status of a non-autonomous territory under the administration of the Portuguese government. Curiously enough, Indonesia had shown no previous interest in East Timor, since its geographic aspirations revolved around the former Dutch East Indies, of which East Timor was not a part. Acting as Minister at the Swedish Embassy to Jakarta back in 1975, Bruno Beijer (cited in Novais, 2010) recognized that until six months prior to the invasion, there was no integrationist pretension or claim on the part of Indonesia. In the same vein, a British press report noted that, even up to two days before the invasion, Indonesian authorities 'reiterated their support for Portugal's orderly and peaceful decolonization policy for the island' (*The Times*, 9 December 1975). Largely, this was so because East Timor was not part of the original territory and did not present the same potential in terms of wealth and natural resources as Aceh and Irian Jaya.

However, the victory of the Frente Revolucionária de Timor Leste Independente (Fretilin or Revolutionary Front for an Independent East Timor: a left-wing party), in the elections and the dense Marxist discourse of the local political parties prompted some doubts whether East Timor would become another Cuba. This was a likely prospect, since Fretilin obtained 55 per cent of votes in the July 1975 elections. It was only at that point that Western powers pushed Indonesia to take action, and East Timor became a military target for Jakarta. Both the Indonesian authorities and their allies regarded the likely prospect of East Timor's independence as undesirable, since the establishment of a left-wing government would pose a security risk in that region as well as trigger a domino effect in other Indonesian areas with ethnic and separatist questions such as Aceh, Irian Jaya, the Moluccas and West Kalimantan.

Five months later, in the aftermath of the civil war resulting from a União Democrática Timorense (UDT or Timorese Democratic Union)-led coup,[1] Fretilin, already apprehensive about an Indonesian invasion,[2] unilaterally declared the independence of the Democratic Republic of East Timor. This Declaration of Independence, according to *The Times* gave 'Indonesia the formal excuse of intervening against a threat of communism' and led Jakarta to persuade 'the Portuguese to keep the UN out of it' (*The Times*, 4 November 1975). For some, such as Michael Leifer (cited in Novais, 2010), Fretilin's move provoked the Indonesians into invading the territory.

Taking advantage of this period of unrest in the former Portuguese colony and prompted by Western countries, Indonesia invaded East Timor on 7 December 1975. Allegedly, the goal was to 'liberate' the territory from Fretilin's oppression at the request of the pro-Indonesian brothers in East Timor. The account reveals that the version from Jakarta, reported by the news agencies (*France Press*, API, Reuters), was that Indonesia had sent its troops to East Timor at the 'request of the four pro-Indonesian parties to help to restore security in Dili' or to 'capture the capital from the leftist Fretilin independence movement'. Among other things, a statement from the Indonesian government said that it could not prevent 'Indonesian volunteers from helping their brothers in East Timor in the struggle to liberate themselves from Fretilin oppression' (*The Times*, 8 December 1975). However, Jakarta concealed the fact that, 'since September of that same year Indonesia had been committed to naval patrolling of the East Timor shore, so that supplies could not reach Fretilin, while training and arming guerrillas' (*The Times*, 4 November 1975 and 9 December 1975). The 'age-old ties of blood brotherhood', against the prior lack of interest in the former Portuguese colony, now served as the excuse to merge East Timor into Indonesia and to justify the Indonesian takeover. Back in 1975, Indonesia took the Timorese issue off the international community's agenda and, from then on, promoted internal development in a way the Portuguese had not done before.

Their military solutions to the problems in East Timor, however, consistently aroused widespread Timorese disapproval.

The motive for the pro-Indonesian positioning by the major powers seems obvious. Jakarta's anticommunist stance in the Cold War scenario, its flexible and cheap labour market, as well as the wealth of natural resources (such as gas, coffee, oil-rich sea beds among others) made it an attractive partner for Western countries. If that was not enough, the Indonesian archipelago's geographical position also improved Indonesia's already distinctive geo-strategic strength. As Alain Dupont notes 'It sits astride the main sea lane connections and trade links between East Asia, Europe and the Middle East and at the southern extremity the region's most important waterway, the South China Sea' (1996: 278). Indeed, lying north of the Island are the Ombai-Wetar straits, a series of extremely deep channels allowing undetected (i.e. submerged) passage of nuclear submarines between the Pacific and Indian Oceans, which otherwise would mean at least eight more days to accomplish the journey (Taylor, 1994: 26–29). Therefore, the establishment of a communist government in a Cold War scenario and at such a geo-strategic location, as pointed out before, was both unwelcome and actively opposed. Thus the natural and geographic conditions of the eastern half of the Timor Island did not favour the Timorese ambition for independence.

Portuguese Timor

East Timor experienced a peaceful cohabitation with Portuguese rulers for over 400 years.[3] In Portugal itself, the fall of the Estado Novo in 1974 led to a dramatic shift in the political direction of the country that was also to affect colonial policy. The 'proudly-alone' Portuguese foreign policy course of action, characteristic of the 46-year dictatoral regimes of Salazar and Caetano, was a refusal to accept the inevitable decolonization process, even if it resulted in international isolation.

In fact, this was to be a distal contributory cause triggering the Carnation Revolution, thereby paving the way for Portuguese decolonization. The African conflicts, far more violent and worrisome at the time, were a priority for the Portuguese. In the case of East Timor, nevertheless, Lisbon sought a compromise solution in order to reconcile the Timorese will for self-determination with Indonesian intentions.

The future of East Timor was, to some extent, divisive at this point. Among the Portuguese political elite many, such as Mário Soares, initially promoted East Timor's integration into Indonesia provided that this was also the will of the East Timorese. At the same time, others, like Almeida Santos, were in favour of it becoming part of Portugal. Thus, in the years immediately after the Indonesian takeover, 'the Portuguese government attempted to renounce its responsibility for political convenience, whilst trying to bury the Timorese case. When this failed, it tried to find an "honorable solution"' (Taylor and Amaral, 1993: 329).

The independence of East Timor was, consequently, regarded as unattainable. In the process, they were to abandon East Timor to its fate and, to some extent, to Indonesian hands. The former Portuguese governor left East Timor for the Atauro Island, which was also under Portuguese control. This, however, can also be understood as merely changing the location of the administration and not abdicating from its legal rights in East Timor. In fact, Atauro was formally a part of the territory of East Timor, along with the islet of Jaco and the enclave of Oé-Cusse.

Unsurprisingly, despite the Portuguese Constitution stating in its article 293 that 'Portugal was still committed to its responsibility, according to international law, of promoting and assuring East Timor's right of independence',[4] until the late 1980s the position of the former Portuguese colony was, at best, 'equivocal' (Ward and Carey, 2001: 55), and remained a minor question for successive governments. Indeed, according to the Foreign Minister at the time, João Deus Pinheiro, it 'did not even constitute a significant burden on our conscience, or it was, at most, a dormant one' (2000). An elucidative example concerns the Portuguese Mission within the United Nations, which between 1976 and 1982 was nothing more than a disinterested, neutral observer (Ramos Horta quoted in Pureza, 2004).

'Globally', notes John Taylor, 'Portuguese foreign policy gave too little, too late. The government's international actions to publicize the situation in East Timor were usually rhetorical statements or small thorns in the side of Indonesian diplomacy' (1994: 185). East Timor only became a priority in Portuguese foreign policy after Portuguse accession to the EC in 1986 and following the authorities' recognition that Indonesia was about to get a supporting vote at the UN Security Council.

The uphill and appeal stages

Portugal, East Timor's former colonial ruler, developed its position on the question as early as the 1980s. Two main factors account for this change by the Portuguese authorities. On one hand, there was Portugal's decreasing influence within the UN's Security Council. In fact, the number of countries that voted in favour of the United Nations General Assembly's resolution concerning East Timor went from 72 (for) and nine (against), back in 1975, to a draw (50 for and against, besides 46 abstentions) in 1982. What is more, in March 1985, the Indonesian view prevailed in voting in the United Nations Human Rights Commission (UNHRC) 41st session debate. In fact, some EU members either abstained or sided with Indonesia to remove the consideration of East Timor from its agenda.

Given this trend, the Portuguese authorities became apprehensive about the prospect of Indonesia getting a favourable vote in the UN Security Council. As a consequence of that, the legal basis for the Portuguese acting as an administrative power would be lost. On the other hand, the Portuguese accession to the European Community (EC) in 1986 also prompted a dramatic change: East Timor went from a footnote reference in the government's consecutive programmes to become a priority issue in Portuguese foreign policy.

In Portugal, the socio-political context significantly contributed to pushing the subject of East Timor into the forefront as a priority issue. The country was going through a period of political stability, which contrasted with the previous parliamentary volatility in the immediate aftermath of the Carnation revolution. This was due to the right-wing Social Democrats' second term in government led by Cavaco Silva. After becoming the country's Prime Minister in 1985, with a minority government, Cavaco Silva had to step down and ask for elections in 1987. With this campaign, he obtained his first majority vote which, coupled with the integration into the EC (1986) and incoming European funds, helped to pave the way for a period of notable economic growth. It was a period in which Cavaco Silva's political popularity was on the rise, as reflected in the October 1991 elections. The Social Democratic Party (PSD) obtained 50.4 per cent of the votes, an unprecedented landslide vote in Portuguese history.

This internal political and economic stability combined with the country's enhanced international status contributed auspiciously to the cause of East Timor. The improvement of Portugal's international position had been a result of its mediating role between the opposing MPLA (People's Movement for the Liberation of Angola) and UNITA (União Nacional para a Independência Total de Angola) in obtaining peace in Angola, as well as its full integration into the EC. After the 1986 accession, and despite omitting any reference to East Timor in the EC accession agreement, Portugal opted for a strategy that combined the willingness to talk alongside international pressure (Gomes, 1995: 112).

Against this backdrop, the Cavaco Silva government's new approach comprised two distinctive phases or moments. The first stage consisted of getting the community's partners acquainted with the question of East Timor. However, this proved to be an uphill struggle since, in his first intervention as Foreign Minister at the EC, João Deus Pinheiro realized that apart from the British Minister, Geoffrey Howe, all the others were completely ignorant regarding the issue (Pinheiro, 2000). This politico-diplomatic attempt to sensitize European co-members to East Timor ultimately met with lack of interest from the major European countries owing to their unwillingness to antagonize Indonesia. The latter was seen as far more important than tiny East Timor, as Indonesia was the fourth most populous country, the major Muslim nation in the world and a geo-strategic partner in that region of the globe. João Deus Pinheiro (ibid.) reckons that it was not an easy task, since the Portuguese Government could barely count on any assistance. At best, the country could only count on support from some European ministers, on a personal level, while the co-members were not willing officially to consider the issue of East Timor.

The Portuguese Government thus changed its approach. This second stage consisted more of a 'guerrilla stratagem', since the Portuguese authorities were determined to obtain some sort of acceptance or, at least, to get the East Timor affair on to the international agenda.

Being part of a multilevel governance system, Portugal now worked with other member states to build up and shape a common foreign and security policy. The initial break-through occurred at the meeting with ASEAN countries held at

Dusseldorf during the German presidency of the EC during the first half of 1988. The agenda and final communiqué required agreement of both ASEAN countries and EC members. The Portuguese Government was determined to demand the inclusion of such an inconvenient issue as East Timor, even if this meant standing up against the will of the remaining counterparts.

To avoid any embarrassment, the German presidency managed to reach an agreement with Portugal to omit East Timor from the Dusseldorf final declaration. This omission was a trade-off for an explicit allusion from the German Foreign Minister Genscher in an intervention at the UN a few days later, as well as a mutually agreed answer to a query raised by a Portuguese journalist during the question-and-answer period at the beginning of the session. Portuguese foreign correspondent António Esteves Martins was willing to perform this 'national service', by being present at the press conference and raising the question. It was in such circumstances that East Timor merited a public mention for the first time by the EC at an international organization level.

The generally indifferent mood of the community's partners was to change with the November 1991 Dili incident, which confirmed the Indonesian authorities' violence in East Timor. Although the issue was still as inconvenient and embarrassing as it had been in the past, in the aftermath of the massacre, and due to its international impact it became politically incorrect not to be aware of the situation in the former Portuguese colony. Understandably, many considered the 12 November episode as the most decisive moment in the modern history of East Timor.

Following the Dili Massacre, the Portuguese presidency of the EC scheduled to take place during the second half of 1992 had the potential to enhance further the country's standing in the international arena. Although unable to reach agreement among its fellow members on a condemnation of Indonesia at the UNHRC, Portugal maintained pressure by permanently boycotting the third-generation agreements with the ASEAN countries, and used the human rights argument in an instrumental fashion, ensuring that East Timor was on the agenda of those meetings. In 1993 Portuguese diplomatic efforts prompted a couple of resolutions from the European Parliament on the need to improve the human rights situation in East Timor (Barroso, 1992–1993: 21), something that was to continue the following year.

Then, in 1995, East Timor assumed a core feature of the new Prime Minister's foreign policy as stated in the government's programme, and acquired a final dimension that proved to be beneficial to the Timorese cause within the 'New Transatlantic Agenda' (MNE, 1995: 112). In June, Portugal sought to challenge the legality of the 'Timor Gap Treaty' signed between Australia and Indonesia to explore petroleum resources in an area of overlapping maritime jurisdiction between Australia and East Timor. The International Court of Justice confirmed East Timor as a non-self-governing territory.

In the Madrid European Council of that same year an explicit reference was made to East Timor while a common single collective position by the EU member states was achieved in June 1996 that called for respect for the interest and legitimate aspirations of the Timorese people (Neves, 2000: 34). This was to coincide with another high profile event that reinforced the visibility of the East Timorese' plight, that is, the awarding of the 1996 Nobel Peace Prize to the political activist, Jose Ramos Horta, and the Head of the Catholic church in East Timor, Bishop Carlos Belo, for their efforts to gain freedom and independence from Indonesian rule.

Then, an EU Troika of Jakarta-based ambassadors visited East Timor in June 1998, leading the way to tripartite talks between the UN, the Portuguese and the Indonesians in New York in August. Such talks, seen by the EU as the key to a lasting settlement for the East Timor affair, eventually resulted in the historic breakthrough of the 5 May 1999 accords in New York. The comprehensive agreement on the future of the territory in turn paved the way for the 'popular consultation' on 30 August 1999 and the establishment of the UN Mission in East Timor (UNAMET). Despite the past record of gross human rights violations by the Indonesian military in East Timor, both the UN and Portugal saw it as a one-off opportunity to be seized, and thus agreed to grant Indonesia's security forces sole responsibility for maintaining peace during the referendum and its aftermath, not without some Portuguese uneasiness about the adequacy of the security guarantees for East Timorese voters (Dee, 2001). By not making provision for a military component in UNAMET when accepting the security assurances of the Indonesian military, as Richard Leaver notes 'the UN essentially acted in innocence of the history of the military's complicity in the humanitarian atrocities' (2001: 4). Concerns not to destabilize Indonesia and its sovereignty considerations further were involved in the ultimate decision.

Despite the intimidating campaigns of 'integration with Indonesia' supporters on 30 August, a 98 per cent turnout rejected political autonomy with Indonesia in favor of independence, since 78.5 per cent of East Timorese voters chose the latter option. (Dee, 2001: 14). Such a result led to widespread violence and ferocious attacks from militias opposed to East Timor's independence, backed by the Indonesian military. In the face of international condemnation, and bowing to foreign pressure – in the form of international isolation and threats to lever IMF, World Bank and other economic sanctions – Jakarta accepted the deployment of the International Force in East Timor (INTERFET) in September 1999.

In October, Indonesia's Parliament formally revoked the 1978 decree incorporating East Timor into Indonesia. It was no longer part of Indonesia and reverted to its 1975 status as a non-self-governing territory and Portugal as the administering power, allowing the UN to take over the territory and prepare the East Timorese for eventual self-government after a suitable transition period. On 25 October, Resolution 1272 was adopted by the UN Security Council establishing the UN Transitional Administration in East Timor (UNTAET), the UN body mandated to oversee East Timor's reconstruction and transformation towards eventual statehood (Suhrke, 2001: 12). Finally, in February 2000, INTERFET handed over to the United Nations Transitional Administration (UNTAET) the authority to administer the new state during the two-year transition period to self-rule. UNTAET was a ground-breaking transitional administration with total executive, legislative and judicial authority and it is frequently touted as the most extensive involvement in peace operations in Asia and the Pacific, as well as one of the organization's great success stories. East Timor's political destiny was formally sealed when constituent assembly elections were held in August 2001, followed by the first presidential election in April 2002, and East Timor was accepted in the UN shortly afterwards as Timor Leste.

The contextual factors: multiple causal for independence

Although, to a great extent, Portugal deserves credit, because this proved to be a long, difficult and quite lonely cause to fight for (Beijer cited in Novais, 2010), East Timorese independence was the result of many other factors over several years. Indeed, despite the Portuguese authorities' efforts and commitment, the emergence of an alternative solution for the continuing question of East Timor was only possible due to the combined factors of the international context and Indonesian internal politics. The economic crisis affecting Indonesia and the Asian rising tiger economies in 1997, as well as changes in Indonesia with Suharto's stepping down in May 1998, were among the factors that further facilitated the solution for East Timor.[5] President Habibie wanted to break with the past and to establish a contrast as being liberal and democratic. East Timor presented itself as favourable ground to display his new predisposition. Unlike his predecessor, Habibie had a different outlook altogether about the twenty-seventh province. He believed that the situation in the territory was no longer worth maintaining due to the high military and economic costs involved. East Timor was, moreover, insulated from the Indonesian general public view. It was never a relevant domestic issue, in the sense that no one really knew what was going on and did not understand all the talk about it (Tirtosudarmo, 1992: 136). Thus, Habibie could handle the matter along a more liberal line without expecting any public backlash. Significantly, the new Indonesian leadership prioritized the country's international credibility. East Timor's newly-acquired visibility as an international issue and a news item within the Western press gave Habibie an additional reason to escape from a situation that had been a source of overriding foreign criticism.

Habibie's openness in talking about autonomy and, later, in allowing for the possibility of a referendum on independence, left no doubts about a redirection in the Indonesian approach *vis-à-vis* East Timor. It also left few doubts that Suharto had been blocking the resolution of the East Timorese affair and, had he remained in power, it would have been most unlikely that East Timor's status would have undergone any alteration. In this vein, it could be argued that to some extent independence and self-determination had more to do with the then current status of Indonesian politics than with the Timorese or the Portuguese will for change.

Politico-economic transformations in Indonesia also led other countries to reassess and, in most cases, redirect their policies towards Jakarta. This was not without repercussions for East Timor. For instance, Australia changed its governmental position in December 1999. Canberra's authorities traditionally regarded East Timorese independence as a lost cause and Indonesia's takeover as irreversible. Such official policy changed to an approach favouring self-determination of the East Timorese, which was also crucial for the future of the territory.

A security or defence priority (i.e. the fear of its powerful neighbour, Indonesia) might have prompted an Australian betrayal of the Timorese, but another possible explanation seems even more plausible. As Noam Chomsky puts it, a major factor secretly emphasized by Australian ambassador to Jakarta Richard Woolcott in August 1975 was that, by going along with the invasion, his country 'could make a better deal on the oil reserves with Indonesia than with Portugal or an independent Portuguese Timor' (1996: 200). In fact, Australian *de jure* recognition of Indonesian sovereignty over East Timor enabled the beginning of negotiations with Jakarta that eventually led to the signing of the Timor Gap Treaty ten years later, concerning Timorese gas and oil resources (Gunn, 1997: 57–68). The pursuit of Australian national interest, therefore, prevailed over ethical and moral values, such as respect for self-determination and human rights. Burchill goes even further commenting that 'since Indonesia's invasion, Australian governments have routinely put commercial and strategic interests before a concern for human rights, forging closer economic relations with the Suharto regime and training Indonesian military' (2001: 170).

For a long time, despite UN resolutions calling for immediate withdrawal and frequent accusations of abuse of the most basic freedoms, the Indonesian occupation benefited from the de facto recognition of some strategic Western allies – the US, Britain and France, to name just a few. It was only by the end of the 1990s that the main Western powers reversed their course regarding East Timor and broke with the past. The political redirection of those powers' attention towards this continuing human rights case, alongside some critical internal changes in Indonesia, created an opening for change. This was not without repercussions for East Timor.

Although at a different level, the UN General Assembly and Security Council's resolutions regarding the integration as illegal[6] and continuously acknowledging Portugal as the administering power, proved decisive for East Timor as well as the organization's own credit (see the different resolutions cited by Gunn, 1997: 107–112). In fact, the recognition of the non-self-governing territory status of East Timor was of great importance. It initially allowed the Portuguese authorities and the Timorese to pursue their lonely campaign for their common cause, and later it legitimized the intervention of the international community. Despite facing a lack of political will from the major powers (i.e. the 'coalition of the unwilling') to improve its resolutions, over the years the UN managed to keep the unfinished issue on the agenda and to set the legal boundaries.

From 1983 to 1991, under the auspices of Perez de Cuellar, the UN encouraged negotiations between Indonesia and Portugal on East Timor. In the late 1990s, mostly due to the innovative diplomacy of Kofi Annan and his special representative on East Timor, Jamsheed Marker, the UN facilitated negotiations between Indonesia and Portugal, and indirectly with the East Timorese resistance, thereby contributing to a solution to the East Timor affair.

Similarly, East Timor remained on the international agenda as a result of the Timorese resistance, and Fretilin in particular, who carried on a determined struggle to keep the issue of East Timor alive. In addition, there was also the persistence of such groups as Amnesty International, the Indonesia Human Rights Campaign based in London (TAPOL), Asia Watch, and a host of East Timorese solidarity groups such as the International Platform of Jurists for East Timor, and East Timor Action.

Finally, it can also be argued that media attention was one of the decisive factors in keeping East Timor alive in the international scenario. Some, such as João Deus Pinheiro (2000), upgraded it to a key role, both before and after the Dili Massacre. Before the 12 November shootings the sporadic coverage devoted to East Timor was highly important in substantiating the Portuguese position and activism in favour of its former colony. In the aftermath of the massacre, the reporting not only reached a wider international audience, thereby unprecedentedly projecting East Timor's problem, but also became more critical in terms of denouncing the human rights violations in the territory (ibid.).

Working both ways: the success of the internationalization and Europeanization stages for East Timor and Portugal

The relevance of East Timor, apart from the historical ties deeply rooted in Portuguese colonial domination, rested on the fact that it had been a longstanding unresolved issue in world affairs as well as a shocking example of the decimation of a people. The former Portuguese colony had to wait for the simultaneous occurrence of particular conditions to break the impasse over its longstanding claims. Among those factors that facilitated change in East Timor were the shifting of interest in the international community, the political and economic changes in Indonesia and the Portuguese 'reconciliation' with its former colony.

Unable to prevent the Indonesian invasion and subsequent takeover, and forced to abandon East Timor to its fate and to Jakarta's hands, the former colonial power was, for a protracted period, nothing more than a marginal reference in the different governmental programmes that consistently advocated self-determination of the territory.

Dwelling on Portuguese foreign policy towards East Timor, it only resumed its proactive interest and enhanced its positioning *vis-à-vis* its former colony after the country's membership in the EC in 1986. Indeed, this was to prompt a dramatic change in the affair, since from then onwards East Timor went from a footnote reference in the government's consecutive programmes to becoming a priority issue in Portuguese foreign policy. Indeed, the importance of East Timor in domestic policy grew hand-in-hand with the consolidation of the Europeanization and internationalization of Portuguese foreign policy. Such a recentring of Portuguese foreign policy would prove to be a decisive option for the visibility of the East Timorese cause, but succeeding in championing the independence of its former colony also resolutely contributed to the affirmation of the country within Europe and the world.

If self-determination and independence was not an easy task for East Timor, the consolidation of democracy and a market economy will be decisive for the survival of the state in a mood of national reconcilaiation.

Notes

1 As Damien Kingsbury points out,

> Fretilin and UDT were initially not radically different in their aims, and managed to come together in alliance in January 1975, seeking independence ... But with Indonesian intelligence conspiring against the more left-wing Fretilin, the UDT was led to believe Fretilin would soon launch a coup. To forestall this possibility, on 11 August 1975, UDT, supported by local police, made a pre-emptive strike against Fretilin in what was called the "Revolutionary anti-communist movement of 11 August" ... Fighting was fierce but it was over within days, costing some 2,000–3,000 lives.
>
> (2000: 155).

2 Following the failure of the coup, Indonesian forces began mounting aggressive border raids from west Timor, attacking Batugade and Balibo.

3 Such cohabitation goes back to 1520. East Timor became a Portuguese overseas province in 1896 and this was confirmed by Portugal in 1926.

4 Author's translation. Since the invasion, Portugal had been urged by the UN to seek a peaceful solution and to cooperate to enable the people of East Timor to exercise their right of self-determination. See for instance, General Assembly resolution 3485 of 12 December 1975 and Security Council Resolution 384 of 22 December 1975 (cited by Gunn, 1997: 107–110).

5 António Monteiro, the Portuguese representative at the UN from 1997 to 2001, argues, likewise, that the fall of Suharto opened a window of opportunity, although the true power holder, the military regime, was still the same (Monteiro, 2001).

6 The military invasion of East Timor by Indonesia falls into The United Nation's General Assembly Declaration of Principles of International Law Concerning Friendly Relations and Co-operation among States. This is also in Accordance with the Charter of the United Nations, General Assembly Resolution 2625, 24 October 1970, principle 1, which determines that 'no territorial acquisition resulting from the use or threat of force shall be recognized as legal'.

References

Barroso, José Manuel Durão (1992–1993), 'A Política externa portuguesa', Lisbon: Biblioteca diplomática Série C, MNE.

Chomsky, Noam (1996), *Powers and Prospects. Reflections on Human Nature and the Social Order*, London: Pluto Press.

Burchill, Scott (2001) 'East Timor, Australia and Indonesia', in Kingsbury, Damien (ed.) *Guns and Ballot Boxes: East Timor's vote for Independence*, Victoria: Monash Asia Institute.

Dee, Moreen (2001) '"Coalitions of the Willing" and Humanitarian Intervention: Australia's Involvement with INTERFET', International Peacekeeping 8 (3): 1–20.

Dupont, Alain (1996) 'Indonesian Defence Strategy and Security: Time for Rethink?', *Contemporary Southeast Asia* 18 (3): 275–297.

Gomes, Ana (1995) 'Timor Leste e o imperativo de uma política de direitos humanos', *Política Internacional* 10: 111–121.

Gunn, Geoffrey C. (1997) *East Timor and the UN: The Case for Intervention*, Trenton: Red Sea Press.

Kingsbury, Damien (ed.) (2000) *Guns and Ballot Boxes: East Timor's vote for Independence*, Victoria: Monash Asia Institute.

Leaver, Richard (2001) 'Introduction: Australia, East Timor and Indonesia', *Pacific Review* 14 (1): 1–14.

MNE (1995) 'Portugal na União Europeia', Décimo ano, Lisbon: MNE.

Monteiro, António (2001) 'A União faz a força', *Nação e Defesa* 115: 187–192.

Neves, Fernando (2000) 'Timor Leste:processo diplomático', *Política Internacional* 21: 29–38.

Novais, Rui Alexandre (2010) *News Factors in Foreign News*, Lisbon: Media XXI.

Pinheiro, João Deus (2000) Portuguese Foreign Minister back in 1991, interview held at Universidade do Minho in Braga, 3 April 2000.

Pureza, José Manuel (2004) 'Who saved East Timor? New references for international solidarity', *South European Society & Politics* 9(2): 191–217.

Suhrke, Astri (2001) Dilemmas of the UN in East Timor, *International Peacekeeping* 8 (4): 1–20.

Taylor, John (1994) *Indonesia's Forgotten War: The hidden history of East Timor*, London: Zed Books.

Taylor, John G. and Amaral, António Sá (1993), *Timor: A História Oculta*, Venda Nova: Bertrand.

Tirtosudarmo, Riwanto (1992), 'Indonesia 1991. Quest for Democracy in a Turbulent Year', *Southeast Asian Affairs Yearbook:* 123–139.

Ward, Eilís and Carey, Peter (2001) 'The East Timor issue in the context of EU–Indonesian relations, 1975–99', *Indonesia and the Malay World* 29 (83): 51–74.

12 Lusophonia and the continued centrality of the Portuguese-speaking community

Paulo Gorjão

Introduction

The former Portuguese Minister for Foreign Affairs, Luís Amado, said in an interview that when the Treaty of Lisbon entered into force in December 2009 Portugal symbolically closed a foreign policy cycle.[1] In other words, the focus given to Portugal's European integration, at least in its previous form, was over.

From the transition to democracy in April 1974 and until 2009, Portugal's foreign policy was structured between three main pillars. Transatlantic relations were one of them, in particular the relationship with the US on a bilateral level, as well as within multilateral structures, such as NATO. Although the transatlantic pillar always went beyond the US, the fact was, and still is, that the US was *primus inter pares*. Portugal's entry into the European Union, on the one hand, and the end of the Cold War on the other, had inevitable consequences regarding the relevance of transatlantic relations, both from a political and an economic point of view.

European integration was the second pillar. Until the transition to democracy, in large measure, Portugal had its back turned on Europe. The regime change unblocked Portugal's strategic approach to Europe. As a consequence, after 1985 and until 2010, Portugal dived into European affairs with its heart and soul. In those 25 years, Portuguese efforts towards full integration within Europe were a source of national consensus. In each stage of Europe's institutional developments – whether economic/financial, political, or military – Portugal was always in the leading group.

Last but not least, Portugal's political, economic and diplomatic relations with Portuguese-speaking countries – Brazil in Latin America, Angola, Cape Verde, Guinea-Bissau, Mozambique and São Tomé and Príncipe in Africa, and Timor-Leste in Southeast Asia – was the third pillar. The historic legacy and in particular the wounds of decolonization regarding the Portuguese-speaking African countries (PALOP) has taken some time to overcome. Indeed, it was only in 1996, more than 20 years after Portugal's regime change and subsequent decolonization, that conditions were met to allow the Portuguese-speaking countries to create a multilateral forum. Thus, as a consequence, this is the least mature pillar and the one still waiting for further consolidation. Inevitably, relations among Portuguese-speaking countries face challenges; but they will also have bilateral and multilateral opportunities in the forthcoming years. Whether they will be addressed successfully remains to be seen.

This chapter is divided into three sections. The first one deals with the period between 1985 and 1996. It begins with Portugal's accession to the European Union and ends with the establishment of the Community of the Portuguese-speaking Countries (CPLP). In large measure, it corresponds to the slow normalization of diplomatic, political and economic relations between Portugal and the PALOP. The second section covers the period between 1996 and 2009. During these 14 years, relations among Portuguese-speaking countries were upgraded and taken to the multilateral level. The third section is a prospective exercise, and aims to provide some leads regarding the path that will be taken in the forthcoming years. The chapter ends with some final remarks.

The years 1985–1996: the slow path towards greater bilateral cooperation

Following the regime change in Portugal, in April 1974, the former Portuguese colonies in Africa – Angola, Cape Verde, Guinea-Bissau, Mozambique, and São Tomé and Príncipe – became sovereign states.[2] Inevitably, the Portuguese colonial war that lasted between 1961 and 1974 left serious political wounds and scars. As a consequence, the following years were devoted to overcoming this historical and political legacy. Unsurprisingly, the period between 1985 and 1996 was characterized by a gradual, although slow, normalization of the diplomatic and political relations between Portugal and the PALOP, a process that was highly dependent on previous developments within each Portuguese-speaking country. If, on the one hand, Portugal was fully committed to European integration as the main path towards democratic consolidation and economic prosperity, the truth was that, in the short term, the prospects for fostering relations with the Portuguese-speaking countries were rather dim. In other words, the primacy of the Portuguese commitment towards European integration was both a deliberate choice, and at the same time, a reaction to circumstances.

After independence in 1975, Angola fought a long and destructive civil war that lasted until 2002. Caught in the whirlwind of the Cold War, it became one of the most important and longest proxy wars between the Soviet Union and the United States and therefore its outcome was dependent on the end of their mutual geostrategic competition. Similar internal strife would also occur in Mozambique until 1992. Thus, the political, diplomatic and economic deepening of bilateral relations with two of the most important Portuguese-speaking countries in Africa faced serious obstacles. Brazil, too, was going through the pains of transition to democracy until 1985, thus complicating the development of bilateral relations.

But despite these constraints, Portugal always followed political events in Portuguese-speaking countries with interest. Thus, unsurprisingly, Portugal seized the opportunity and acted as the mediator of the Bicesse Accords in 1991, which laid out a transition to multi-party democracy in Angola under the supervision of the United Nations. The Bicesse Accords stipulated that presidential elections should occur within one year. The first round of the presidential elections took place in September 1992 but, without a winner, war broke out once again. In 1993 the US deserted UNITA (National Union for the Total Independence of Angola), which prompted the movement to sign the Lusaka Protocol with MPLA (the People's Movement for the Liberation of Angola) in October 1994. Once again, peace would not last long.

Meanwhile, in Mozambique, an equivalent tale was unfolding. The duelling conflict between Marxist-ruling FRELIMO (Mozambique Liberation Front) and anti-Communist RENAMO (Mozambican National Resistance) combined with constant neighbourly interference (from former Rhodesia and Apartheid-ruled South Africa), disastrous central planning and economic collapse, quickly led the country to a desperate situation. After President Samora Machel's plane crash in 1986 and the rise of Joaquim Chissano at the helm of the country, Mozambique finally began to see some hopeful signs in its future with the beginning of peace negotiations with RENAMO. With the promulgation of a new constitution in 1990, an auspicious framework for a multi-party political system, a market-based economy and free elections was provided, paving the way for the Rome General Peace Accords in 1992, which would bring an end to the civil war. As an observing party in these talks, Portugal strongly emphasized the need for an international mission that would oversee the implementation of the agreements. ONUMOZ, the United Nations Operation in Mozambique – totalling 6,500 troops and military observers – was thus deployed and helped to ensure the 1994 first multi-party elections in the country, opening a new chapter of political stability in Mozambique.

As for Brazil, the military regime came to its end during this period. With the election of José Sarney in 1985 and the new constitution in 1988, civil liberties, fundamental rights as well as free and direct elections were restored. Nevertheless, an uncontrollable economic crisis and high inflation would dictate harsh times for successive civilian governments, until the arrival of Fernando Henrique Cardoso's Plano Real in early 1994, which would stabilize the Brazilian economy and launch Cardoso's successful presidential campaign by the end of the same year. Although symbolizing a new stage for Brazilian foreign policy, the country's relations with the Portuguese-speaking world would remain, at this point, rather bland as political efforts were clearly focused on the consolidation of democratic order and economic stability.

As for the remaining Portuguese-speaking countries, Guinea-Bissau endured the rule of a revolutionary council led by João Bernardo 'Nino' Vieira until the first free elections in 1994, which Vieira would eventually win, thus providing a sense of stability, albeit short-lived. São Tomé and Príncipe would, on the other hand, open itself to the world sooner, with a new constitution in 1990 and the election of Miguel Trovoada as President. A similar move would also be taken by Cape Verde, with significant constitutional reforms both in 1990 and 1992, aiming towards the implementation of a pluralistic and free society.

Still, the gradual democratization and stabilization of most Portuguese-speaking countries – with the notable exceptions of Angola's civil war and the Indonesian rule of Timor-Leste – prompted a generalized recognition of a favourable climate for greater cooperation with each other. Taking advantage of Portugal's EU membership, Brazil's growing regional weight and Africa's increasing pacification, the Portuguese-speaking countries began in this period to take cautious but steady steps towards creating a viable institutional mechanism that would be based on the common historical and linguistic background, which they all shared. In many ways similar to the approaches taken by other organizations – the Commonwealth of Nations or the French Francophonie – the emphasis fell on the promotion of a common language and the political and economic possibilities that it could present to each and every country as well as their repositioning, as a concerted and unified bloc, in the international community.

In this context, and from the start, Portugal stood out as one of the main advocates for such initiative, since it was the ideal solution to tie its former colonies into some sort of preferential relationship, this time not based on subordination, but on common respect for each other, valuing, and not denying, their common past.

To that end, the first summits of heads of state and government began to take place during this time, aiming to pave the way for the institutionalization of an effective new Portuguese-speaking organization.

The years 1996–2009: the new multilateral dimension

Although this period symbolizes a landmark for Portuguese-speaking cooperation, it is important to take into consideration the seeds of the formalization of such a bond. As such, already in 1989, at the first meeting of Heads of State and Government of Portuguese-speaking countries held in São Luís do Maranhão, Brazil, the seven participants – Angola, Brazil, Cape Verde, Mozambique, Guinea-Bissau, Portugal and São Tomé and Príncipe – recognizing the political and economic potential of a common language, agreed to create the *Instituto Internacional da Língua Portuguesa* (IILP, or International Institute of the Portuguese Language), as a first step towards a future unified approach. This would eventually result years later, in the institutionalization of the *Comunidade dos Países de Língua Portuguesa* (CPLP or Community of Portuguese-speaking Countries), officially created on 17 July 1996 in Lisbon.

With this new multilateral mechanism in place, the possibilities for common foreign policies grew exponentially. Previous attempts to consolidate bilateral relationships between the designated countries, which had often stagnated due to lack of opportunities, were now preferentially encompassed in a joint framework that would ideally provide for the development of a trans-world bloc and at the same time encourage the deepening of existing political, economic and cultural ties among the various Portuguese-speaking states.

However, every multilateral organization needs a leading player, able to maintain the pace and the political will focused on the nurturing of relations between all parties, and although Portugal had European Union member status, all eyes were set on Brazil's level of interest towards CPLP. Although at first enthusiastic about the opportunities of such project, the Brazilian authorities quickly realized that the easiest path for greater regional and international preponderance – despite all the good-will rhetoric frequently demonstrated[3] – did not necessarily involve the Portuguese-speaking countries. Therefore, in the following years, Brazil channelled its foreign policy to its fellow developing countries – India, South Africa and China – as well as to South American regional integration and reform of major international organizations, while at the same time heavily investing in a new relationship with the African continent – including the creation of 15 new diplomatic missions – without a specific focus on its Portuguese-speaking connections.

Nevertheless, such a pragmatic posture towards the international community did not prevent Brazil from enhancing its ties with Portugal. Marking a new era in the relations between the two countries, the Consultation, Cooperation and Friendship Treaty (2000) paved the way for significant bilateral economic investments, allowing for a steady growth of trade that eventually enshrined Brazil as one of the biggest sources of imports for the Portuguese market. Another example of the existing good relations was the establishment of a Strategic Partnership between Brazil and the EU, during Portugal's presidency, a token of the benefits associated with the Portuguese-speaking trump card, skillfully played by the Portuguese.

In fact, Portugal has ended up becoming the primary advocate of Portuguese-speaking cooperation and one of the main promoters of increased interactions. Quickly understood by Portuguese policymakers as a key element of the traditional foreign policy triad mentioned above, CPLP gradually developed an indisputable position in the country's international approach.

Beyond the crucial lobbying included in the cited EU–Brazil partnership, Portugal also made use of its credentials with Portuguese-speaking Africa when pushing for the realization of both EU–Africa Summits, in 2000 and 2007, while holding the European Council's presidency. Such occasions reflected the positive outcomes the country had drawn from its resolve in investing its resources in public cooperation with Portuguese-speaking African countries, thus obtaining widespread praise and respect from the rest of the continent.

On the other hand, independent since 2002, Timor-Leste was immediately welcomed as the newest CPLP member state, thus further enlarging the official number of Portuguese-speaking citizens in the world, while adding international weight and publicity to the bloc's purposes and stances.

The CPLP would also be brought to the spotlight when the political situation in Guinea-Bissau escalated to a full-blown civil war in 1998, with elected-President Nino Vieira opposing Brigadier Ansumane Mané. Intending to stabilize the civil unrest in a state member's territory, a CPLP delegation managed to ensure a truce between the warring parts. Nevertheless, this episode would also demonstrate the shortcomings of the incipient organization, since it had eventually to rely on the Economic Community of West African States

(ECOWAS) and on the deployment of its Cease-Fire Monitoring Group's interposing forces to implement peace on the ground. This, however, would not definitely resolve the structural problems of Guinea-Bissau's society, and successive crises continued to unfold through the years, with the Portuguese-speaking community unable to provide a common and reliable solution to one of its peers.

But if Guinea-Bissau remained a troublesome member, Angola, on the other hand, managed to end its long-lasting internal strife. With all the CPLP states backing international sanctions on the UNITA movement, President, José Eduardo dos Santos took the opportunity of rebel leader Jonas Savimbi's death to reach a truce with his opponents, thus finally bringing peace to the country. Now with a stable political and social framework, Angola began to grow as a significant African player, as well as a major world oil provider – with the inherent international financial muscle – strategically inserted in a security and energy 'hot zone'. With such new-found status, Angola saw relations with some of its peers, in particular Brazil and Portugal, rise exponentially as the increasing economic relations between all parties demonstrate – Angola soon became one of the leading destinations of the majority of Portuguese exports.

Mozambique, on the other hand, experienced a fragile but enduring equilibrium between FRELIMO and RENAMO that created a propitious climate for reconstructing and developing the country. On the political front, however, Mozambique appeared to centre its foreign policy in the country's entry into the Southern African Development Community (SADC) and in the Commonwealth of Nations, rather than reinforcing its ties with the Portuguese-speaking world, perhaps because it took the realistic view that the CPLP lacked the means to tackle some of the country's problems effectively. Nevertheless, the country is bound to attract greater attention – once again, from Angola, Brazil and Portugal – as local stability consolidates and economic opportunities continue to arise.

All in all, since 1996 the Portuguese-speaking countries have managed to construct a multilateral mechanism of cooperation that has reinforced bilateral relations between them.[4] Despite the shortcomings that inhibit the CPLP from reaching its true potential as an effective multilateral organization, the institution has managed to encourage its member states towards greater cooperation and projection within the international community. Nowadays, the CPLP is becoming a source of interest for other countries, and future enlargements are possible. Gradually, between 1996 and 2009, Portuguese-speaking countries became a cornerstone for Portuguese foreign policy. But will it continue to be so in the coming years?

Prospective exercise

With the above-mentioned natural ties to the four corners of the world, Portugal's external credibility is undoubtedly connected with developments in its relations with the countries with which it shares a common historical and cultural background. However, in order to continue to invest a significant part of its foreign policy in such countries, expecting to generate further political, economic or cultural advances between them, Portugal will necessarily need to rethink the existing strategies and priorities in order to evaluate how to generate dividends sooner and more consistently.

First of all, at a political level, Portugal will inevitably have to focus better its efforts in concerting positions among its Portuguese-speaking peers in major international forums. Portugal's diplomatic efforts were, until recently, chiefly directed to its candidacy for a non-permanent seat on the Council for the 2011–2012 period, a goal successfully secured, in part due to the unanimous support of the CPLP and the active campaign by its members. Nevertheless, such timely pledges of solidarity towards a country's foreign agenda can be considered under-achievements owing to the vast potential for political cooperation among the various countries practically going to waste in the UN's range of action. Even if the usual disparity of national interests in such multilateral platforms is taken into account, the lack of a better-coordinated approach is still striking. In fact, a better use of such preferential relationships could consist of a concerted campaign that would influence the respective voting caucuses and systematically reserve a seat for a Portuguese-speaking country at the UN,[5] thus allowing the permanent continuance of Portuguese-speaking influence and visibility in the world, and further accentuating Portugal's role as intermediary with important and diverse regional partners.[6] Furthermore, Portuguese foreign policy could also focus on gathering support for Brazil's candidacy for a permanent seat, due to the natural advantages of partnering with a growing regional actor, with global aspirations, which can in turn sympathize and align more easily in a near-future scenario, with Portugal's own national interests and objectives in the continuous evolution of the international community. The same line of thought can be considered when covering the subject of voting resolutions and decisions that naturally arises in bodies such as the General Assembly, where the opportunities for showcasing a unity bloc with fellow countries can probably appeal to Portuguese diplomacy. However, these possible increased consultations should not be restricted to the UN alone. Taking advantage of the multiple memberships of the significant multilateral institutions that Portugal holds could result in a deepening of existing relationships with the Portuguese-speaking community. In fact, as an active EU member, Portugal is in a position to encourage further institutional ties with some of its areas of natural influence, as the EU–Brazil partnership and the EU–Africa Summits, mentioned previously, have already proved.

On the other hand, the benefits inherent to sharing a common language and history should receive greater focus in Portuguese diplomacy as a way to promote the cultural, economic and political aspects of a supposedly unified community with over 260 million speakers. Although commonly emphasized in official declarations from national authorities, cultural cooperation could be highlighted even more through increased efforts to advocate the use of Portuguese in international organizations, particularly in the long-lasting struggle to make it a United Nations official language, as well as demonstrating the possibilities that the recent Spelling Agreement between Portugal and the remaining countries can bring to raise the profile of the language and consequential outcomes in terms of economic benefits and advantages.

Indeed, it is precisely this mutual cultural background that could also lead the way to the next step in fostering a new and sustainable economic environment. It is already safe to assume that imports of oil and gas will rise exponentially in the near future, and due to its significant external dependence, Portugal is obliged to foresee a scenario where the continuous escalation of high prices will force it to search for new economic partners, which are able to provide for its needs. As potential frontrunners, one can cite the likely (and already growing) preponderance of Brazil and Angola in Portugal's future trade balance, in which we can include the viability of developing truly transnational companies that could benefit from the expertise, financial capability and political good-will from these three countries, to grow in their respective markets. Such probable exchange of Foreign Direct Investment (FDI) is expected to start with the energy sector (where the shared interests between Brazil's Petrobrás, Angola's Sonangol and Portugal's Galp Energia are just the beginning) but could certainly comprise other activities, such as transportation (such as a feasible fusion between the three countries' airlines) or communications (where the long-cherished ambitions of creating a Luso–Brazilian operator could finally come to life).

All these economic breakthroughs would therefore be encouraged by the competitive advantages that a common language brings to the table. Such specific features should then be based in existing cooperation mechanisms, under the auspices of CPLP, where Portugal can easily share the risks with its fellow members and reap the benefits in its economy, namely as a result of an increase in export demand from these countries.

The premises in the economic and trade sector could also eventually spill over to affect the military realm positively. With a small number of relevant industries dedicated to weapons equipment production and maintenance, Portugal could try to seek further external investments that would allow the sharing of state-of-the-art technology and precious know-how, thus bringing considerable development to this specific sector. Searching across the Atlantic for such a scenario is the likely path, since Portugal's OGMA was privatized and bought by a consortium led by Brazil's EMBRAER, which opened the doors to further future investment and possibilities for cooperation in designing and manufacturing new military projects,[7] and thus create common and profitable defence industries with considerable gains to both countries' economies.

Another aspect of military cooperation inviting investment is the growing relationships between the Portuguese military and its CPLP states' counterparts. Already with official military agreements with Brazil[8] and Portuguese-speaking Africa,[9] Portugal is likely to continue and even accentuate its support for the professionalization and adequate formation of the respective armed forces, so as to prepare them for the endangering challenges of the new century. A concrete step would be to increase the quantity of joint exercises between the several countries' military forces, like the existing 'Felino', seen as a perfect vehicle to transmit precious knowledge and build trust among the different parties. Likewise, another possibility worth analysing by Portugal's military and political hierarchies would be the development of compatible procedures that would entail a shared capability to actively deploy a common force in areas of interest, where Portugal by itself does not normally have the necessary capability. The lessons gained by the CPLP-based *Centro de Análise Estratégica* (CAE or Centre for Strategic Analysis), designed as a platform for the exchange of joint strategic thinking and military doctrines, could then be better put to use.

Nevertheless, every window of opportunity faces obstacles down the road. Portugal's desire for reinforced and externally visible cooperation with Portuguese-speaking countries, will, at times, probably be supplanted by the economically driven bilateral relationships with major regional powers – Brazil and Angola. These two countries will also want to pursue their own particular foreign agendas that, by focusing on regional and occasional world preponderance, can eventually bypass or even jeopardize existing and future ties with Portugal and the remaining Portuguese-speaking world.

At the end of the day, Portugal will simply have to present the best case for the development of its foreign relations with these countries, proving that, through cooperation in a number of critical sectors, multiple gains are available to all parties.

Conclusion

Several reasons explain the lack of equilibrium between the three main pillars of Portuguese foreign policy. In the last 25 years, this disequilibrium has been working against transatlantic and Portuguese-speaking relationships. It is this imbalance that nowadays some wish to correct in the forthcoming years. Thus, they emphasize correctly that Portugal needs to pay more attention to the North and South Atlantic, that is, the strategic square that connects Portugal to the US, Brazil and Angola.

This rebalancing is more than welcome, since as it is also recognized and pointed out that Portugal's relevance within Europe will reflect its influence elsewhere. Thus, the main challenge nowadays consists in identifying strategic, political, diplomatic and economic niches that Portugal can fill in the forthcoming years. The deepening of transatlantic and Portuguese-speaking relations fits into this overall assessment and approach. In particular, Portugal must renew its emphasis on strategic relations with Angola, Brazil and the US.

As explained above, within its overall foreign policy, even at its lowest point, Portugal has never ceased to pay particular attention to Portuguese-speaking countries. Even when the political diplomatic and economic dividends did not justify it, Portugal focused particularly on them. Having overcome the wounds of decolonization, currently the relationship between the Portuguese-speaking countries is more mature and more consolidated. Their partnership will continue to grow in the forthcoming years, reflecting their increasing common interests. Still, it is their common language that is the main glue that creates a common identity. It is this glue that, despite geographic distance, fluctuations in their economic relations, or short-term political agendas, keeps them together. If the past tells us something about the future, then in the forthcoming years the Portuguese-speaking countries will continue to play a central role within Portugal's foreign policy.

Notes

1 Teresa de Sousa (2010): 2–4.
2 Regarding other Portuguese-speaking territories: Brazil was an independent state since 1822; Goa, Damão and Diu were integrated into India in 1961, but only recognized as such by Portugal in 1974; Macau's sovereignty was transferred to China in December 1999; and Timor-Leste would become an independent state in 2002.
3 See Miyamoto (2010): 8–12.
4 CPLP's working organization comprises a biennial meeting of the Conference of Heads of State and Government, an annual meeting of the Council of Ministers, sector Ministers' Meetings, a Committee of Permanent Consultation and an Executive Secretariat. The IILP and a Centre for Strategic Analysis are also included.
5 In addition to the latest term, Portugal has already occupied the seat as a non-permanent member twice, in 1989–1990 and 1997–1998, while Angola held the same position during the 2003–2004 period, On the other hand, Brazil has had a presence in the Security Council nine times, in 1946–1947, 1951–1952, 1954–1955, 1963–1964, 1967–1968, 1988–1989, 1993–1994, 2004–2005, and 2010–2011. Furthermore, Cape Verde also managed to secure a seat in 1992–1993.
6 See Paulo Gorjão, (2010). p. 6.
7 'Brasil busca parcerias em Portugal para fabricar novo avião militar' (*Público*, 27 January 2010).
8 Foreseen in the Consultation, Cooperation and Friendship Treaty (2000), and further reinforced by the Agreement over Cooperation in the Domain of Defence (2005).
9 Technical–Military Cooperation Agreements with Cape Verde, São Tomé and Príncipe and Mozambique in 1988, Guinea-Bissau in 1989 and Angola in 1996.

Bibliography

Burges, S.W. (2009) *Brazilian Foreign Policy after the Cold War*, Gainesville, FL: University Press of Florida.

Chabal, P. and Vidal, N. (eds) (2008) *Angola: The Weight of History*, New York, Columbia University Press.

De Sousa, Teresa (2010) 'Portugal será agora na Europa o que conseguir ser fora dela', *Público*, 3 January.

Gorjão, P. (2002) 'Regime change and foreign policy: Portugal, Indonesia, and the self-determination of East Timor', *Democratization*, 9: 142–58.

Gorjão, P. (2003) 'The legacy and lessons of the United Nations transitional administration in East Timor', *Contemporary Southeast Asia*, 24: 313–33.

Gorjão, P. (2010) 'Lusophone countries must devise a grand strategy towards the Security Council', *IPRIS Lusophone Countries Bulletin*, 4, February.

Gorjão, P. and Monteiro, A. (2009) 'Is Timor Leste a Failed State?', *Portuguese Journal of International Affairs*, 1: 12–21.

Manning, C.L. (2002) *The Politics of Peace in Mozambique: Post-Conflict Democratization, 1992–2000*, Praeger Publishers.

Miyamoto, Shiguenoli (2010) 'Brazil and the CPLP: Discourse and practice', *IPRIS Lusophone Countries Bulletin*, 4, February.

Oliveira, R.S. (2007) *Oil and Politics in the Gulf of Guinea*, New York, Columbia University Press.

Pazzanita, A.G. (1991) 'The Conflict Resolution Process in Angola', *The Journal of Modern African Studies*, 29: 83–114.

Pitcher, A. (2008) *Transforming Mozambique: The Politics of Privatization, 1975–2000*, Cambridge, Cambridge University Press.

Seabra, P. and Gorjão, P. (2010) 'Portugal and Angola: Ties that bind?', *IPRIS Policy Brief*, 4: 1–8.

Seabra, P. and Monteiro, A. (2010) 'Portugal and São Tomé and Príncipe: Beyond oil expectations towards real cooperation', *IPRIS Lusophone Countries Bulletin*, 6: 6–10.

Teixeira, N.S. (1998) 'Between Africa and Europe: Portuguese Foreign Policy, 1890–1986', in A.C. Pinto (ed.) *Modern Portugal*, Palo Alto, CA: The Society for the Promotion of Science and Scholarship.

Thaler, K. (2009) 'Avoiding the Abyss: Find a Way Forward in Guinea-Bissau', *Portuguese Journal of International Affairs*, 2: 3–14.

13 Relations between Portugal and Spain

Three decades after accession

Sérgio Caramelo

The Iberian countries have many features in common in their recent history, of which the second half of the twentieth century is an excellent example. From the simultaneous periods of dictatorship to the transition to democracy and, more recently, their integration into the European Union, the two countries have travelled many roads together. However, this does not mean that cooperation between the two states has always been strong. In fact, for many years relations were kept to the minimum necessary to avoid major tensions and, at the same time, ensure that there was sufficient distance to keep the two countries separate, especially their economies. Democratic normalization in Portugal and Spain and, particularly, accession to the European Economic Community (EEC) created the conditions that fundamentally changed relations between the two states.

This chapter seeks, first, to explain how the political changes in Portugal and Spain during the period of transition from dictatorial regimes to democracy ushered in a new paradigm of bilateral relations, a model that would be consolidated following the accession of both countries to the EEC. Second, the chapter presents a summary of the main elements of concern in Luso–Spanish relations in the period of accession to the 'European Club'. There is a particular focus not only on relations in the European and international arenas, but also the more obviously bilateral issues, the mechanisms employed in the design of an increasingly extensive and deep cooperation and the way in which accession to the EEC influenced the process as a whole.

Finally, and in order to understand the progress made in Luso–Spanish bilateral relations, concrete examples are provided of the development of coordination and integration in addressing specific matters such as cross-border transport infrastructures, joint management of water resources and economic relations.

Luso–Spanish relations prior to accession to the European Union

Despite the similarity of the political regimes in Portugal and Spain, their peaceful transitions to democracy during the 1970s were very different from each other. In Portugal the military coup of 25 April 1974 put an abrupt end to the previous system, bringing about a social and economic transformation of the country. Conversely the Spanish transition was a more gradual process, in which a range of factors played a part. These included the increasing frailty of the aging dictator, Franco, on whom the whole political system was built (which his successor, Carlos Arias Navarro, proved unable to emulate), and the consequent deterioration of the situation with the death of the *Caudillo* on 20 November 1975; factionalisms within the regime itself, notably between the more radical Falangists and the reformist wing; the opening of Spain to the outside world, not only economically but also socially and culturally; the possibility of restoring the monarchy together with democracy; and, finally, the political changes that were taking place in Portugal itself.

However, before democracy was established in the two countries, there were a number of difficult moments in their bilateral relations. Spain recognized the new Portuguese regime following the 25 April revolution, with regular contact initiated between the two countries once General António de Spínola took office. Nevertheless, this did not stop support from within Portugal for those who were seeking to overthrow the Franco dictatorship, or Spanish support for those who wanted to roll back political developments in Portugal.

Thus, there reappeared 'in 1974, in the context of the degeneration of the Spanish dictatorship, a situation similar to that which existed in the peninsula between April 1931 and November 1934' (Oliveira 1995: 201), in which both countries, facing antithetical political regimes, fear of 'ideological contamination' and threats to their internal cohesion, supported and gave refuge to political exiles from the other. It was impossible to engender a lasting coexistence between 'an authoritarian and radical power of the right (in Spain) and a radical political situation hegemonized by forces of the left and embraced by elements of the armed forces (Portugal)' (Oliveira 1995: 208), and these incompatibilities intensified as the respective political regimes became more politically radicalized, especially the Portuguese regime.

These circumstances led to a number of incidents that further jeopardized what were already very delicate relations between Portugal and Spain. Among these incidents the most obvious and important were the alleged support for and refuge in Spain of those behind the attempted military coup of 11 March 1975, including General Spinola, and also the attack on and looting of the Spanish Embassy in Lisbon on 27 September 1975. In this latter case, a group of civilians, supposedly members of extreme leftist groups and including elements of ETA (*Euskadi Ta Askatasuna*) and FRAP (Revolutionary Anti-Fascist Patriotic Front) (D'Abreu and Calvo 2007: 422), broke into the premises of the Spanish embassy in the Portuguese capital, which they destroyed and looted, without any effective action against them on the part of the Portuguese security forces. Even though the Portuguese government accepted responsibility for the incident, the Spanish government felt it had to respond formally. Diplomatic representation was withdrawn, trading in the escudo was suspended, some border crossings were closed and border security was stepped up (Gómez 2004: 164).

It became clear that the political radicalization of Portugal following the events of 11 March 1975, together with the entrenched authoritarianism of the final years of the Franco regime, meant that for a considerable time relations between the two countries gradually became more difficult and delicate – 'the more Portugal moved to the left, the further Spain moved to the right' (Cervelló 2000: 179). It was only with the Spanish transition to democracy at the end of 1975 and the gradual consolidation of the democratic regime in Portugal that bilateral relations started to improve and the difficulties around the attack on the Spanish Embassy began to be addressed.

In an effort to defuse the tensions that arose in late 1975, the two Ministers of Foreign Affairs met in Guarda in February 1976, an event known as the 'Spirit of Guarda'. This was a symbolic moment in the history of the two Iberian countries. It produced no surprising or immediate results in bilateral arrangements between the two states, but given the prolonged absence of cultural and economic relations 'it drew a line under the mutual suspicion between those who governed the two states and was indeed the beginning of the process of constructing democracy both in Spain and in Portugal' (Oliveira 1995: 211). From this point on, even though they had different interests and strategies in many cases, the two countries were committed to a common goal – membership of the EEC. This objective required them gradually to define common understandings and positions, not only in a general sense but also in relation to particular sectors (as is evident in the Luso–Spanish Summits, which started in 1983).

It was in this context of the push for membership of the EEC and following extensive contacts between representatives of the two states that during the course of his first official visit to Portugal in May 1978 King Don Juan Carlos of Bourbon ratified the new Luso–Spanish Treaty of Friendship and Cooperation (signed previously by Mário Soares and Adolfo Suarez in November 1977), which finally replaced the 'Iberian dictators' pact' (the Friendship and Non-Aggression Treaty of March 1939) and supported the gradual consolidation of a new paradigm for relations between the two countries.

Cold and hot spots in bilateral relations following European accession

In 1977 the two Iberian countries formally applied for membership of the EEC and negotiations began in October 1978 for Portugal and in February 1979 for Spain. The accession negotiations were central to the increase in bilateral relations between the two countries (Oliveira 1995: 217; Alves 2000: 37; Martins 2008: 30), since they involved not only the shared aim of both countries and societies, but also the need to achieve greater levels of coordination and agreement between the two states in order to ensure speedy and successful entry into the 'European club'.

At the same time, and as a result of the agreements between Spain and the European Free Trade Association (EFTA) of 1980, the Luso–Spanish Bilateral Trade Agreement was signed (Appendix P of the Spain–EFTA agreement), which aimed to stimulate trade within the Iberian peninsula. With the implementation of this agreement the way was clear for the gradual integration of the Iberian market, since the reduction and elimination of legal barriers and tariffs, together with the liberalization of world markets and the need for companies of both countries to internationalize, brought significant increases in economic relations and investment volumes between Portugal and Spain (Alves 2000: 37). It can be said that the impact of this agreement on Luso–Spanish trade was almost immediate and in 1981 the Portuguese import coverage ratio for imports from Spain dropped almost 100 per cent compared to the previous year (Oliveira 1995: 216). Portugal therefore saw the first practical manifestations of the opening of the Iberian markets in the second half of the twentieth century, and the response of the government was robust. Two years later an interim period was established 'to allow adjustments to be made to Appendix P of the Agreement between EFTA and Spain, with the aim of reducing the trade imbalance' (Martins 2006: 71) between the two countries.

These two factors, the accession process and the bilateral trade agreement, were in fact crucial to the increase in political and economic relations between the two countries. However, at the start of the 1980s there was still a great deal of caution in moves towards an effective and permanent bilateral cooperation that could start to resolve internal problems by beginning to address the adverse consequences of several decades of extreme separation, such as the very low levels of territorial, economic and social coordination between the two countries (Caramelo 2002: 343). The institutional response to these limited bilateral relations came in 1983 with the creation of the Luso–Spanish Summits.

In 1983 the Portuguese Prime Minister, Mário Soares, suggested to his Spanish counterpart, Felipe Gonzalez, that the two states should start regular summits at the highest level, to be held annually and to alternate between the two countries. This model of bilateral relations and cooperation was formally ratified in the first Luso–Spanish Summit, in Sintra, with the signing of an additional protocol to the Luso–Spanish Treaty of Friendship and Cooperation of 1977, which shaped the principles that would frame relations between the two countries and institutionalized the annual meetings.

In essence the Luso–Spanish Summits 'had, and continue to have, the aim of facilitating greater political coordination between the two States in the international organizations of which they are members and a joint approach to bilateral problems' (Alves 2000: 38). Today, and given the fact that up to the end of 2009 25 Luso–Spanish Summits had been held, we can state categorically that of themselves these meetings strengthened Iberian relations and bilateral efforts within the context of integration and cooperation between the two countries. However, they also enable us to identify the issues that were priorities for the governments (Martins 2006: 67). In fact, the summits and all the negotiations that preceded them have been the key forum for understanding between Portugal and Spain, not only for addressing issues of a bilateral nature, but above all in the search for agreement on European and international questions.

Through analysis of the development of the summits and of their content, we can identify four major phases (Pedrosa 2008: 45): an initial phase (1983–1986), a phase during which relations were normalized (1987–1995), a phase of consolidation of bilateral cooperation (1996–2004), and a phase of coordination and concerted action (2005 to the time of writing, i.e. 2012).

The period before accession to the EEC, the initial phase, was marked by the accession negotiations that involved both countries and also by a certain fear of moving forward with more extensive bilateral agreements, particularly where they touched on more delicate issues such as the fisheries sector. Hence, these meetings tended to be highly circumscribed and addressed issues of a somewhat limited relevance for Iberian relations (such as protection of endangered species and the construction of an international bridge).

The following phase (1987–1995) was the period of normalization of relations, during which understanding started to be established between the respective institutions and political leaders towards an increasingly coordinated response to international and European issues (such as European Regional Policy, the Common Agricultural Policy, the Schengen Agreement, the Single Market, the independence of East Timor and relations with the Mediterranean, Africa and Latin America). In bilateral terms agreements of much greater significance were reached in Iberian relations, particularly with regard to the construction of road and railway infrastructures, finance for cross-border cooperation, police and judicial cooperation and water resources.

The phase of consolidating bilateral cooperation (1996–2004) was no longer characterized by noticeable developments in Luso–Spanish understanding on European and international issues but by a more mature bilateralism, in which it became possible to reach agreement on highly problematic and delicate issues such as the Iberian Electricity Market (MIBEL), the protection and sustainable exploitation of Luso–Spanish hydrographic basins, the high-speed railway and cross-border cooperation between territorial entities.

Finally, the phase from 2005 to the present day (2012) is a period in which relations between the two countries appeared to reach 'cruising speed', characterized by a gradual increase in the number of people involved in bilateral relations (a growing presence of political representatives, no longer solely of the central administrations but also of regional governments) and by an expansion of the issues addressed in each of the Summits, as they became increasingly multisectoral (simultaneously dealing with issues from very different areas, such as health, research and development, education, defence, culture, environment, civil protection, infrastructure and employment).

This brief analysis of the Luso–Spanish Summits enables us to verify that in spite of the faltering start to this model of bilateral relations centred on annual summits, over the course of 25 years they have established methods and procedures for mutual understanding and also, above all, relationships of trust between institutions and individuals, a fact that has enabled agreements to be reached and problems, some of which were very longstanding, to be solved.

Some examples of coordination and integration

The development of formal bilateral relations between Portugal and Spain provide a number of examples of the enormous progress it has been possible to achieve in coordination and integration between the two countries. These are areas in which important – we could even say revolutionary – developments took place compared to the situation prior to EU accession, a prime example being the cross-border transport infrastructures and the related permeability of the border.

For many years both states maintained a concerted policy of control and containment of movement between Portugal and Spain. Whether based on defence strategies or with the aim of effective management of the border, to contain and control the movement of people and trade (legitimate commerce and, particularly, contraband activity), the two dictatorships clearly chose not to develop their infrastructures towards cross-border coordination. As a result, by 1986 there were even fewer rail links than in the first half of the twentieth century (only four) and there were only 25 cross-border asphalted roads (on a frontier about 1,300 km long), with no motorway sections and none engineered for speeds greater than 90 km/h.

Beyond the infrastructures themselves (or the lack thereof) there was also the control of the border. In 1986 between Portugal and Spain there were only 76 legitimate crossing points along the border, among which 61 functioned on an occasional basis or during particular periods and only four were open 24 hours a day (Valença, Vilar Formosa, Beirã and Caia). These figures give us a very clear picture of the highly impermeable nature of the border as accession to the EEC took place and of the difficulties that restricted traffic between the two countries, as there were many stretches of the border that had no permanent crossing points (for instance, the whole north and northeastern sector and the south of Portugal). In spite of the border between Portugal and Spain not being 'equipped with large-scale separation infrastructures, such as walls, fences, minefields, etc. and mostly lacking any physical means to stop the flow of traffic' (Caramelo 2002: 331), in fact in terms of road permeability it was far more closed than most of the Central European borders of the time – it was much more tightly sealed, for instance, than some politically sensitive European borders, for example between Italy and Yugoslavia (Caramelo 2007: 322).

This was undoubtedly an enormous obstacle to the development of the Luso–Spanish border regions and to an increase in trade, cultural and social relations between the two countries; and border permeability therefore came to occupy a prominent place in the Luso–Spanish summits. In this context issues were addressed and agreements reached on railway links (1987, 1988, 1990 and 1993), road infrastructure (1990, 1996, 2000, 2001 and 2006) and on the future high-speed train between the two countries (1991, 1997, 1998, 2000, 2001, 2002, 2003, 2005, 2006 and 2008) (Martins 2008: 32–33).

As a result of these efforts on both sides today's cross-border infrastructures linking the two countries are very different. There are four motorways, the number of asphalted roads has more than doubled, improvements have been made to almost all railway lines and there are concrete plans for the construction of a high-speed rail link. Although there are still peripheral areas of the border that remain very isolated, from a cross-border perspective it is undeniable that the obstacles to the free movement of people and goods between Portugal and Spain have been substantially reduced.

Another area of bilateral relevance and in which it has been possible to reach an almost historic understanding, which is even a point of reference internationally, is the management of water resources. This is a historical–geographical question of huge magnitude in Luso–Spanish relations, since the two countries share five hydrographic basins (the rivers Minho, Douro, Lima, Tagus and Guadiana) which constitute the main water resources of a large part of peninsular Spain (42 per cent) and, above all, of the continental territory of Portugal (64 per cent of the total).

The Luso–Spanish hydrographic basins, apart from the fact that they are located in areas characterized by wide seasonal and spatial asymmetries (with peak shortages in the hottest months and frequent episodes of extreme precipitation), nonetheless have quite distinct geographies. The upstream stretches of the rivers are all located in Spain, with the downstream areas belonging to Portugal while the vast majority of the area covered by the basins (78 per cent of the total) is located in Spain.

In short, it is well-known that shared water resources are absolutely indispensable for the two countries and constitute around 45 per cent of the surface water resources produced in the Iberian Peninsula (MAOT 2002: 3). However, their importance is even greater for Portugal as shared basins constitute the country's main water resources, a fact that has historically led to tensions in Luso–Spanish relations.

Efforts to find a solution to this problem are longstanding and many agreements have been signed on the exploitation of water resources (such as the Appendix to the Treaty of Limits of 1864 and the agreements of 1927, 1964 and 1968). Nevertheless, the geographical spheres of intervention and the procedures envisaged in these agreements were limited to the development of integrated and co-coordinated management of the Luso–Spanish hydrographic basins. Furthermore, in the 1980s and 1990s changes took place on the Spanish side that decreased the regularity and quality of the flows of water arriving in Portugal, including for instance, a substantial increase in the number of dams and transfers of water to other hydrographic basins, growth in public and industrial consumption, increased discharges of sewage and the consequent organic and chemical pollution, and increased irrigation and consequent salinization.

A real effort to find a solution to this problem came through the 'Agreement on Cooperation for the Protection and Sustainable Use of the Waters of the Spanish–Portuguese Hydrographic Basins' of 1998. This new agreement is much more far-reaching than previous agreements, and 'translates into legislative terms an environmentalist and holistic perspective on the problem of relations between Portugal and Spain with regard to their international rivers' (MAOT 2002: 16). That is, it is not limited to the management of cross-border stretches and their related use, but also includes the surface water, groundwater and the respective ecosystems of all the hydrographic basins, the activities and uses that can affect water quality and also actions to mitigate the effects of drought and floods. The aims of this agreement were very wide-ranging and addressed issues such as continuous information sharing on water flows, water quality and infrastructure and the creation of permanent bodies for joint working, the coordination of activities to protect water resources and ecosystems, pollution monitoring and coordinated responses to the more extreme hydrological situations of flood and drought (MAOT, 2002: 16).

This was clearly a very delicate issue in Luso–Spanish relations, and one that was politically and technically complex. Nonetheless it was possible to reach an understanding that has brought positive results, such that in April 2008 the two countries approved the Revision Protocol to the 1998 Agreement to continue the process.

Finally, we can mention another area that has seen a radical transformation over the past 25 years – economic integration. Along with the historical fear of political annexation, fear of economic *colonization* was probably the ghost that loomed largest over Luso–Spanish relations in the past. Consequently, the attitude (and politics) of Portugal towards its neighbour during the second half of the twentieth century was largely marked by the 'culturally rooted fear of the potential threats from a large country with a "great" economy (Spain) beside a small country which, like Portugal, had a weak economy' (Oliveira 1995: 213). The results of this position led, above all, to an almost total absence of economic relations between the two dictatorial regimes (between 1960 and 1974 the average annual level of exports from Portugal to Spain amounted to 2 per cent of total exports, with Spain registering a similar level). However, from the 1980s and as a result, *inter alia*, of the Luso–Spanish Bilateral Trade Agreement of 1980 and accession to the EEC, this scenario began to change radically, as can be seen in the following data:

- In 1960 Spain accounted for less than 1 per cent of Portuguese imports; in 1980 this figure was 5.5, in 1986 10.9, in 2000 25.9 and in 2008 30.8 per cent;
- Portuguese exports to Spain in 1960 were 1 per cent of total exports. By 1980 this figure was 3.6, in 1986 6.6, in 2000 19.3 and in 2008 27.2 per cent;
- In Spain, imports from Portugal in 1960 amounted to less than 1 per cent of total imports. In 1980 this figure was 0.5, in 1986 1.3, in 2000 2.7 and in 2008 9.5 per cent;
- Spanish exports to Portugal in 1960 were less than 1 per cent of total exports. In 1980 this figure was 2.7, in 1986 3.4, in 2000 5.0 and in 2008 11.6 per cent.

As we can see, from a situation where trade between Portugal and Spain was completely irrelevant or residual (the 1960s and 1970s), Spain was both the main customer and provider in the Portuguese economy throughout the 2000s, with Portugal being Spain's third largest export market and the seventh in terms of imports.

However, analysis of the development of Luso–Spanish trade shows an unequal position between the two economies. For example, if we consider the coverage of trade between the two countries, we find that in the last quarter of a century this has always been very favourable to Spain (the Portuguese/Spanish balance of trade has had a negative value of over four billion Euros since the mid-1990s).

Numerous factors help us to understand this imbalance in terms of the benefits derived from Iberian economic integration which include 'a more proactive approach by Spanish companies to operating in the Portuguese market, with the rapid establishment of distribution networks for their products and brands and the consolidation of their positions in key sectors' (Pires 2008: 187); the specialization profiles of the two countries are disadvantageous to Portugal, as areas of dependence in the Spanish economy do not match the areas of expertise in the Portuguese economy, while Spain's specialist sectors match the dependent sectors of Portugal's economy (Caetano 1998: 108). In addition, geographical location – Spain is closer to its other European partners and has to be crossed for Portugal to trade with the rest of Europe (Ferreira 2008: 152); while, finally, the comparative disadvantages of the different sizes of the two markets, since with the opening of the Iberian market Portuguese companies have seen their market greatly expanded but have to make a far greater strategic, productive and logistical effort than Spanish companies (Pires and Teixeira 2002: 303), for whom entry into the Portuguese market is often possible without major adjustments to production processes or logistics.

The evolution of economic flows between Portugal and Spain in the last three decades has moved from a stage where economic relations were residual to a diametrically opposite reality of deep economic interdependence, and shows that in all probability, economic 'fusion' between the two countries could only ever be a side effect of the implementation of a free trade model. This process actually shows that the fears of economic *colonization* have some justification. These fears were expressed *inter alia*, by the political leaders of the Portuguese dictatorship, who were only able to keep the two economies apart through specifically targeted restrictive administrative and customs policies.

There is no doubt that economic relations between the two countries and their level of economic interdependence has changed radically since accession to the EEC. However, they did not have the same starting point and the Portuguese economic fabric failed to keep pace with Spanish companies in exploiting the opportunities brought about by the geographical expansion of markets, something that has caused some unease among the economic elites. Nevertheless, data from recent years show that Portugal is slowly but steadily starting to make up for some of the delay in entering the Spanish market.

Bibliography

Alves, R.P. (2000) *Portugal: as relações ibéricas no âmbito da globalização e liberalização dos mercados*, Lisbon: Ordem dos Economistas – GEPE.

Caetano, J.M. (1998) *Portugal-Espanha: relações económicas no contexto da integração europeia*, Oeiras: Celta.

Caramelo, S. (2002) 'Fronteiras e regiões fronteiriças na União Europeia: processos, dinâmicas e singularidades do caso luso-espanhol', in M. Ribeiro (ed.) *Identidade europeia e multiculturalismo*, Coimbra: Quarteto.

Caramelo, S. (2007) *União Europeia, fronteira e território*, Porto: Campos das Letras.

Cervelló, J.S. (2000) 'Las transiciones democráticas', in H.T. Gómez (ed.) *Portugal y España contemporáneos*, Madrid: Marcial Pons.

D'Abreu, C. and Calvo, E.R. (2007) 'O Espírito da Guarda no relançamento das relações luso-espanholas', in A.Infestas *et al.* (eds) *Territórios e Culturas Ibéricas* II, Porto: Campo das Letras.

Ferreira, R. (2008) *Comércio interregional ibérico*, Portalegre: Associação de Desenvolvimento Regional do Instituto Politécnico de Portalegre.

Gómez, H.T. (2004) 'Portugal e Espanha: o problema peninsular na época contemporânea', in: J.Medina (ed.) *História de Portugal*, Lisbon: Ediclube.

Manuel, P.C. and Royo, S. (eds) (2004) *Spain and Portugal in the European Union: the first fifteen years*, London: Routlege.

Martins, C. (2006) 'Estratégias de desenvolvimento no contexto de afirmação numa Europa alargada: as cimeiras luso-espanholas', in I.M. Pires (ed.) *As relações entre Portugal e Espanha: oportunidades criadas no contexto europeu*, Lisbon: Centro de Estudos Geográficos.

Martins, C. (2008) 'Contextualização teórica do processo de integração dos mercados ibéricos no contexto da União Europeia' in I.M.Pires (ed) *A integração dos mercados ibéricos: um processo dependente e territorialmente diferenciado*, Lisboa: Centro de Estudos Geográficos.

MAOT (2002) *Plano Nacional da Água*, Lisbon: Ministério do Ambiente e Ordenamento do Território.

Martins, C. (2008) 'Contextualização teórica do processo de integração dos mercados ibéricos no contexto da União Europeia' in I.M. Pires (ed.) *A integração dos mercados ibéricos: um processo dependente e territorialmente diferenciado*, Lisbon: Centro de Estudos Geográficos.

Oliveira, C. (1995) *Cem anos nas relações luso-espanholas: política e economia*, Lisbon: Cosmos.

Pedrosa, M. (2008) 'las cumbres luso-espanõlas', in I.M. Pires (ed.) *A integração dos mercados ibéricos: um processo dependente e territorialmente diferenciado*, Lisbon: Centro de Estudos Geográficos.

Pires (2008) 'A integração do mercado ibérico – um processo dependente e territorialmente diferenciado?', in I.M. Pires (ed.) *A integração dos mercados ibéricos: um processo dependente e territorialmente diferenciado*, Lisbon: Centro de Estudos Geográficos.

Pires, I.M. and Teixeira, J.A. (2002) 'A integração do mercado ibérico: novos ventos, que casamento?', in C. Cavaco (ed.) *Repensar Portugal na Europa: perspectivas de um país periférico*, Lisbon: Centro de Estudos Geográficos.

Royo, S. (2005a) *Regional integration and economic development in the Iberian Peninsula and Mexico*, CIES e-Working Paper, Lisbon: CIES-ISCTE.

Royo, S. (ed.) (2005b) *Portugal, Espanha e a integração europeia: um balanço*, Lisbon: Imprensa de Ciências Sociais.

14 Portugal's experience in the European Union

Lessons for newcomers

Sebastián Royo

Introduction

After decades of relative isolation under an authoritarian regime the success of the Portuguese democratic transition in the second half of the 1970s paved the way for full membership of the European Community. For Portugal, and its European Community (EC) partners this momentous and long-awaited development had profound consequences and set in motion complex processes of adjustment.[1]

There was no dispute that Portugal belonged to Europe. This was not just a geographical fact. Portugal shared its traditions, culture, religion, and intellectual values with the rest of Europe. Moreover, Portugal had historically contributed to the Western and Christian conceptions of mankind and society that were dominant in Europe. Without Portugal the European identity would be only a reflection of an incomplete body. It belonged to Europe. Its entry into the European Community was a reaffirmation of that fact.

The purpose of this chapter is to use the experience of Portugal in the European Union (EU) to draw some lessons that may be applicable two Eastern European countries. Portugal's experience will illustrate some of the opportunities and challenges associated with EU and European Monetary Union (EMU) membership.[2]

Portugal's lessons for newcomers

Portuguese integration into the EC/EU provides useful feedback for the new member states as regards the consequences of membership. *What are the Portuguese integration lessons for post-Communist Europe?*

An incentive to democratize

First, Portugal shows that democratization as a pre-requisite for membership is a powerful incentive to democratize and promote institutional reform. Indeed, European integration had a very important effect on the Portuguese democratization process. Europe had a symbolic impact on "the identification of the EU with liberal democracy and political freedom." The pressures induced by the democratization pre-requisite for membership, the effect of membership prospects on domestic policies and policy direction, and the involvement of political and economic elites in European institutions during negotiations as well as their participation in European transnational networks, all had a very positive impact on the transitions to democracy (Pridham 2002). Moreover, the EC had important indirect levers, particularly during the negotiations for accession, for influencing the direction of events and the decisions of policymakers and economic actors (i.e. economic incentives). As a result Portugal undertook fundamental processes of institutional, social and cultural reforms. Hence, from a political standpoint EU integration has been an unmitigated success, as Portugal has consolidated its democratic regimes and institutions. The two processes – European integration and democratization – were thoroughly intertwined.

Benefits from reintegration into the global community

EU membership paves the way for the complete incorporation of new member states into the major international structures of Europe and the West, as well as the normalization of their relations with their European partners. Portugal has become, again, an important player in Europe. More importantly, accession has allowed the country to influence European policies from within, as Portugal now participates in decisions taken at the European level that affects it, and over which before accession it had little influence, and in any case, no voting power. This is very important because some of the decisions adopted by the EU have an even greater impact on countries than some decisions of their national administrations.

Focus on strategic coalition building

The Portuguese experience also illustrates that any negotiations within the EU should not be based on an "us against them" approach but on a "them versus them" stance. The new member states should take advantage of divisions among older member countries. Portugal's experience shows that despite similar interests and objectives, after two decades of membership, there has been no consistent approach to EU negotiations between Portugal and Spain. They have often cooperated, but they have also worked separately and with other EU members. Portugal and Spain choose alliances depending on the issue at stake. Hence, although the new members (like Portugal and Spain earlier) will find themselves on the same side on many issues (such as social questions, EU structural funds and the concept of cohesion), each new member should develop its own ad hoc coalitions with other members based on common interests.

The Portuguese experience also shows that the aim of the new entrants should be to find the best ways to maximize the benefits of membership once they are in. Countries should remember that negotiations are not final. There are always future rounds. A nakedly selfish strategy that satisfies only particular needs is also bound to fail. The new members also need to look at their potential contribution to the EU and the model of European integration they want to build. Paraphrasing President Kennedy, they should ponder, not only what the EU can do for them but also what they can do for the EU. This should not be a zero-sum-game but instead a positive-sum-game.

Accept that there are both benefits and costs

Portugal also shows that EU membership has both benefits and costs. EU membership has improved the access of countries to both the European common policies and the EU budget. At the same time Portugal's trade with the Community has expanded dramatically over the last two decades, and foreign investment has flooded in. One of the main consequences of these developments has been a reduction in the economic differentials that separated the country from the European average. Since 1986, Portugal's average per capita income has grown from 56 percent of the EU average to about 76 percent. The culmination of this process was the participation of the country as an original founder of the European Monetary Union in 1999. EU integration, however, has also brought significant costs in terms of economic adjustment, loss of sovereignty, and cultural homogenization. In addition, accession has also brought more integration but also fears (exacerbated by issues such as size, culture, and nationalism).

Membership's impact upon public opinion

The Portuguese experience also illustrates that economic success drives public opinion. Indeed, Eurobarometer polls consistently indicate that the overwhelming majority of the Portuguese people support the process of European integration. Originally, this support hinged largely on the expectation that EC membership would increase economic growth and standards of living. Subsequently these polls indicate that this support has become somewhat instrumental because many Portuguese citizens have a utilitarian concept of the European Union – that is, they evaluate the consequences of membership in terms of costs and benefits. Up to this point, since the membership benefits have been explicit (i.e. EU funds) and much larger than the costs, it is not surprising to find a comparatively high level of consistent support for the EU among Portuguese citizens.

Membership supports modernization

An additional lesson is that membership may give countries a better competitive position. Indeed, EU integration has been a catalyst for the final conversion of the Portuguese economy into a modern Western-type economy. The idea of Europe became a driving force that moved reforms forward and it was a fundamental factor for bringing together political stabilization and economic recovery. One of the key consequences of the country's entry into Europe has been that it has facilitated the modernization of its economy, as well as the implementation of the micro- and macro-economic reforms that successive Portuguese governments undertook throughout the 1980s and 1990s (Tovias 2002). In the context of strong support among Portuguese citizens for integration, membership became a facilitating mechanism that allowed successive governments to prioritize economic rather than social modernization and hence, to pursue difficult economic and social policies (i.e. to reform their labour and financial markets), with short-term painful effects. Moreover, as a result of enlargement Portuguese producers gained access to European and world markets, which provided additional incentives for investment and allowed for the development of economies of scale, resulting in increasing competitiveness, and thus attracting investment, which has helped to build these new industries.

Nominal convergence takes place faster than real convergence

Portugal's economic record also shows that nominal convergence is faster but that real economic convergence is a slow process (Tovias 2002).[3] The process of financial liberalization, economic reforms, and the significant decline in real interest rates permitted Portugal to meet the Maastricht convergence criteria (see Table 14.1). Hence, on January 1, 1999 Portugal became a founding member of the European Monetary Union and the country, which as late as 1997 had been considered an outside candidate for joining the Eurozone, fulfilled the inflation, interest rates, debt, exchange rate, and public deficit requirements established by the Maastricht Treaty. This development confirmed the nominal convergence of the country with the rest of the EU.

However, the country's income levels still remain behind the EU average (see Table 14.2). The data show that nominal convergence has advanced at a faster pace than real convergence. Indeed, twenty-five years have not been long enough. Portugal's European integration has revealed both convergence and divergence, nominal and real. In Portugal real convergence has been slowing down each year since 1998, actually turning negative in 2000. Since the accession of Portugal to the EU in 1986, per capita income has increased "only" 14.2 percent. Ireland's, in contrast, has increased 38 percent. In the first fifteen years after integration only Greece with an increase of 6.8, and

Table 14.1 Compliance with EMU convergence criteria, 1996–2009

	1996	*1997*	*2004*	*2009*
Inflation	2.9	1.9	2.6	–0.902
General government deficit	3.2	2.5	–3.496	–7.813
General government gross debt	65.0	61.4	66.3	75.8
Long-term interest rates	8.6	6.4	3.64	4.0

Sources: IMF, European Commission and EMU Reports.

Table 14.2 Divergence of GDP per capita, 1980–2008

	1980 (%)	*1985 (%)*	*1990 (%)*	*2000 (%)*	*2005 (%)*	*2008 (%)*
EU totals	100.0	100.0	100.0	100.0	100.0*	100.0*
Portugal	55.0	52.0	55.7	74.0	73.0	76.0

Source: European Union.

Note
* EU25.

Spain with 11.5 percent have had a lower real convergence than Portugal. A possible explanation for this development has been the fact that while Portugal grew between 1990 and 1998 at an average of 2.5 percent, Ireland grew 7.3 percent over the same period. This growth differential explains divergences in real convergence. Other explanations include the higher level of unemployment, the relatively low rate of labor participation, the inadequate education of the labor force, low investment in R&D and information technology, and inadequate infrastructure. The inadequate structure of the labor market, with high dismissal costs, a relatively centralized collective bargaining system, and a system of unemployment benefits that guarantees income instead of fostering job searching, have also hindered the convergence process. The recent global financial crisis, however, shows that Ireland and Spain's growth was unsustainable, as it was largely based on a real estate bubble.

Migration patterns can be reversed

In addition, the Portuguese experience also shows that patterns of migration can be reversed. Portugal (like Spain) was made to wait for accession until the 1980s, partly over immigration fears that never materialized. As in 1986, the new treaties of accession have established a period of seven years before citizens of the new member states of Central and Eastern Europe may move freely to all member states. Fears of uncontrolled migration were not substantiated after 1986 (or even after the seven-year transition period). On the contrary, as a result of improved economic conditions in Portugal, one of the key results of EU access was that by 1995 there were 110,000 fewer Portuguese living in other EU member states than before enlargement. Furthermore, the reverse process took place, with thousands of Europeans (particularly from Germany and Britain) migrating to Portugal. Such concerns are likely to prove to be unfounded again.

Indeed, the European Commission estimates that from 70,000 to 150,000 workers (of a population of 350 million) could migrate from Eastern Europe to the older member states. This is hardly a large number. The continuing existence of language, cultural, and structural barriers will most likely continue to hinder labor mobility in an enlarged Europe. In addition, the rapid economic growth of

Eastern European countries is likely to have the same effect that it had on migration patterns in Portugal after 1986. Finally, given the EU's aging population and its low fertility rates it will be important to facilitate the migration of young people from Eastern Europe. In the end, instead of displacing local people from the labor market or lowering wages, immigrants from the new member states should contribute to the host country's economy by adding value, creating jobs, and pushing up wages because they will be able to work legally (as several hundred thousand workers are currently working illegally in the EU).[4]

European Union funds did help

It is also important to highlight that the relative economic success of Portugal was influenced by the support that the country received from EU funds. During 1994–99, EU aid accounted for 3.3 percent of Portugal's GDP. EU funding has allowed rates of public investment to remain relatively stable since the mid-1980s. The percentage of public investment financed by EU funds has been rising since 1985, reaching average values of 42 percent. Moreover, the European Commission has estimated that the impact of EU structural funds on GDP growth and employment has been significant. For instance in 1999, these funds added 9.9 percent to GDP growth. These funds have contributed significantly to reduce regional disparities and foster convergence within the EU. As a result, major infrastructure shortcomings have been addressed and road and telecommunications networks have improved dramatically both in quantity and quality. In addition, increased spending on education and training have contributed to upgrading the labor force. In sum, these funds have played a prominent role in developing the factors that improve competitiveness and determine the potential growth of the least developed regions of the country. The new member states should not expect the same level of aid. Therefore, adjustment costs will be higher and it will take them longer to catch up.

EU funds are not the panacea

Indeed, receiving EU funds is by no means a guarantee of success. Ireland received a larger transfer per head than the other three cohesion countries (Greece, Portugal and Spain). Yet its GDP per head grew only from 52 percent of the French levels to 60 percent in 1990. Then in 2000 it surpassed France. Why did it take two decades to accomplish this goal? The key was the process of reforms of the 1990s. In Spain GDP per head grew from 62 to 74 percent and in Portugal it grew from 53 to 69 percent of the French levels from 1986–2001. Greece, for its part, received millions of Euros in EU funds but experienced more than a decade of decline after accession. While it had a higher GDP per head than Ireland until 1986 and a higher one than Portugal until 1987, by 2004 it was the EU's poorest country.

What really matters is not how much money you receive but how you spend it. This evidence illustrates that success is contingent on the good use of regional projects and structural funds (i.e. transport projects). Spain is perceived as a case of success based on its regional policy and structural projects. Portugal, in contrast, has suffered from insufficient matching funds and implementation challenges. This will be particularly critical for the new member states because they will have fewer resources available: the EU allocated only 10.3 billion euros to the new states during the first three years in regional aid and farm subsidies, and Poland has received 67 euros per capita and Hungary 49. In contrast, Greece received 437 per head and Ireland 418.[5]

Success is not automatic: the key is to exploit membership opportunities

The experience of member states also shows that while access to markets is important, EU membership is not enough. Success is not automatic. On the contrary, it is determined largely by how countries exploit the advantages of membership, namely, access to EU markets and the free movement of labor and capital. For instance between 1985 and 2002 the ratio of the stock of inward FDI to GDP grew in Spain from 5 to 33 percent, in Portugal from 19 to 36 percent, whereas in Greece it fell from 20 to 9 percent. In addition, fiscal and monetary discipline and planning, as well as reforms, are also critical. The countries that have performed the best within the EU are the ones that have followed this policy mix. This is so because stability influences the rate of growth and gives confidence to investors. For instance, Greece, one of the worst performers, ran fiscal deficits close to 10 percent until 1996, and its public debt increased from 48 percent of GDP in 1986 to 111 percent in 1996. On the contrary, in Ireland, one of the best performers, debt fell from 112 percent in 1987 to 38 percent by 2000. It is also critical not to use funds to prevent economic reforms and support failing industries. The best models are Ireland with its investment in education (technical colleges), low corporate taxes, and flexible industrial relations,[6] and Finland with its focus on innovation. Finally, it is also important to minimize expectations. Austria, for example, generated too many expectations to oversell EU membership to its citizens, and when they failed to materialize, it created a backlash.

A focus on dynamic effects

While Portugal had feverishly pursued its integration into the Community, the effects of EU integration have not always been favorable. Indeed, in manufacturing and in agriculture there has been both trade diversion and trade creation, implying further adjustment problems, since greater import penetration led to a contraction in domestic production. This was particularly true in the case of the Portuguese manufacturing sector. Factors such as exchange rate movements and the strategies of multinational companies with subsidiaries in the country also played a critical role in the final outcome of integration. This analysis proves that the expected static effects, which were not always favorable to Portugal, should not be the main economic expectation behind the Eastern European countries' entry to EU membership. Based on the Portuguese experience, dynamic effects, on the contrary, provide an important rationale for supporting integration.[7] Over the long term, they will affect the new member states' rate of economic growth, which will be largely influenced by investment patterns, by the efficiency with which these resources are used and, finally, by their distributional effects among regions.

It is essential to prepare for EMU

The Iberian enlargement also shows that prior to monetary integration, candidates must carry out a process of modernization and nominal convergence without fixing their exchange rate. An additional lesson is that the reform of financial institutions does not necessarily bring about institutional changes in other areas (such as the labour market and fiscal policies). The virtual collapse of the European Monetary System in 1992, caused in part by successive devaluations of the Iberian currencies, showed the limitations of financial and monetary instruments to impose institutional reforms in other areas and to balance domestic and external economic objectives. Institutional reforms require active policies by governments that are willing to pay the short-term political price for unpopular policies. The jury is still out regarding the domestic institutional impact of EMU.

Fiscal policies matter

Lax monetary policies played a significant role in the slowdown of the convergence process prior to EC accession (Barry 2003). However since Portugal became a founding member of EMU, monetary policies were no longer in the hands of its national governments. Yet, differences in fiscal policies, within the constraints imposed by the Growth and Stability Pact, have played a central role in economic performance within EMU. It is now widely accepted that increases in government consumption adversely affect long-term growth, and also that while fiscal consolidation may have short-term costs in terms of activity, these costs can be minimized if consolidation is credible, by implementing consistent decisions that deliver solid results.

The Portuguese economy experienced a boom in the second half of the 1990s, boosted by the considerable fall in interest rates, when nominal short-term interest rates converged to those set by the ECB – they fell sharply from an average of 12.3 percent in 1991 to about 6 percent in 1996–2000. They fell more rapidly than inflation and the simultaneous processes of financial liberalization and increasing competition that took place at the same time, which contributed to increasing domestic demand, and in particular housing demand, further boosted their impact. The expansion in these years was driven largely by internal demand. This boom coincided with a period of international expansion. This growth, however, would have required a concomitant prudent fiscal policy, which in the case of Portugal did not take place. On the contrary, the cyclically adjusted primary balance fell from 1.2 percent of GDP in 1994–96 to –0.6 percent in 1999–2001. At the same time, the combination of expansionary fiscal policies and insufficient structural reforms did not prepare the country for the economic downturn.

Indeed, one of the fundamental reasons for the poor performance of the Portuguese economy prior to the 2008 crisis, between 1999 and 2006 was the lack of fiscal discipline and the failure in the adoption of ad hoc measures to control the deficit (see Table 14.3).

Indeed, there is widespread consensus that Portugal's biggest mistake was its "chronic fiscal misbehaviour."[8] Vítor Constâncio, Governor of the Bank of Portugal, has acknowledged that:

> when in 2001 we had these big shocks to growth, tax revenues dropped and suddenly we were in a situation of an excessive deficit … The sudden emergence of budget problems led to an extensive revision of expectations about the future.[9]

Largely as a result of this revision of expectations, the Portuguese economy contracted by 0.8 percent in 2003. The deficit reduction, on the contrary, is credited by Fernando Teixeira dos Santos, Finance Minister, with restoring "Portugal's credibility in international markets and strengthening confidence in the economy."[10] The improvement in the financial position of the budget allowed the government to cut Value Added Tax from 21 to 20 percent in July 2008 to stimulate the economy.

The Portuguese experience shows that countries wishing to join the Eurozone need to have a "comfortable budget position because that will allow room for manoeuvre once inside."[11] Not surprisingly, of the cohesion countries, the ones that have done better in the decade prior to the current global financial crisis have been those who have maintained fiscal discipline, namely Ireland and Spain, which either maintained a budget surplus or reduced their budget deficits to comply with the SGP, while reducing their total expenditures *vis-à-vis* GDP. Portugal, as we have seen, was the exception.

Conversion rates at the time of EMU accession matter

In the case of Portugal, an economic downturn coincided with the country's accession to the EMU, and the adoption of the Euro in 2002. EMU, however, cannot be blamed for the poor performance of the Portuguese economy. If that were the culprit, it would be hard to explain how the other cohesion countries performed much better. Yet, it is important to note that there was a significant difference in the conversion rate of the escudo *vis-à-vis* the euro, which further hampered Portugal's competitiveness (see Goucha Soares 2008: 5). When the national currencies were fixed to the euro at the end of 1998 the Portuguese rate was fixed at 200 escudos to one euro, while the Spanish peseta was converted at a rate of 166 pesetas to one euro). Yet, in the years previous to the final

Table 14.3 General government balance, 2000–2008

	Units	*Scale*	*2000*	*2001*	*2002*	*2003*	*2004*	*2005*	*2006*	*2007*	*2008*
Portugal	General government balance	Percentage of GDP	–2.919	–4.268	–2.839	–2.882	–3.352	–6.124	–3.919	–2.585	–2.611

Source: International Monetary Fund, World Economic Outlook Database, October 2009.

conversion of exchange rates there had been a significant devaluation of the peseta *vis-à-vis* the euro. It had devalued about 30 percent, while the escudo had devalued only 12 percent (in the early 1990s the exchange rate was 128 pesetas to one euro, and 179 escudos to one euro, respectively). In other words, the fixed exchange rate at which Spain joined EMU was significantly more favorable than Portugal's. This problem was compounded by the appreciation of the real effective exchange rate in the 1990s due to wage increases. While it depreciated by approximately 15 percent in Spain, in Portugal it appreciated by the same amount. According to the European Commission, the Portuguese real effective exchange rate is approximately 20 percent higher than it was in the early 1990s (while Spain's is at the same level). This is an important consideration when trying to account for the loss of competitiveness of Portugal.

EMU membership carries risks

Portugal provides interesting insights into the pitfalls of integration into a monetary union. As noted by Vítor Constâncio, Governor of the Bank of Portugal, one of the main lessons from Portugal's experience is that "countries previously used to high inflation and high interest rates are likely to experience an explosion in consumer spending and borrowing" upon joining the monetary union. This spurt will make a downturn inevitable, particularly in cases such as Portugal that are vulnerable to higher oil prices and increasing competition from developing countries like India and China. In Portugal the strong demand stemmed from the sharp fall in interest rates and it was further fuelled by expansive fiscal policies. Demand, however, was not followed by a parallel increase in supply, as it was hindered by low productivity growth, which led to a significant increase in imports and high external deficits and debts. External indebtedness in turn has led to lower available income domestically.

For a decade, Central and Eastern European countries have seen EMU membership as a prize and have been willing to do anything to join. However, the current global financial crisis has exposed the weaknesses of the EMU. While Eurozone countries like Portugal, which no longer have the option to devalue their currencies, are undergoing massive fiscal tightening and a brutal internal devaluation, lowering real wages and prices to regain competitiveness and growth, non-Eurozone countries like Poland and the Czech Republic have allowed their currencies to fall (i.e. Poland's real effective exchange rate fell almost 20 percent between 2008 and 2009), thus boosting their competitiveness and evading recession.[12]

While these countries have currencies that are too small to thrive independently and they have high levels of Euro borrowing, there are potential lessons from Portugal's experience for future EMU applicants (Abreu 2006: 5). The most important lesson is that lower interest rates and the loosening of credit is likely to lead to a credit boom, driven by potentially over-optimistic expectations of future permanent income, which in turn may increase housing demand and household indebtedness, and lead to overestimations of potential output and to expansionary fiscal policies. The boom will also lead to higher wage increases, caused by the tightening of the labour market, higher inflation and losses in external competitiveness, together with a shift from the tradable to the non-tradable sector of the economy, which would have a negative impact on productivity.

In order to avoid these risks new entrant countries should tighten budgetary policies in the case of a boom in demand and/or strong credit expansion. At the same time, they should guard against potential overestimation of GDP, and measure carefully the weight of consumption on GDP, because they may inflate revenues in the short-term and create an unrealistic perception of the budgetary accounts. Furthermore, to avoid unsustainable external imbalances, countries should also carry out the necessary structural reforms to increase flexibility and productivity, in order to allow their productive sectors to respond to the increasing demand and to ensure that their economies can withstand the pressures of membership. They should also set wages based on Eurozone conditions to ensure wage moderation, and not on unrealistic domestic expectations (Abreu 2006: 5–6). New EMU members should also take the opportunity presented by the boom to move into higher value-added and faster growth sectors and towards a more outward-oriented production structure. Finally, the current global crisis has illustrated the need for tight financial supervision to avoid excessive lending and misallocation of resources.

The need to control labor costs to remain competitive

The experience of Portugal within the EMU also shows that there have been lasting performance differences across countries. These differences can be explained at least in part by a lack of responsiveness of prices and wages, which have not adjusted smoothly across sectors, and in the case of Portugal have led to accumulated competitiveness losses and large external imbalances. While Germany (and other EMU countries) implemented supply-side reforms to bring labor costs down, through wage restraint, payroll tax cuts, and productivity increases, making it the most competitive economy with labour costs 13 percent below the Eurozone average, Portugal continued with the tradition of indexing wage increases to domestic inflation rather than the European Central Bank target, and they became the most expensive ones, with Portuguese labour costs 23.5 percent above average (followed by Spain with 16 percent, Greece with 14 percent, and Italy with 5 percent).[13]

Awareness of new players in world trade and the erosion of comparative advantage

A problem for Portugal has been the dramatic erosion of its comparative advantage. The emergence of major new players in world trade, like India and China, as well as the Eastern enlargements of the European Union have been particularly damaging to the Portuguese economy because these countries have lower labor costs and they competed with Portugal's traditional exports (as an exporter of relatively unsophisticated labor-intensive products), which led to losses in export market shares (aggravated by the appreciation of the Euro, and the increase of unit labor costs relative to those in its trading competitors). At the same time Portugal's attempt to specialize in medium- and higher-technology products was also hindered by the accession of the Eastern European countries into the EU, which were moving into those sectors and also specializing in these products.

In the end, the country's ability to keep the lid on unitary labor costs was insufficient to generate enough growth in exports to compensate for decreasing domestic demand. While easy access to cheap credit had boosted domestic demand in households, it also caused a shift of resources from the tradable to non-tradable (services). This shift was further hastened by high wage increases, also in the public sector, caused by a tighter labor market in the second half of the 1990s, which further hampered external competitiveness and productivity. The result was an imbalanced economy sustained by strong domestic demand that translated into higher imports (and external deficit).

Until 2000 the impact of wage increases was offset by high productivity growth (it grew yearly at an average of 2.2 percent between 1996 and 2000), thus limiting the growth of unit labor costs. After 2000, however, the international expansionary cycle started to reverse, particularly in the EU (the leading market for Portuguese exports), where growth slowed to 1.4 percent between 2001 and 2003 (compared to 2.8 percent between 1995 and 2000). This deceleration of the international economic cycle hit Portugal severely and affected expectations among consumers and businesses.

Furthermore, some Portuguese sectors of the economy did not prepare well for the WTO liberalization of sectors with major economic impact in the country, particularly footwear and textiles. The situation was compounded by the Asian crisis of the late 1990s, which led to the devaluation of these currencies, further eroding the competitiveness of Portuguese exports. As a result, Portuguese exports of footwear and textiles fell from almost two-thirds of total exports of goods between 1995 and 1996, to a little more than one-third between 2004 and 2005, with the concurrent wave of job losses and closures, which further dampened expectations and caused social problems, particularly in the north of the country, where these industries are based (Abreu 2006: 3–4).

Political stability is essential

There is consensus that one of the key problems in Portugal prior to 2006 was the lack of political stability. Indeed, there have been more changes at the prime ministerial level (there were four PMs between 1995 and 2005), and the previous three prime ministers (before Sócrates) resigned before their terms were over for different reasons. These constant changes up to 2005 made economic policy continuity more problematic and, more importantly, made the implementation of reforms in the face of popular opposition very difficult.

Furthermore, the minister of finance position became a revolving door, bringing instability to the economic policy portfolio, with ministers often resigning in protest at their inability to hold sway over their colleagues and control fiscal policies and expenditures. Between 1990 and 2005 there were ten ministers of finance, and on average they have been less than two years in the position. The problem was compounded by the finance minister's limited powers over the budget. Indeed, according to a recent study (Halleberg *et al.* 2004) of all the EU-15 finance ministers the Portuguese one has the lowest control over the formulation, approval, and implementation of the budget.

This problem extends to other critical areas, such as education, where Maria Isabel Girão de Melo Veiga Vilar Alçada, the Minister of Education (as of 2009), was the twenty-eighth education minister in thirty-three years.

In the end, the credibility of economic policies (and fiscal policies in particular) was undermined by the relative political instability that prevailed in Portugal in the first half of the 2000s. It is not surprising, therefore, that once some stability has been achieved in the position (Fernando Teixeira dos Santos has been in the position for over four years, the longest tenure in the past eighteen years), the government has been able to implement substantive reforms and pursue fiscal consolidation. The fact that the Socialist Party had an absolute majority in parliament until September 2009 was also an important factor in facilitating the implementation of reforms.

Conclusion

For Portugal and the new member states, the EU symbolizes modernization and democracy. In Portugal the European integration process has facilitated the reincorporation of the country into the international arena, has contributed to the legitimacy of the new democratic regime, acted as a buffer in controversial issues (such as the implementation of economic reforms), and facilitated and accelerated the process of convergence and modernization of financial, commercial, and manufacturing structures. The idea of Europe became a driving force that moved reforms forward and was a fundamental factor in bringing together political stabilization, economic recovery, and democratic consolidation.

Table 14.4 Portuguese Ministers of Finance, 1990–2010

July 21, 2005–June 21, 2011	Fernando Teixeira dos Santos
March 12, 2005	Luís Campos e Cunha
July 17, 2004	António Bagão Félix
April 6, 2002	Maria Manuela Ferreira Leite
July 3, 2001	Guilherme d'Oliveira Martins
October 25, 1999	Joaquim Augusto Nunes de Pina Moura
October 28, 1995	António Luciano Pacheco de Sousa Franco
December 12, 1993	Eduardo Almeida Catroga
October 31, 1991	Jorge Braga de Macedo
January 4, 1990	Luís Miguel Beleza

Yet, despite all the significant progress accomplished over the last two decades, Portugal still has considerable ground to cover to catch up with the richest EU countries. The current global crisis is illustrating even further the country's vulnerability. Although EU membership will facilitate (and in many cases ameliorate) adjustment costs, and provide the impetus for reforms, the experience of Portugal shows that this is no substitute for the domestic implementation of reforms, which should proceed further in areas such as labor, production, and capital markets. The success of the EU member states will hinge to a considerable degree on the ability of their leaders to implement reforms in the face of domestic resistance and increasing scepticism about EU/EMU membership.

Notes

1 References to the European Economic Community (EEC) or the European Union (EU) can be misleading if the historical period covered extends back to 1991. This chapter addresses themes in the European Economic Community prior to the introduction of the European Union label in the Maastricht Treaty of 1991. The terms "the European Community" (EC) or "the European Union" (EU) are used indistinctly to refer to the European integration process and institutions throughout the chapter. Similarly, "Europe" is here always used to refer to the countries that are members of the European Union, either before or after the Maastricht Treaty.

2 This chapter borrows from Royo and Manuel (2003), Royo (2003), Royo (2006) and Royo (2012).

3 While there is significant controversy over the definition of real convergence, most scholars agree that per capita GDP is a valid reference for measuring a country's living standards.

4 See: "UK leads way on opening borders to new workers," in *Financial Times*, December 13, 2002, p. 2, and "Fears of big move west may be unfounded," in *Financial Times*, December 2, 2002, p. 4.

5 See: "EU novices hope to roar like Irish 'Celtic tigers' rather than star in Greek tragedy," in *Financial Times*, April 22, 2004, p. 3, and "Coming Together: a small step for Europe's economy but a giant leap for the continent," in *Financial Times*, April 26, 2004, p. 11. It is also important to place all this in context: Ireland and Spain also made dubious investment decisions, as shown by the 2008 crisis.

6 The Irish model was also based, however, in a real estate bubble and poor risk management on the part of the Irish financial institutions. In the end these factors led to the virtual collapse of the Irish economy, which had to be rescued by the EU/IMF in the winter of 2010.

7 Static effects refer to trade creation and diversion, while dynamic effects refer to foreign direct investment.

8 Martin Wolf, "Struggling to tackle bad fiscal behaviour," in *Financial Times*, April 8, 2008, pp. 1–2 (special section on *Investing in Portugal*).

9 "Concerns about divergence 'overlook ability to change'," interview with Vítor Constâncio. Governor of the Bank of Portugal in *Financial Times*, May 16, 2008, p. 2.

10 Interview in *Financial Times*, See "Tough cuts to strengthen confidence," in *Financial Times*, April 8, 2008, p. 2 (special section on *Investing in Portugal*).

11 "Concerns about divergence 'overlook ability to change'," interview with Vítor Constâncio. Governor of the Bank of Portugal in *Financial Times*, May 16, 2008, p. 2.

12 Neil Buckley, "Eastern nations ready for long wait to tie knot with the euro," in *Financial Times*, May 24, 2010.

13 Stefan Collignon, "Germany keeps dancing as the iceberg looms," in *Financial Times*, January 20, 2009, p. 13.

Bibliography

Abreu, Orlando (2006) "Portugal's boom and bust: lessons for euro newcomers," in *ECFIN Country Focus*, 3 (16), December 22.

Barry, Frank (2003) "Economic integration and convergence process in the EU cohesion countries," in *Journal of Common Market Studies*, 41 (5), pp. 1–25.

Goucha Soares, António, (2008) "Portugal: The Incomplete Europeanization," paper presented at the 2008 Annual Meeting of the American Political Science Association. Boston, MA, August 29.

International Monetary Fund (2009) World Economic Outlook Database, October.

Halleberg, M., R. Strauch, and J. von Hagen (2004) "The Design of Fiscal Rules and Forms of Governance in European Union Countries," *ECB Working Paper* No. 419, December.

Pridham, Geoffrey (2002) "European Integration and Democratic Consolidation in Southern Europe," in António Costa Pinto and Nuno Severiano Teixeira (eds), *Southern Europe and the Making of the European Union*. New York: Columbia University Press, 185–86.

Royo, Sebastián (2003) "The 2004 Enlargement: Iberian lessons from Communist Europe," in Sebastián Royo and Paul C. Manuel (eds), *Spain and Portugal in the European Union*. London: Frank Cass.

Royo, Sebastián and Paul C. Manuel (eds) (2003) "Some lessons from the fifteenth anniversary of the accession of Portugal and Spain to the European Union," in Royo, Sebastián and Paul C. Manuel (eds), *Spain and Portugal in the European Union*. London: Frank Cass.

Royo, Sebastián. (2006) "The Challenges of EU Integration," in Joaquín Roy and Roberto Domínguez (eds), *Towards the Completion of Europe: Analysis and Perspectives of the New European Union Enlargement*. Miami: Jean Monnet EU Chair, University of Miami.

Royo, Sebastián (2012) "Portugal and Spain in the EU," in Sebastián Royo (ed.), *Portugal in the Twenty-First Century: Politics, Society and Economics*. New York: Lexington Books.

Tovias, Alfred (2002) "The Southern European Economies and European Integration," in António Costa Pinto and Nuno Severiano Teixeira, eds., *Southern Europe and the Making of the European Union*. New York: Columbia University Press.

15 In the eye of the storm

Portugal and the European crisis

André Azevedo Alves

Introduction: the international crisis and the Portuguese economy in 2010

The Portuguese crisis came at the culmination of a decade of economic stagnation and mounting internal and external imbalances. The first years of EU membership were relatively successful for Portugal. In the first decade as a member of the EU (1986–1996), the Portuguese economy exhibited an average real GDP growth rate of 3.6 per cent, well above the 2.4 per cent average experienced in the same period by the countries that currently make up the euro area (OECD, 2011a). The process of convergence continued until the end of the 1990s, although in the later years of the decade it was already losing steam. Additionally, in 2000 several key imbalances were already visible, namely the extremely rapid growth of public social expenditure – an expansion from 12.5 per cent to 18.9 per cent of GDP in just 10 years (OECD, 2011b) – and a negative current account balance that surpassed 10 per cent of GDP (OECD, 2011a). What followed in the next decade was essentially a prolonged period of economic stagnation that created the setting for a perfect storm when the international crisis finally hit the Portuguese economy at full strength in 2010.

The international financial and economic crisis had a significant impact on Portugal essentially from late 2008 onwards. The Portuguese economy experienced zero growth in 2008 and contracted by 2.5 per cent of GDP in 2009. But the most severe consequences came in 2010, when widening spreads on sovereign debt reached an unsustainable level. The persistent inability of Portuguese governments to reign in public deficits (since 2001 there was only one year – 2002 – when the public deficit was contained within the 3 per cent limit) reached a climax in 2009, with the fiscal imbalance surpassing 10 per cent of GDP (OECD, 2011a). As would be expected, the persistence of high levels of public deficits had consequences in terms of the Portuguese government's gross financial liabilities: a rapid rise from about 60 per cent of GDP in 2000, to 73 per cent in 2005 and 103 per cent in 2010.

In addition to the accumulation of unsustainable imbalances in public finances, by 2010 the Portuguese economy also suffered gravely from a long period of gradually deteriorating conditions in terms of international competitiveness. The average growth of unit labour costs in the Portuguese economy since 1986 surpassed by a substantial margin the euro area average and, unsurprisingly, this coincided with a rise in the structural unemployment rate from a 6.1 per cent average in the 1996–2005 period to 8.1 per cent in 2010 (OECD, 2011a). The lack of competitiveness combined with the much easier (public and private) financing conditions that came (until the crisis) with membership of the European monetary union resulted in a persistent current account negative balance that stood at about 10 per cent of GDP from 2005 to 2010.

By 2010, the Portuguese unemployment rate stood close to 11 per cent – above the eurozone average of 9.9 per cent – which compared with unemployment of only 4 per cent at 2000 – at a time when the eurozone average was 8.3 per cent (OECD, 2011a). Furthermore, the Portuguese unemployment problems are compounded by a markedly dual labour market setting where insiders holding regular contracts enjoy some of the strongest legal protections in the world, while outsiders – mostly young and/or unskilled workers – stand at the margins holding temporary contracts or working under other formal and informal arrangements that aim to circumvent the extremely rigid conditions of 'normal' contracts (OECD, 2010).

The overall conditions of the Portuguese economy were therefore already quite grim before the impact of the international crisis, but these weak conditions also meant that the crisis had a more devastating impact than in other euro area countries. Additionally, the Portuguese government's austerity measures enacted in 2010 proved insufficient to consolidate Portuguese public finances and substantially reduce the external deficit. The combination of weak growth prospects, severe fiscal imbalances and international uncertainty in financial markets led investors to demand progressively wider spreads on Portuguese debt, and the bail-out requests by Greece in April 2010 and then by Ireland in November of 2010 made the prospect of a bail-out request by Portugal in the following months increasingly likely.

The request for emergency assistance and the June 2011 elections

With pressing financing needs, weak economic growth prospects, and growing unrest in international financial markets, the rising interest rates quickly reached an unsustainable point for the Portuguese governmment. Faced with a quickly deteriorating scenario, in early March 2011 it compiled a set of additional internal emergency measures to control the budget deficit. Although these were assessed positively by the European Commission and the European Central Bank, they were not approved by the Portuguese Parliament. Given that the then leader of the Socialist Party José Sócrates had linked his own political survival as prime minister directly to his ability to avoid resorting to an external financial rescue, it was not surprising that following the parliamentary rejection of what would have been his government's fourth internal austerity package on 24 March, he handed in his resignation and called for early elections (*Economist*, 2011a).

The further surge in Portuguese sovereign debt yields – with two-year bond yields surpassing 10 per cent – led the caretaker government to request emergency financial assistance from the UE and the IMF on 7 April 2011 (European Commission, 2011a, p. 14; *Economist*, 2011b). The €78 billion bail-out deal was negotiated with the European Commission, the European Central Bank and the IMF (the so-called 'Troika'), and the agreement was reached with Sócrates acting as caretaker prime minister but sponsored also by the Social Democratic party, PSD, the main party in the opposition, and by the smaller opposition party, CDS.

The campaign leading up to the 5 June legislative elections was – as would be expected – dominated by discussions about the precarious economic and financial situation of the country, and the heavy defeat imposed on the ruling Socialist party (which fell from a result of over 36 per cent in 2009 to just 28 per cent in 2011) came as no surprise. For its part, PSD increased its level of support from 29 per cent in 2009 to close to 39 per cent in 2011. Despite the substantial rise in support, PSD fell short of achieving an absolute majority in parliament, but still had enough seats (108) to surpass the 115 threshold necessary to form a majority parliamentary coalition with CDS-PP which gathered close to 12 per cent of the vote and 24 seats.

The new centre-right government led by Pedro Passos Coelho has framed its objectives in very ambitious terms, outlining a reform agenda that openly seeks to go beyond the requirements imposed by the bail-out package agreed with the Troika and dramatically reshape the Portuguese economy (*Economist*, 2011c):

> 'We will be much more ambitious', he insists, outlining plans for social security, health and education reforms that go beyond the rescue package. He wants to meet deficit-reduction targets ahead of schedule and extend the privatisation programme to include water utilities and the postal service. The aim is to 'surprise' investors so that Portugal can resume borrowing in the capital markets.

Although backed by a parliamentary majority, the new government faces a tremendous task. In addition to the very difficult economic and financial circumstances, the executive will also have to deal with a political culture that – notwithstanding the 2011 election results in the context of a severe crisis – is in large part shaped by a long tradition of anti-liberalization sentiments and dependence on the state by influential sections of Portuguese society, including important segments of the new prime minister's own political party (Alves, 2011; *Economist*, 2011c).

Regardless of the extent to which the new government will be able to fulfill its rhetoric, one thing appears fairly certain: the developments in Portuguese politics and in the country's position within the European Union and the eurozone and will be closely linked with the conditions established in the bail-out agreement reached with the Troika and the degree of success in their execution.

The Troika's memorandum: main guidelines and implementation

The terms of the rescue package provided to Portugal were set in the May 2011 'Memorandum of Understanding on Specific Economic Policy Conditionality' (European Commission, 2011a: 58–93). The key fiscal objectives were set as follows:

> Reduce the Government deficit to below EUR 10,068 million (equivalent to 5.9% of GDP based on current projections) in 2011, EUR 7,645 million (4.5% of GDP) in 2012 and EUR 5,224 million (3.0% of GDP) in 2013 by means of high-quality permanent measures and minimising the impact of consolidation on vulnerable groups; bring the government debt-to-GDP ratio on a downward path as of 2013; maintain fiscal consolidation over the medium term up to a balanced budgetary position, notably by containing expenditure growth; support competitiveness by means of a budget-neutral adjustment of the tax structure.

The proposed path to achieve the fiscal consolidation goals and simultaneously reignite economic growth sets out a vast range of measures and specific targets. In terms of cost reductions, the Troika's memorandum outlines the main expenditure cuts to be achieved in education, the health sector, pensions and social benefits, transfers to local authorities, state-owned enterprises and also reductions in capital expenditure. On the receipt side, the main measures outlined in the memorandum are increases in VAT revenues (through reductions in VAT exemptions and changes in the categories of goods and services subject to lower rates) and excise taxes, as well as reductions in both corporate and personal income tax deductions, benefits and special regimes. Additionally, the memorandum puts forth changes in property taxation directed at increasing revenue, and stresses the need to reduce tax evasion, fraud and informality.

In what concerns the financial sector, the main concerns outlined in the memorandum are directed at sustaining the stability and liquidity of the financial sector and strengthening banking regulation. A number of policies are also directed at improving efficiency levels in Portuguese public administration and streamlining existing structures and budgets. Further cost reductions are expected from measures targeted at reviewing existing public–private partnerships, and the Portuguese government is required to eliminate special rights in private firms ('golden shares') and to speed up its privatization programme, which is supposed to include a range of state-owned firms and state participation in transportation, energy, industry and communications.

The memorandum also puts forth several ambitious objectives in terms of labour market reform to stimulate job creation and enhance flexibility and competitiveness but the recommendations in terms of actual legislative changes and Active Labour Market Policies are for the most part vague. Largely the same can be said about the memorandum's objectives in terms of reforming the housing market, improving the operation of the judicial system and increasing competition in energy markets and in the services sector. At best, these may serve as guidance principles for reform; at worst, they risk being mostly statements of wishful thinking.

As of October 2011, implementation of the memorandum has been the main driving factor in the Portuguese government's policy. The August 2011 joint assessment by an EC/ECB/IMF mission deemed the programme's execution to be on track, and praised the Portuguese government's commitment to fulfilling its objectives and its quick and determined reaction to shortfalls and hidden debts in public finances that had emerged (European Commission, 2011b).

Notwithstanding the Portuguese government's commitment and a positive first review by the Troika, the challenges faced in late 2011 by the Portuguese economy are truly tremendous, some would say overwhelming. So far, the measures with the most impact have been a range of tax increases and public sector wage cuts. An extraordinary one-off tax of 50 per cent on the extra one month's salary received as a December bonus has been enacted for all (private- and public-sector) workers and VAT and other tax increases – as well as wide-ranging reductions in deductions and benefits – have been announced. To achieve the 5.9 per cent budget deficit target in 2011, pension funds from the banking sector are to be transferred to the state social security system – also a one-off measure that, at best, only buys time while more structural fiscal reform is enacted. For the time being, the 'fiscal devaluation' strategy outlined in the memorandum (reducing social security contributions to cut labor costs) has been postponed and replaced by an increase of 30 minutes a day in private sector working hours. But quite possibly the most significant measure so far has been the announcement that the extra two months' pay normally received as Summer and Christmas bonuses will be cut for most public sector workers and pensioners for the duration of the external assistance programme (*Economist*, 2011d). With this additional measure, the accumulated wage cuts for a substantial part of public sector workers are now in the region of 25 per cent.

However, even though the Portuguese government appears to be determined to meet the targets set in the memorandum, it remains to be seen if it will be able to achieve the necessary public expenditure cuts in a way that is both economically and socially sustainable. With the Portuguese economy expected to continue in recession throughout 2012 and unemployment reaching record highs, the potential for social and political unrest is correspondingly on the rise, and much will depend on whether economic reforms are able to foster increased competitiveness quickly, under very difficult internal and international conditions.

The Portuguese crisis in context

A mix of internal and external factors have contributed to the current Portuguese situation (Alves, 2011). The favourable conditions – in terms of EU transfers, investment flows and low interest rates – that came with membership in the EU and the eurozone were associated in the Portuguese case with a rapid expansion of public expenditure (particularly social transfers and benefits) and of public and private debt levels. While part of this evolution can be explained by convergence trends in terms of public expenditure that were to be expected (Tavares and Alves, 2006), the actual increases were of such a magnitude that internal political and social factors must also be factored in (OECD, 2011b; Alves, 2011, pp. 47–48).

After an initial period of relatively successful reforms and economic convergence from 1986 until the late 1990s the Portuguese economy has basically stagnated from that point onwards. Excessive growth of wages with low productivity growth (Blanchard, 2007), labour market and regulatory rigidities, an inefficient justice system (Alves, 2011, p. 49) and increased competition from Asian and Eastern European economies, are all likely to have played a part in Portugal's disappointing economic performance, in conjunction with the difficulties experienced in the process of adjustment to the new monetary regime (Aguiar-Conraria *et al.*, 2010).

An additional significant factor – and one that has been fuelled partly by the political competition for EU funds – is the persistence of high levels of cronyism and rent-seeking activity in Portugal. Problems continue to arise from lack of trust in Portuguese government officials and regulators (Rego *et al.*, 2006) and the salience of this issue can be evidenced, for example, by the fact that the Troika's memorandum includes an explicit reference to the need to 'ensure a level playing field and minimise rent-seeking behaviour' (European Commission, 2011a, p. 90).

Several of Portugal's main structural problems outlined above are similar to those of Greece, Spain, Italy, and, to a lesser extent, Ireland, but there are also important differences. On the one hand, Portugal experienced a comparatively small real estate bubble and the banking sector's exposure to toxic assets has been relatively limited. On the other hand, the Portuguese case is quite possibly the most serious within the group in terms of sluggish economic growth and lack of competitiveness.

Debt figures are not easily comparable because implicit and indirect obligations often distort figures, but net debt interest payments provide a reasonably objective indication of how Portugal stands in comparison with Greece, Italy, Ireland and Spain. According to OECD (2011a) estimates, Portuguese general government net debt interest payments are expected to rise from 4.2 per cent of GDP in 2011 to 4.8 per cent in 2012. In the euro area, and for 2012, only Greece is expected to face a heavier burden with government net debt interest payments of 5.6 per cent of GDP, while projections for Italy stand at 4.7 per cent, for Ireland at 3.9 per cent, and for Spain at a rather less menacing figure of 1.9 per cent of GDP.

Future prospects for Portugal in the European Union

Discussing possible scenarios in such a volatile setting is a high-risk, speculative endeavour but nevertheless some considerations can be made about the most likely options and outcomes as of late 2011. International developments – particularly in the European Union – will, of course, be crucial not only to future prospects for Portugal but even in terms of defining the options that will be realistically available to Portuguese policy makers and to the Portuguese economy.

At this point there would seem to be essentially three main scenarios for Portugal. The first would be an exit from the single currency (propelled either by external or internal factors or by a combination of both). This would almost certainly entail a substantial currency devaluation and a default on Portuguese debt denominated in euros. As in the pre-euro past, the effects of shortcomings in competitiveness would be addressed through monetary policy and meaningful structural reforms would probably be avoided. A variation of this first scenario would be a German exit from the euro (possibly accompanied by a handful of other eurozone members). The main effects in this variation would not differ much for Portugal, regardless of whether a weaker and devalued euro would persist or collapse entirely leading to the outcome already described above.

A second scenario would consist in Portugal staying in and somehow managing to enact the adjustment programme successfully, while at the same time relaunching economic growth. This seems a difficult triangulation, and one that would require bold and decisive structural reforms. Even so, the Portuguese external debt burden is so high that the only possible execution of this second scenario may well be one that also includes some form of haircut.

A third scenario would involve Portugal staying in the eurozone on the basis of the establishment of some form of transfer union within the eurozone. This could be achieved either through fiscal transfers or through a further loosening of the ECB's monetary policy, and would necessarily entail greater economic and political centralization as well as a substantial additional loss of national sovereignty. Although this would seem to be the preferred approach of large segments of the EU's political elites, its feasibility is far from certain and the broader question of how to integrate the very different economies of southern Europe with those of the northern and central part of the Continent remains an open one.

The difficult path ahead for Portugal

The discussion about the tensions in the European integration project that arise from the coexistence of a northern core and a southern 'flaky fringe' are far from new (Verney, 2009) but the debt crisis in the eurozone has brought it to the forefront of European politics.

Community cohesion policies were designed mostly to address this gap but the observed patterns of economic divergences and the crisis has made it clear that they have largely failed in that key objective. The establishment of a fully fledged transfer union seems unlikely in the near future given the resistance of German and northern European electorates.

On the other hand, an exit by Portugal (or Germany) from the euro, while certainly possible, is likely to remain as a last-resort option since the general position among the EU's political elites seems to be that this would be an outcome with potentially disastrous and wide-reaching political implications.

In Portugal's case, the decisive factor for the medium-term outlook would appear to be the enactment of the adjustment programme and its economic and social consequences. If the adjustment measures are successful and the international situation does not deteriorate to the point where collapse of the euro becomes inevitable, a staying-in scenario would seem to be more likely. At the same time, given the lack of competitiveness in the Portuguese economy and the public and private debt levels, it is hard to see how some form of partial default can be avoided, so perhaps a mix of continued external assistance with a structured creditor's haircut is a more realistic prospect. In any case, the degree of enactment and success in achieving structural reforms and reducing fiscal imbalances to a manageable level will be crucial.

In addition to achieving credible fiscal consolidation, other factors likely to be decisive for the sustainability of Portugal's position in the European integration process are the increasing flexibility of labour markets, the promotion of a more open, competitive environment and substantial foreign investment flows. Partly due to specificities in the Portuguese administrative tradition, state reform has generally been a slow and cumbersome process (Tavares and Alves, 2006). In such a context, a credible external push for structural reforms does not ensure a successful outcome, but may be quite useful and, in many important regards, the best external assistance that can be provided to Portugal at this point.

References

Aguiar-Conraria, L., Alexandre, F. and Pinho, M. C. (2010) 'O euro e o crescimento da economia portuguesa: uma análise contrafactual', *NIPE Working Paper*, 37, 1–21.

Alves, A. A. (2011) 'The Portuguese Malaise: Structural Causes of the Crisis and Lessons for the Eurozone', *Economic Affairs*, 31 (2): 47–52.

Blanchard, Olivier (2007) 'Adjustment within the euro. The difficult case of Portugal'. *Portuguese Economic Journal*, 6 (1): 1–21.

Economist, The (2011a) 'Portugal's government collapses: The death of Sócrates', 23 March (online edition). www.economist.com/blogs/newsbook/2011/03/portugals_government_collapses. Accessed 16 October 2011.

Economist, The (2011b) 'Sócrates' poison: A deal is agreed, but will it work?', 5 May (print edition). www.economist.com/node/18651749. Accessed 17 October 2011.

Economist, The (2011c) 'A grim inheritance: The next Portuguese prime minister promises much, but promises are cheap', 9 June (print edition). www.economist.com/node/18805349. Accessed 16 October 2011.

Economist, The (2011d) 'In the mire: Austerity, austerity – always austerity', 22 October (print edition). www.economist.com/node/21533438. Accessed 26 October 2011.

European Commission (2011a) 'The Economic Adjustment for Portugal', *European Economy Occasional Papers*, 79, Directorate-General for Economic and Financial Affairs. http://ec.europa.eu/economy_finance/publications/occasional_paper/2011/op79_en.htm. Accessed 23 October 2011.

European Commission (2011b) 'The Economic Adjustment Programme for Portugal. First review – Summer 2011' *European Economy Occasional Papers*, 83, Directorate-General for Economic and Financial Affairs. http://ec.europa.eu/economy_finance/publications/occasional_paper/2011/op83_en.htm. Accessed 23 October 2011.

OECD (2010), *OECD Economic Surveys: PORTUGAL, September 2010*. www.oecd.org/dataoecd/34/20/46062172.pdf. Accessed 16 October 2011.

OECD (2011a), *OECD Economic Outlook 89 database*. www.oecd.org/oecdEconomicOutlook. Accessed 14 October 2011.

OECD (2011b), 'Social Expenditure – Aggregated Data', OECD Stat, www.stats.oecd. Accessed 10 October 2011.

Rego, A., Sarrico, C. S. and Moreira, J. M. (2006) 'Trust in Portuguese Public Authorities', *Public Integrity*, 8 (1): 77–92.

Tavares, L. V. and Alves, A. A. (2006) 'The Future of Portuguese Public Administration and a New Agenda for Public Administration Sciences in the 21st Century', *Public Administration*, 84 (2): 389–406.

Verney, Susannah (2009) 'Flaky Fringe? Southern Europe Facing the Financial Crisis, South European Society and Politics', 14 (1): 1–6.

16 Conclusion

Laura C. Ferreira-Pereira and A.J.R. Groom

This volume has so far reflected an essentially sectoral approach, with chapters on agriculture, trade and various other issues of a political, economic or social nature. Portugal's history in the period that we have covered has been full of movement and its experiences before that were even more so, as it managed to move from being a country of Empire to a post-colonial European state like many others. Initially, Portugal found this transition more difficult than most others, but there was subsequently a catching up, as we can see from the chapters in this volume. To be sure, Portugal's 25 years' experience of integration is an integral part of the complex and multidimensional historical process of redefining the country's contemporary identity and international role. EC/EU membership, along with the consolidation of democracy and subsequent adaptation of policies and institutions to meet European standards, constitutes two sides of the same coin.

As this study has hopefully confirmed, after 25 years of full engagement in the European integration process, Portugal has made a shift from being a nation state *tout court* to being a member state. Be that as it may, the chapters appraising the impact of EU membership upon Portuguese foreign and security policy suggest that this shift has not been all-encompassing or unconditional. This is reflected in the continued zeal for the safeguarding of autonomy in the formulation and implementation of foreign, security and defence policy.

EU membership in perspective: not a leap of faith, but a stark reality

The application for membership in 1977 was not a leap of faith. By then, the EEC was synonymous with democracy (with all its inherent political and civil freedoms), prosperity, stability and modernity. As some chapters of this book have demonstrated, the first decade or so of Portugal's membership experience can be said to correspond to a 'golden' period, particularly for the national economy with the country being able to modernize itself and catch up with its more affluent European partners. Yet, before the beginning of the new century, Portugal was already distancing itself from the latter thereby moving to the bottom of the averages for the GDP per capita. In fact, the country's gap with the

EU average in terms of growth rates, GDP per capita, budget deficits, levels of productivity, competitiveness and unemployment has increased over the last decade. Such a poor performance against the backdrop of continued material support substantiated in European structural funds has fostered legitimate perceptions of both disappointing failures and missed opportunities for a sound 'leap forward' in the direction of sustainable economic growth and social development.

Participation in the EMU and subsequent credit boom created the illusion that 'good times' would endure and, ultimately, could only get better. The context is marked by the lack, or intermittent application, of structural reforms (namely, in the domains of justice, health, education, the social security system and public administration), continued low productivity and higher labour costs. At the same time the new Eastern European member states have emerged as Portugal's direct competitors in trade and investment whilst fierce competition for its traditional exports has come from such emerging powers as China and India. All this has contributed to the erosion of the country's position in European and international trade and also to a deep contraction of the national economy. This became irrefutable and virtually impossible to address alone when the country was caught in the eye of storm of the economic and financial crisis that followed the collapse of the Lehman Brothers in 2008. Eventually, after the Greek and the Irish bailouts, in May 2011, the Portuguese government requested financial assistance from the EU and the IMF, which led to an emergency bailout to deal with a soaring sovereign debt.

As part of the successive austerity programmes starting in 2011, the government has made draconian cuts by reducing employment subsidies, retirement pensions and economic assistance measures, and also by freezing the extra salaries traditionally paid at Christmas and in the summer holidays. All this, but especially the rising unemployment, has increased the number of Portuguese leaving the country and becoming economic migrants. The new wave of migrants in search of stable employment and better living conditions has headed to Brazil, Angola and Mozambique alongside such more classic destinations as Britain, Switzerland, France and Germany. To be sure, if during the last decade or so of the twentieth century, Portugal saw its status changing from that of a 'country of emigrants' to a 'country of immigrants', the economic hardship that has been fiercely hitting both the state and people after the bailout is leading to a reversal of this trend. A considerable number of those migrants comprised youngsters educated in national universities, which is enormously detrimental to the country's future.

While the current economic hardship has challenged the relative success of Portugal's experience of European integration, there is no doubt that in the last 25 years its fully-fledged participation in the EU has contributed substantially to the country's convergence with European norms and standards. The same can be said about the political and economic spheres as a result of the governing elites merging with their European counterparts inside and outside the EU's institutions. As such, as many of this book's contributions have highlighted, participation in the Community-building process has been from the outset a critical driver of change and transformation of contemporary Portuguese society. This sound legacy is a critical asset as Portugal faces extremely trying times dictated by the external assistance programme. This is so despite the economic and financial adversity that has led some to call for the country's exit from the Eurozone – and from the EU for that matter. Nevertheless, there has been general recognition that by being within the European family Portugal is better equipped to face the economic and financial storm.

Therefore, the political and strategic choice made in the mid-1970s to be part of the political and economic European project has been ultimately, a wise one. After all, in 1976 the Portuguese leadership applied for EC membership with two major goals in view: the consolidation of democracy and the overall modernization of the country and economic development. As elucidated by the chapters in this volume (particularly from the first and second parts), both goals have been achieved in their essentials. There was also the realization of economic and social benefits arising from EC membership that eventually materialized as a result of massive financial transfers from the structural funds and cohesion policies. All this fostered a general euro-optimism among the population – a feature that has characterized the Portuguese case throughout the period considered in this book. Furthermore, both the political and economic elites have sustained an instrumental allegiance to the EU based on the belief that the country has benefited from European integration. In this regard, historically speaking, these governing elites have successfully conveyed this message to public opinion as the Portuguese themselves have exhibited a similar outlook in mass opinion surveys.

That being said, Portugal's experience of integration, has nevertheless, witnessed various setbacks, flaws and unforeseen side effects. The economic, financial and budgetary crisis has put the traditional Portuguese euro-optimism to the test whilst fuelling a more pronounced wave of euro-scepticism. This started to be felt particularly against the backdrop of the preparations leading to Eastern enlargement, which entailed the partial transfer of cohesion and structural funds to the countries admitted to Europe in the enlargements of 2004 and 2007; and even more so upon the impact of the austerity measures imposed by the European institutions, which gave rise to a strong impression of a grave imbalance between the costs and benefits of being part of the EU. Consequently, after enjoying for more than two decades an overwhelming popularity, a sort of 'state of grace' in the eyes of the Portuguese public opinion, the country's participation in the European integration process has entered a period of unparallelled contestation.

The 'good student' and the quest for credibility: implications and limitations of a metaphor

This book has shown that all along the Portuguese authorities have exhibited a particular concern in promoting the credibility of the country's membership. This can be related with the metaphor of the 'good student', which has more or less accompanied the Portugal's quest for a credible place within the EU's fold.

In fact, in the early years of membership, the country's European strategy was devised to lend credibility to its capacity to meet the challenges stemming from belonging to a club of prosperous democratic states that abided by international human rights law. During the first decade of the twenty-first century, the national strategy has shifted towards boosting credibility in the country's ability to contribute in a tangible way to the advancement of the European integration process. This could be seen in the way the Portuguese EU Presidencies of 2000 and 2007 were devised and implemented. On these two occasions, it can be said that the Portuguese foreign policy makers have endeavoured to make the country transcend the 'good student' metaphor and profile itself as a 'good player'. The approval of the Lisbon Strategy (2000) and the signing of the Lisbon Treaty (2007) are illustrative manifestations of this.

The continued quest for credibility in the eyes of Portugal's European partners helps to explain its Europeanization, notably the so-called 'downloading' dynamics that took place in public and sectoral policies as a result of legislative changes required by EU Treaties. Equally important is the evolution that took place in the country's foreign policy outlook, which moved from an orthodox Atlantic stance to an Euro-Atlantic posture. Such an evolution started its full expression during the first Portuguese Presidency of the Council of the EU in 1992, under the aegis of which the country participated, for the first time since the First World War, in multilateral military operations. The need for credibility moved the country to engage itself in and contribute to the advancement of the political and security integration process by means of participation in virtually all relevant developments in the CFSP/CSDP realms. Incidentally, it is worth noting that Portugal has been reaping the fruits of its post-colonial links and affinities in playing the 'lusophone card' based on areas of natural expertise and influence comprising more than 250 million people. Examples of this include the organization of two EU–African Summits, in 2000 and 2007; the establishment of an EU–Brazil strategic partnership and a special partnership with Cape-Verde, both in 2007; and the launching of a ESDP civilian mission in Guinea-Bissau in 2008. As a result, the country has been able to punch above its weight, while gathering further credibility and respectability in the eyes of its European peers. The current technical and military cooperation arrangements, economic partnership and linguistic identity founded on a Spelling Agreement, holds the potential for greater enhancement of Portugal's role as promoter of the EU's links with the lusophone world, especially with Brazil, Angola and Mozambique. Indeed, on the back of the rise of both Brazil and Angola as economic powers, Portuguese authorities have been looking for and seizing new opportunities for business and investment. In this perspective, the country's economic woe is likely to engender deepened ties with the Portuguese-speaking world, while giving additional arguments for Lisbon to bring the lusophone countries to the negotiating table in Brussels and highlight their relevance in the promotion of global economic development and security.

Not unsurprisingly, since the beginning of the assistance programme, the question of credibility has become more critical than ever, with Portugal having to present itself before the European institutions as a credible partner capable of tackling simultaneously diverse challenges, dilemmas and hurdles in order to continue to get economic assistance in the current trying times. Therefore, under different circumstances, history has seemed to repeat itself, and not without with a measure of irony. In the 1980s, Portugal received financial assistance to secure both its democratization and modernization, a process that in due course has allowed the country to participate in all the principal European integration-oriented ventures, notably the functioning of the EMU. Since 2011, the country has been receiving assistance to undertake structural reforms that lingered for decades as unfinished business. It has also had to cope with multiple difficulties posed not only by the financial constraints resulting from the adoption of the Euro, but also the political challenges brought about by the establishment of an imperfect Economic Union; and, finally, it has had to overcome the financial and budgetary indiscipline that has contributed to the soaring sovereign debt crisis.

Portugal and the Eastern and Central European enlargement

In addition to the continued quest for credibility, albeit linked to it, Portugal's engagement within the EU has been characterized by continual efforts to overcome its small size and peripheral position while safeguarding issues and regions related to its national interests. This was mainly done through its efforts in being part of the *avant garde* group leading the major integration ventures and consequently placing itself at the centre of a critical decision-making process that would ultimately affect the country. In fact, since its accession Portugal has been involved in all the most crucially important milestones of the European economic and political project, notably in the completion of the Single Market, the foundation and functioning of the EMU, the establishment of the Schengen Agreement, the historic enlargement to Central and Eastern Europe and the launching of crisis management missions around the world under the CFSP/CSDP. On the other hand, national authorities have been successful in drawing its European peers' attention and resources not only to regional actors corresponding to areas traditionally linked to the country's key national strategic interests, but also to ethical and normative issues in international relations. The militancy around East Timor's self-determination and the emphasis placed upon the need to deepen relations with India, Brazil and the African continent are cases in point. Incidentally, it was under the Portuguese Presidencies that the first ever EU–Brazil and EU–Africa Summits took place, and strategic partnerships with these major actors were signed up. Finally, Portuguese leaders have seized the windows of opportunity generated by the country's Presidencies of the Council of the EU further to invoke an intra-European consensus around new visions about the role that the EU should play in the world, such as those enshrined in both the Lisbon Strategy and the Lisbon Treaty.

In the post-2004/2007 enlargement landscape, it is, therefore, not surprising to see Portugal being looked to both by newcomers and those still on the road to membership while the country's earlier positive experience as part of the

European project may be taken as a source of inspiration and emulation for those who are coming to terms with the manifold challenges generated by the increasingly demanding integration dynamics. Furthermore, given its consolidated position in Europe, Portugal has been already identified as a potential supporter of an eventual future membership for countries like Turkey and even the Ukraine and Georgia.

Furthermore, viewed through the prism of the Eastern and Central European members states and candidate countries – but also of those that aspire to join the EU – there are lessons to be learned from Portugal's 25 years of integration experience. Entering into the EU's fold can function as a fundamental driver for, and anchor of, a reformist and transformative multifaceted process in engendering both macro and micro economic reforms and modernizing financial, commercial and manufacturing structures. An enhancement of infrastructure, notably in roads and telecommunications networks, can be also expected under the impetus of European structural funds. There can also be dividends to be reaped in the domains of trade and foreign investments. On the other hand, in general, the Portuguese experience has shown that EU membership carries with it a mixed bag of constraints, dilemmas and problems. A concrete lesson that stands out clearly is that the EU structural and cohesion funds do not constitute a guarantee of success for recipient states, since such success is contingent on their effective use. Economic success is furthermore derived from how countries exploit the advantages springing from access to a vast European market founded on the free movements of goods, persons, capital and services. This can only be attained by means of structural reforms to increase productivity and competitiveness, which are critical for securing comparative advantage in the fiercely competitive markets in world trade.

Incidentally, Portugal's trajectory within the EU, particularly in the context of the financial turmoil, provides topical insights into the pitfalls of both the European project overall and the economic and monetary integration process, in particular. In fact, it proved the major weaknesses – if not the virtual failure – of the Eurozone during a sovereign debt crisis. And, related to this, it also exhibited the dramatic implications of monetary policies being no longer in the hands of national governments, which, for that reason, are now unable to devalue their currencies to redress imbalances.

Portugal in a wider historical context

If this book had been devised in 1910, rather than in 2010 it would have been dominated by a world which was divided up into great empires, chiefly, but not exclusively, European empires, in which Portugal was a major imperial power. Most empires formally came to an end in a remarkably short period of time, due to the impact of the two world wars on Europe's status in the world, the growth of nationalism and the growing middle class in colonial territories, the incompatibilities of establishing a democratic welfare state at home with an authoritarian colonial policy, and above all, the ability of the colonial powers to mobilize societies, but not to assimilate the mobilized people into a new framework that those people would then legitimize. Their wish was to have a European-style bourgeois national state, not to be part of a cosmopolitan quasi-global entity. There was also the economic factor, in that free trade gave the former colonial powers the benefits that they wished to have without having to pay the administrative costs of Empire. Moreover, they were under very great pressure from the United States to open up their colonial territories.

Perhaps the turning-point was the surrender of Singapore by the British to the Japanese, because it was symbolic of the victory of an Asian power (although one that considered itself to be, in some senses, Western) – Japan – over all the major imperial powers with interests in Asia, whether it was the Americans in the Philippines, the French in Indo-China, the Dutch in the East Indies, or the British in Burma, Malaya and Singapore. It was the first time a non-European power had defeated the full range of the Western colonial powers in a major war. The myth of Western superiority was punctured.

However, the end of Empire was not at all smooth, especially not for Portugal. Britain and France conceded independence in the 1960s, when Prime Minister Macmillan made a famous speech on the 'winds of change' in Africa, to the Parliament in Cape Town, and General de Gaulle offered the French African territories the possibility of independence. Portugal did not take part in this general movement. Rather, it decided to stay and fight, and Portuguese society was rent asunder by the consequences of this, giving rise to the Revolution of the Carnations, and a period of political and economic change, which did not finally reach a safe harbour until Portugal eventually became a member state of the European Community.

Most of the European powers were faced by the necessity to follow a policy that was really a policy of decline. Former US Secretary of State Dean Acheson caused a furore in Britain by stating the obvious, that Britain had lost an Empire, but had not yet found a role. The same was true of France; and the same was true of course, of Portugal, as well as the other major colonial powers. For the most part, Britain departed quietly, often leaving catastrophic situations behind, as in the Indian subcontinent, and in Palestine. The French stayed to fight in Indo-China, as to a lesser degree did the Dutch in the Dutch East Indies. The French were defeated, not only in Indo-China, but also in Algeria, while the Dutch came to terms with their new global situation. It is true that the British did fight a major colonial war in Malaya, but the other major colonial military engagements were not large-scale, although they were sometimes bloody, as in Cyprus, Aden and the Mau Mau revolt in Kenya.

The reactions of the colonial powers differed. Britain was clearly a victor, or at least on the victorious side in the Second World War, and it was treated for the first decade thereafter as one of the 'big three', but it had been deeply wounded and was concerned primarily with building a welfare state at home. France had suffered defeat and occupation in the war, as had Germany, and the reaction of these three powers differed. Britain was following a policy of decline, where all the choices were unfortunate ones, and everything was less than it used to be, and it failed to adopt a policy of renewal or rebirth. The French, after the catastrophic defeats in Indo-China and Algeria, did follow a policy of renewal and rebirth, and the Germans, after their defeat and occupation did likewise. Portugal was initially in a similar category to France, in that it had an assimilationist social and political policy, and fought a number of major wars, not least in Angola and Mozambique, but following the failure of a military solution and the Carnation Revolution, it looked to Europe, as did France, as a way of escaping from the politics of decline. Britain, perhaps because it had not been defeated and occupied, failed to carry out such a reassessment of its position, as the furore over Acheson's statement suggests.

At the end of the colonial conflicts the Portuguese communities, particularly in Angola and Mozambique, quickly returned to metropolitan Portugal, or went to South Africa. As we have seen in many of the chapters above, the Portuguese policy following the Revolution of the Carnations was to move from an Atlanticist position to a European one. As France and the Netherlands realized that their colonial past was over, and therefore played an active role in the construction of a new European entity, so Portugal with similar reasoning joined the EU and its major activities, whether being part of the Eurozone, or in terms of military contribution to EU military operations.

Whereas the Atlantic dimension of Portugal's place in the world was extremely relevant in the Second World War, and subsequently in the Cold War, it was no longer the case when the Cold War was over as the prime goals were decolonization, democracy and modernization. Portugal determined that it should be a good European state, and indeed, for a decade, it really was a good European state, but then it all turned sour, and Portugal became a European problem. It seems as though the Portuguese state and society had sleep-walked into a dream world in which it felt that by joining the EU it could relax, since all would be well after a period of social and economic adjustment. Portugal had been recognized and accepted as a full European partner but it was not able, after its initial success, to put the opportunity of membership of the EU to best use. It thought that it had got to heaven and that was enough, since it would automatically stay there, and it used some aspects of its new relationships to strengthen areas such as health and education and to build an impressive road infrastructure, but it did not manage to modernize its traditional industries and agriculture. After the end of the Cold War it therefore became a ready victim of the undercutting by the new members of the EU, which had a low paid but well educated labour force; and externally it was under pressure from Chinese exports in traditional industries such as textiles. Even in wine there was a difficulty, as bottles now had screw-tops or plastic corks, rather than traditional cork, the production of which was part of Portuguese life and culture.

As the difficult period set in at the turn of the millennium, Portugal was able to reinvigorate its former colonial ties, and act as a bridge between Europe and the new great power, Brazil, as well as major oil-producing countries, such as Angola. It managed successfully to move from the hatred and abuses of colonial war to develop new and cherished linkages with its former Empire. It was able to do this in an exemplary manner. Young Portuguese, (and indeed, not only young Portuguese, in the times of the great economic difficulty with which Portugal is now faced) are willing to go to Africa where they are accepted, or to Brazil, to seek their fortune and help in the modernization of those countries. In short, once again Portugal is making itself useful, with its political, cultural and social, as well as economic, contribution to Europe's relations with Brazil and Africa.

It cannot, however, be denied that Portugal is in deep trouble. It is cutting its spending, and asking its people to bear real hardships; but they are a people who have a degree of resilience, and a strong sense of social cohesion and their nearness to the land and the traditional society of the countryside may enable some to move and bear the adjustment necessitated by the economic cuts. Moreover there are assets: tourism is clearly one of them. There is now a much better educated elite, which includes large numbers of women. There is an international spirit, which still survives. Expectations are not unreasonably high, and socially the country is much freer than it was. Moreover, Portugal has paid its European dues, and it merits the solace of the EU and the former Empire. Half a millennium ago Portugal was the first global leader. The final act of that global leadership was their disastrous colonial wars in Africa and now that they are clearly in the past, and there are resonances that are beneficial both to African states and Brazil, and to Portugal. Despite its failure to maximize on the possibilities that the EU had to offer in the first 25 years of Portugal's membership, nevertheless, its participation does bring with it some resources and a residual capacity to face the present difficult times.

At the time of writing, the foul weather of recession and the demands of the financial aid programme are bringing about stringent austerity measures with dramatic social costs. They have inaugurated an unprecedented critical political, economic and financial juncture that has left no stone unturned, whose implications remain to be seen in the future. In the meantime, the Portuguese authorities remain dependent upon the systemic performance of the international economy and markets, and are hostages to European difficulties in bringing the protracted Eurozone crisis to an end.

Index

Page numbers in *italics* denote tables, those in **bold** denote figures.